Home Networking For Dummies, 4th Edition

S0-BZP-651

Networking Jargon at a Glance

Tear out this handy list of frequently used networking terms and stick it to a wall, the dog, or anything else that doesn't move much.

administrator: The person in charge of maintaining the network — probably you.

backup: A copy of the files on your computer (stored on a removable device) that can be used to restore data in the event that a computer in your network meets with disaster.

CAT-5 cable (Category 5): Ethernet network cable. Also called *twisted pair cable*.

client: A computer that uses hardware and services on another computer (called the *server*).

client/server network: A network model in which one computer (the *server*) provides services for the other computers (the *clients*).

concentrator: The home base of an Ethernet network to which all lengths of cable from the network computers are attached. The concentrator can be a hub or a switch (including a switch that is built into a router).

dial-up networking: A feature in Windows that enables your modem to connect to the Internet through an Internet Service Provider.

driver: Software that enables the operating system to communicate with the hardware in your computer.

IP address: A number that identifies a computer's location on the Internet.

IRQ (Interrupt Request): A communication channel assigned to a device so that it can communicate with the PC's processor.

ISP (Internet Service Provider): A company that provides Internet access to individuals and businesses.

LAN (Local Area Network): Multiple computers connected as a network in one general location.

Mbps (Megabits per second): One million bits per second. A measurement of the speed at which data can be transmitted.

NetBIOS (Network Basic Input/Output System): A network communication system that enables the various applications running on computers in the network to communicate with other computers on a network.

network: Two or more computers connected to each other with hardware (network adapters) and networking software to communicate and exchange data.

NIC (Network Interface Card): A hardware device, also called a *network adapter,* that enables networking by providing the features necessary for cable (or wireless) communication.

peer-to-peer network: A network model in which each computer has the same capabilities as the others, and each computer can communicate with all the other computers.

protocol: A set of rules (sometimes referred to as a *language*) that computers use to communicate with each other across networks.

RJ-45: The connector at the end of Ethernet cable. It looks like the connector at the end of telephone cable, but it's slightly fatter.

router: A hardware device that lets network computers connect to a single DSL/cable modem.

server: A computer that provides services for other computers (called *workstations* or *clients*) on a network. Also called a *host*.

shared Internet connection: A system that permits all the computers on a network to be connected to the Internet at the same time using a modem attached to one of the computers.

shared resources: Resources such as files, folders, printers, and other peripherals that are attached to one computer and configured for access by users on other network computers.

TCP/IP (Transmission Control Protocol/Internet Protocol): The basic suite of communication languages *(protocols)* of the Internet. TCP/IP can also be used as the primary protocol for home networks.

workstation: A network computer that uses the resources of one or more servers. Also called a *client*.

Home Networking For Dummies, 4th Edition

Stuff I Need to Know about My Network Computers

A time may come when one of the computers on your home network goes down, and you have to reconnect the network settings. Rebuilding your network settings is a lot easier if you don't have to start from scratch — you shouldn't waste time trying to find the original documentation if you don't have to. You can find the essential information you need to get in, set up the connection, and get out again by double-clicking the Network icon in the Control Panel. Then select each item and click Properties to see that item's settings. Write down the specifications and keep them in a safe place — just in case Murphy's Law comes a-calling.

Computer 1

Computer name: _____

NIC brand and type: _____

Network components installed: _____

_____

Computer 2

Computer name: _____

NIC brand and type: _____

Network components installed: _____

_____

Computer 3

Computer name: _____

NIC brand and type: _____

Network components installed: _____

_____

Stuff I Need to Know about My Network Printers

Every day, you have a list of important things you need to remember. (You remember that you need to fill the car up with gas, but you can't remember where you left your car keys, where you left the car, and you sure as heck don't remember why there's a list of networking terms pinned to the dog.) Simplify your life — write down the important stuff once (and only once), leave the list in a handy place (don't forget where you put it!), and go on with your life until you really need to know about toner and shared resources.

Printer 1

Printer manufacturer and model: _____

Ink or toner cartridge part number: _____

Attached to Computer #: _____

Shared as (share name): _____

Printer 2

Printer manufacturer and model: _____

Ink or toner cartridge part number: _____

Attached to Computer #: _____

Shared as (share name): _____

For Dummies: Bestselling Book Series for Beginners

Home Networking

FOR

DUMMIES®

4TH EDITION

Home Networking FOR DUMMIES® 4TH EDITION

by Kathy Ivens

BICENTENNIAL
1807
WILEY
2007
BICENTENNIAL

Wiley Publishing, Inc.

Home Networking For Dummies, 4th Edition

Published by
Wiley Publishing, Inc.
111 River Street
Hoboken, NJ 07030-5774

www.wiley.com

Copyright © 2007 by Wiley Publishing, Inc., Indianapolis, Indiana

Published by Wiley Publishing, Inc., Indianapolis, Indiana

Published simultaneously in Canada

For general information on our other products and services, please contact our Customer Care Department within the U.S. at 800-762-2974, outside the U.S. at 317-572-3993, or fax 317-572-4002.

For technical support, please visit www.wiley.com/techsupport.

Wiley also publishes its books in a variety of electronic formats. Some content that appears in print may not be available in electronic books.

Library of Congress Control Number: 2007920007

ISBN: 978-0-470-11806-1

Manufactured in the United States of America

10 9 8 7 6 5 4 3 2

WILEY

About the Author

Kathy Ivens has written more than 50 books about computers and has spent lots of years installing corporate networks. She's a Senior Contributing Editor for *Windows IT Pro Magazine* and runs multiple computer networks in her own home.

Dedication

This book is dedicated to Sarah, Amy, and Leah, with love from Grandma.

Author's Acknowledgments

A great many very talented people worked hard to make sure this book provided information in a way that makes it easy for you to perform all the technical tasks involved in setting up a home network. Some of them really have to be acknowledged specifically, because their expertise and influence is reflected on every page of this book.

It's always a great pleasure to work with Acquisitions Editor Melody Layne, who is exceptionally personable, thoroughly professional, and makes it much more pleasant to face the task of revising this book whenever Microsoft decides to release a new version of Windows. Project Editor Blair Pottenger is so proficient, knowledgeable, and efficient that all the work involved in producing a book flowed beautifully. Even when I provided bumps in the road, he smoothed everything out with the dexterity of a magician. Copy Editor Andy Hollandbeck covered for me so you'll never know about the paragraphs where my writing rambled, broke grammar rules, or lacked accurate punctuation. Technical Editor Matt Goletz made sure I didn't get away with skipping details, taking shortcuts that create technical mistakes, or giving bad information.

Publisher's Acknowledgments

We're proud of this book; please send us your comments through our online registration form located at www.dummies.com/register/.

Some of the people who helped bring this book to market include the following:

Acquisitions, Editorial, and Media Development

Project Editor: Blair J. Pottenger

Acquisitions Editor: Melody Layne

Copy Editor: Andy Hollandbeck

Technical Editor: Matt Goletz

Editorial Manager: Kevin Kirschner

Media Development Manager: Laura VanWinkle

Editorial Assistant: Amanda Foxworth

Sr. Editorial Assistant: Cherie Case

Cartoons: Rich Tennant
(www.the5thwave.com)

Composition Services

Project Coordinator: Lynsey Osborn

Layout and Graphics: Stephanie D. Jumper, Laura Pence, Heather Ryan

Proofreader: Aptara

Indexer: Aptara

Anniversary Logo Design: Richard Pacifico

Publishing and Editorial for Technology Dummies

    Richard Swadley, Vice President and Executive Group Publisher

    Andy Cummings, Vice President and Publisher

    Mary Bednarek, Executive Acquisitions Director

    Mary C. Corder, Editorial Director

Publishing for Consumer Dummies

    Diane Graves Steele, Vice President and Publisher

    Joyce Pepple, Acquisitions Director

Composition Services

    Gerry Fahey, Vice President of Production Services

    Debbie Stailey, Director of Composition Services

Contents at a Glance

Table of Contents

Introduction

*I*f you have more than one computer in your home, you should have a network. I used to consider that statement an opinion, but it's so logical that I now think of it as a fact of nature. Nobody has ever presented a convincing (to me) argument that supports keeping multiple computers isolated from each other.

Using and managing multiple computers is easier if you create a network. You don't have to remember which computer you were using when you started that letter to Uncle Harry because you can just reach across the network to finish it, using any computer in the house. A home network allows you to do the work you have to do better and more efficiently.

One of the best reasons to set up a home network is to share an Internet connection so you don't have to listen to, "I need the modem, tell Tommy to give me a turn!"

And then of course, there are the wonderful psychological rewards. Because you're the one reading this book, you'll probably be the person who installs the network. This means you become the *network administrator,* the person who controls which files your family members can access, as well as which printers they can use. Talk about power! And the wonderful thing about being a network administrator is that the title makes it sound like you do a lot of hard work (but you don't — you'll be amazed at how easy all of this is).

About This Book

This book isn't a novel or a mystery, so you don't have to start at page one and read every chapter in order — you can't spoil the ending. This book is meant to be digested on a subject-by-subject, not a chapter-by-chapter, basis. Each chapter is self-contained, covering a specific subject.

However, because the process of creating the network requires that tasks be performed in a certain order, I recommend that you check out the chapters in either Part I or Part II before you go to any of the other chapters.

After you get up to speed on the basics, you can decide which chapters you want to look at next and figure out which network features you want to add to your home network.

Conventions Used in This Book

Keeping things consistent makes them easier to understand. In this book, those consistent elements are *conventions*. Notice how the word *conventions* is in italics? In this book, I put new terms in italics and then define them so that you know what they mean.

Here are some other conventions I use in this book:

- ✔ When you have to type something in a text box, I put it in **bold** type so that it is easy to see.

- ✔ When I cite URLs (Web addresses) within a paragraph, they appear in monofont: `www.symantec.com`. Similarly, all text formatted as *code* (commands you have to type) also appears in monofont.

- ✔ Regarding the differences between the various versions of Windows, I discuss the operating systems separately when a difference exists in the way they work. Otherwise, I just use the term *Windows*.

What You Don't Need to Read

I've learned that some people are really curious about why some computer functions work the way they do. Other people don't care why; they just want to find out *how* to perform those functions.

I put technical explanations that you don't need to read, but that may be of interest to the little computer geek in your head, in sidebars or passages of text marked with a Technical Stuff icon. You can safely skip this information if you don't care about those details. (I'll never know.)

Foolish Assumptions

I make several assumptions about you:

- ✔ You use PCs that run either Windows XP or Windows Vista.

- ✔ You want to share computers on a network, whether they're desktop computers or laptops.

- ✔ You have more people in the household than computers, so more than one person may use any single computer.

How This Book Is Organized

This book is divided into five parts to make it easier to find what you need. Each part has a number of chapters (some have more than others).

Part 1: Network Basics

Part I helps you plan and install your home network. You have some decisions to make and some hardware to buy. You also have to play architect as you design the placement of computers around the house. This part shows you how to put it all together.

- ✔ Planning your network and buying the hardware (Chapter 1)
- ✔ Installing the network hardware in your computers (Chapter 2)
- ✔ Cabling your house to connect the computers (Chapter 3)
- ✔ Using wires that already exist in your home: telephone lines and electric lines (Chapter 4)
- ✔ Connecting computers without wires (Chapter 5)

The information you find here may seem geeky and complicated, but it really isn't as complex as it sounds. If you perform each step in the right order, building a network is no harder than assembling a complicated toy for your kids. To make things as easy as possible, I take you through each task one step at a time.

Part II: Configuring Computers for Networking

After you've installed all the network hardware, you have to perform some software tasks, including the following:

- ✔ Installing the files that Windows needs for networking and sharing an Internet connection (Chapter 6)
- ✔ Setting up each computer to share stuff — and keep other stuff private (Chapter 7)
- ✔ Setting up users and learning about logins (Chapter 8)

This part tells you how to fine-tune your network — getting the computers to talk to each other and setting up users so everyone can maintain his or her own, personalized computer-configuration options.

Part III: Communicating Across the Network

This part introduces you to the meat of networking. Here's where you get to put all your setup work into action.

- ✔ Setting up network printing (Chapter 9)
- ✔ Accessing the other computers on the network (Chapter 10)
- ✔ Using files from other computers while you're working in software (Chapter 11)

The fun of networking is actually doing stuff across the network. Time to test it all out. Sit in front of any computer on the network and get stuff from any other computer. Ahhh, the power!

Part IV: Network Security and Maintenance

If you're going to create a network, any network, whether in the office or at home, that makes you the network administrator. After all the work you do creating this network, you'll want to make sure the network is safe and happy. The chapters in Part IV cover the following:

- ✔ Protecting the computers against harm from viruses and Internet intruders (Chapter 12)
- ✔ Preparing for disaster by making sure you don't lose your data when a computer dies (Chapter 13)
- ✔ Keeping computers healthy with the aid of some nifty tools (Chapter 14)

Part V: The Part of Tens

In true *For Dummies* style, this book includes a Part of Tens. These introduce lists of ten items about a variety of informative topics. He find additional resources, hints, and tips, plus other gold nuggets of edge. The Part of Tens is a resource you can turn to again and again.

Icons Used in This Book

To make your experience with this book easier, I use various icons in the margins to indicate particular points of interest.

Pay attention to the text this icon flags if you want to make setting up and using your network easier (and who wouldn't want that?). Think of this cute little target as a gift from one network administrator (me) to another (you).

This icon is a friendly reminder or a marker for something that you want to make sure that you cache in your memory for later use.

This icon means "Read this or suffer the consequences." You find it wherever problems may arise if you don't pay attention.

This icon points out technical stuff that computer geeks or highly curious people may find interesting. You can accomplish all the important tasks in this book without reading any of the material next to these icons.

Where to Go from Here

Go ahead — check out the Table of Contents to see which neat networking feature you want to install first. But I do suggest that you check out Parts I and II for some networking basics.

It's quite possible that members of your family have opinions about the order in which you should install networking features — especially the kids, who seem to be born with an advanced knowledge of computing. Have a family meeting and listen to everyone's opinions — make sure the person who has the strongest views about which features should be implemented "volunteers" to help you install and maintain your network. (In my family, when one of my children urged the family to do something, I listened carefully and then said, "Great idea, honey, you do it, and don't forget to let us know how you're doing.")

Creating a home network is satisfying, fun, and incredibly useful. Have a good time. You're on the cutting edge of computer technology. By reading this book, you prove that you're a networking geek — and as far as I'm concerned, that's a compliment.

Part I
Network Basics

"If it works, it works. I've just never seen network cabling connected with Chinese handcuffs before."

In this part . . .

Part I of this book covers all the planning and hardware purchases required for building a network. You can't jump into this project willy-nilly; you have to design your network before you actually build it. The stuff you need to know isn't complicated, and the hardware installation is very easy — anyone can do it.

Lots of different types of hardware are available, so you need to decide what hardware to use in your network; Chapter 1 helps you through that process. After you make your hardware decisions, you have to install the hardware, which you find out how to do in the other chapters in this part.

You're starting a great adventure, and when you cross the finish line, you'll be a network expert. You'll even be able to throw technical jargon into your conversations — words like *NIC, Ethernet,* and *switch.* (Don't worry — before you finish Chapter 1, you'll know what those words mean.) Then all of your non-expert friends, who have no idea how easy this stuff is, will be amazed by your geekiness.

Chapter 1

Planning the Lay of the LAN

● ●

In This Chapter

▶ Deciding to create a home network

▶ Homing in on the right operating system

▶ Understanding how networks work

▶ Figuring out what hardware you need

▶ Purchasing kits or individual components

● ●

A network is a system of two or more computers that are connected in some manner (you have lots of choices about the "manner") and the commonly used term for a network is *LAN,* which stands for Local Area Network. Each computer on the network has access to the files and peripheral equipment (such as printers or modems) on all the other computers on the network. You create those connections with the following elements:

✔ Hardware in each computer that permits the computer to communicate.

✔ A cable or a wireless technology that sends data between the computers (using the hardware you installed).

✔ Software (called a *driver*) that operates the hardware. (I cover drivers in Chapter 6.)

Believe it or not, installing the hardware and software you need on each computer is not complicated at all. Start with the first computer and go through the process one step at a time. After you finish setting up that first computer, you'll see how logical and simple the tasks are.

In fact, anyone who knows how to turn on a computer and use the keyboard and mouse can create a network in an amazingly short amount of time. Many people who installed their own home networks found it so easy and satisfying that they helped neighbors, friends, and relatives. Some have gone on to neighborhood fame and fortune as part-time consultants to other households who want home networks. They never give away the secret that all of this is extremely easy to do.

In this chapter, I explain some reasons you might want to set up a network in your home, explain your software and hardware alternatives, and tell you more about how different networks *work*. I also discuss some of the technology that's available for your network.

The particulars and the installation steps for all the different types of networking hardware and software are found throughout this book — look for the appropriate chapter titles or check the index to find the particular pages you need.

Why Would I Want a Home Network?

I believe that anyone who has more than one computer in the house should definitely have a network. That belief has its roots in the fact that I'm generally lazy and miserly, and I believe everyone should do everything in the easiest and cheapest way. Here's a list of just some of the ways a home network can benefit your whole household:

✔ **You can work anywhere in the house, even in bed if you want to.** Suppose that you have an important presentation for your boss, and it's due tomorrow morning. But it's Sunday morning, and you're having your second cup of coffee in your bedroom. It would be so cozy and comfy to use your laptop, in bed, to finish the presentation. Then you realize that when you were working on the presentation *yesterday*, you were sitting at the kitchen computer, slaving away at the presentation while eating a turkey sandwich. You don't have to leave your cozy bed and stumble downstairs to find the most recently saved version of the document — you can open the file that's on the kitchen computer right on the laptop in your bedroom.

✔ **Your kids won't argue as much.** Sally doesn't have to stop using the computer in the den because Bobby needs to retrieve his homework assignment from it. Bobby can go to the computer in the basement and open the file that's on the computer in the den right on the computer in the basement. There's no need to copy the file to a floppy disk; it's as available and handy as it would be if it were residing on the basement computer.

✔ **You can put an end to the demands for the computer that has the Internet connection.** Because you can set up your network so that everyone in the household can be on the Internet at the same time, those arguments about whose turn it is to surf the Net are a thing of the past.

✔ **You can buy yourself an expensive piece of jewelry with the money you save on peripherals.** Okay, not quite, but you will save money because you won't have to buy a printer and modem every time you buy a computer because everyone shares those tools across the network. Even better, the sharing is simultaneous, so you can avoid "It's my turn!" arguments.

✔ **You can become a god (or goddess).** Another benefit of setting up a home network is that when you install it, you become the *network administrator* (that's what the people who installed the network at your office are called). You may even get to invent usernames and passwords. You'll be in charge of decisions about whether Mom can see Bobby's files or Bobby can see Mom's files. All of this knowledge and power makes you a computer geek. Because I think that being called a computer geek is a compliment, I offer my congratulations to you.

Network Operating Systems (Nothing to Do with Surgery)

You don't have to start creating your network with computers that already contain the hardware and software required for networking because you can easily install that stuff yourself (with the help of this book). However, you must have computers that already run on an operating system that can participate in a network environment.

For this book, I assume that all the computers in your home run Windows XP or Windows Vista. As a result, you won't see specific instructions for performing tasks on any other (earlier) versions of Windows. However, if you happen to have a computer running Windows 98SE or Windows 2000, the instructions in this book should work for you, it's just that you may have to figure out how to open the dialog boxes and windows I refer to because sometimes the menus are different.

Check out the Introduction of this book for other assumptions I've so flippantly made about you.

Network Types — Just Like Personality Types

You can configure networks to operate in any of several *modes,* or *configuration types.* Like personality types, some network configuration types are interested in controlling computer users; other network types are more relaxed about controls. You can choose a mode for your current needs and then easily change your network to another mode if the circumstances warrant. The basic hardware and configuration stuff that goes into creating a network (all of which I cover in this book) are the same for all network types, so your choices depend mostly on how you want to communicate among computers.

Client/server networks for control freaks

Networking schemes that operate in *client/server* mode are almost always found only in businesses. These schemes include a main computer (a *server*) that controls users and holds files and peripherals shared by all the other computers (called *clients* or *workstations*).

One of the most important reasons to install a client/server network is *user authentication,* which is a security feature. The server on a client/server network checks to see if a SuzieQ user is who she says she is and controls whether she can join the network. If she's eligible, the server continues to control her network tasks, determining what she can do. For example, perhaps she can read files but not delete them. The good news is that if you set up the network, you can control *everything.* (Heh, heh, heh.)

All the client computers are connected in a way that gives them physical access to the server. Everyone who works at a client computer can use files and peripherals that are on his or her individual computer (the local computer) or on the server. Look at Figure 1-1 to see the communication between computers in a client/server environment.

Even though all the computers are connected to each other, each client usually communicates with the server. However, you can configure the network so that the users on client computers can also access the other client computers on the network.

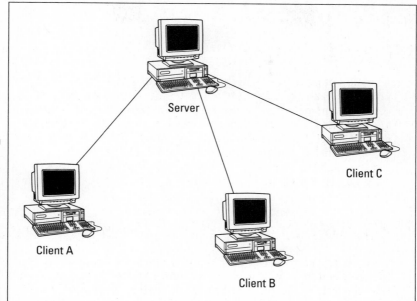

Server

Client C

Client A

Client B

Figure 1-1:
In a
client/server
network, all
the client
computers
have to
check in
with the
server.

Large client/server networks (usually found in the workplace) frequently have multiple servers, and each server has a specific job. For example, one server is used for authenticating users, one manages everyone's e-mail, one contains the accounting software, and yet another has the word processing software. The common network operating systems used for servers on client/server networks are Windows 2000, Windows Server 2003, Novell NetWare, and UNIX/Linux. These kinds of networks may be a *little* more than you need — unless you're thinking of running an enormous enterprise-like business out of your home.

Peer-to-peer networks are more relaxed about controls

Peer-to-peer networks permit all the computers on a network to communicate with each other. In Figure 1-2, you can see a typical peer-to-peer network communication structure.

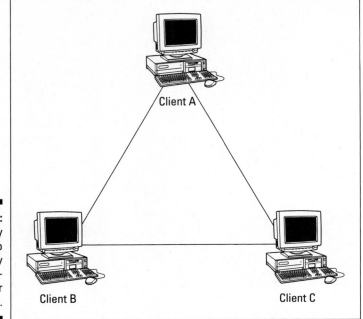

Figure 1-2:
Everybody
talks to
everybody
in a peer-
to-peer
network.

Windows has built-in support for peer-to-peer networks. In fact, this book is really about creating a peer-to-peer network in your home.

With a peer-to-peer network, as long as your network is composed of computers running Windows XP and Windows Vista, you can impose all the security features you want to. You can control files, Windows utilities, and all the other uses of a computer that might be dangerous for some users to access.

Mixed networks fit all types

Just so that you don't think the computer world is rigid, I'll point out that some networks are both client/server and peer-to-peer at the same time. Users log on to the network server and then use it to access software and store the documents that they create. Because the peer-to-peer network is built into the operating system, users can also transfer files from other clients and access printers connected to other clients. A mixed network is the best-of-all-worlds scenario for many businesses.

The Nuts and Bolts of Hardware

To create a network, the primary hardware device that you need is a *network adapter,* also called a *network interface card (NIC).* A NIC must be installed in each computer on the network. It's actually the NICs (not the computer boxes) that are connected to create a network. NICs are traditionally connected via cable. I say *traditionally* because wireless solutions are also available for small networks, and you may prefer to take that route.

Also, even though the term NIC is still commonly used, not all network interface devices are cards anymore. Today, you can connect a network interface adapter device to a *Universal Serial Bus (USB).* However, because of the widespread use of the jargon *NIC,* I use that term generically throughout the book.

The only rule for creating a network is that you must have a NIC in each computer. Beyond that, you have enough choices to make your head spin. I'll try to slow the spin rate by explaining the options before I drag you into the actual installation process (which you can find in Chapter 2).

NICs come in lots of flavors, and when you buy NICs, you must match them to two important elements:

✔ The type of network interface device that your computer accepts.

✔ The type of network cabling that you want to use. (See the section, "Connections: Cables, wires, and thin air," later in this chapter.)

Network connection types

Computers have one or more NICs built right into a chip on the motherboard. These built-in devices are called *embedded network cards* or *embedded network controllers.*

Although motherboard NICs are the most common type of network connections, you have several other options available.

USB Connectors

Most of today's computers come with a USB port (in fact, most come with a bunch of USB ports), and you can buy NICs that plug into a USB port. The best part of a USB connection is that you don't even have to open your computer because USB ports are external. Look for USB port connectors that look like those shown in Figure 1-3.

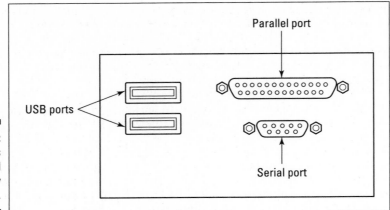

Figure 1-3:
USB ports
are identical
in every
computer.

USB connectors are available for all types of network cabling and wireless connections.

NIC Controller Cards

Another way to add a NIC to a computer is to install a card inside the computer, using a PCI slot (your computer has several PCI slots available for installing controllers). Follow the manufacturer's instructions for installing the hardware and drivers.

Connections: Cables, wires, and thin air

You have one more decision to make before you go shopping for your hardware — you have to choose a cabling system. Your decision affects not only the type of cable you buy, but also the type of NICs you buy. The NIC has a device that accepts the cable connector, so the NIC must be built specifically for the cable you choose.

You have several choices for cabling your computers into a network:

- ✔ Ethernet cable
- ✔ Telephone wires already in your house
- ✔ Electrical wires already in your house
- ✔ None (wireless connections)
- ✔ Mixed (using more than one type)

In the following discussions, I mention the speeds at which cable types transfer data among computers. Network speeds are rated in *megabits per second (Mbps)*. A *megabit* is a million binary pulses, and the best way to put that into perspective is to think about a modem. The fastest telephone modems are rated to transmit data at the rate of 56,000 bits per second (56 kilobits per second, or 56 Kbps).

Don't pooh-pooh the notion of speed; it is important. Everyone who uses computers changes his or her definition of the word *fast*. If you started using computers years ago, think about how fast the computer seemed at first, and then how impatient you became whenever you had to wait for a task to complete. Soon after, you bought a faster computer. Then you got over the feeling that this was the fastest machine you'd ever seen, and impatience set in again. Waiting a long time for a file to open in an application or for a file to be copied from one machine to another can drive you nuts.

Ethernet cable

Ethernet cable is the connection type of choice. It's fast, accurate, pretty much trouble-free, and simply the best. Ethernet can transfer data across the network at up to 1000 Mbps, depending on the rated speed of the NICs and the hub or switch. The commonly sold NICs and Ethernet cable operate at 100 Mbps. Most Ethernet equipment can determine the speed of individual devices on the network and automatically drop or raise the speed to match the device's capabilities.

Ethernet is the cable that you find in business networks. The commonly used variety of Ethernet cable is *twisted-pair cable* or *Category 5 UTP cable* (nicknamed *CAT-5*). Although Ethernet cable looks like telephone wire, it's not the same thing. Ethernet cable is designed to transmit data rather than voice. Using Ethernet cable requires the purchase of a *concentrator,* a device that collects all the Ethernet connections in one place. Concentrators are usually sold as devices called *hubs* or *switches.* All the network computers are connected to the concentrator, which distributes the data among the connected computers, as shown in Figure 1-4.

The connector at the end of the cable looks like the connector at the end of your telephone cable, but it's actually slightly fatter. The 10Base-T cable connectors are *RJ-45 connectors* (telephone connectors are *RJ-11 connectors*).

Telephone line cable

Telephone line cable is another option you can choose for wiring your home network. It transmits data at the rate of about 10 Mbps, which isn't nearly as fast as the speed of Ethernet cable. Telephone line networking is increasing in popularity, especially because most of the computer and device manufacturers have developed and accepted standards. Having standardized technology makes it easier to buy equipment; you know it all works together. You can find out more about the technology at www.homepna.org.

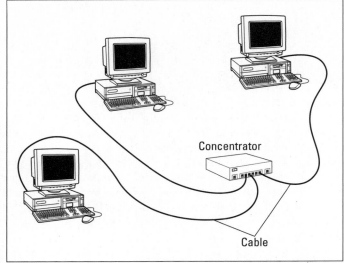

Figure 1-4:
Each
computer is
connected
to its own
port in the
concen-
trator.

Concentrator

Cable

To use telephone cable for home networks, you just connect a regular tele-phone cable between the telephone-cable NIC you install in your computer and the telephone wall jack. Telephone cable is inexpensive and available everywhere, including your local supermarket. The networking process uses a part of your telephone line that voice communication doesn't use, so your telephone lines are still available for normal household telephone use as well as for modem use.

You can use your wall jack for both a telephone and a network connection at the same time. You just have to adapt the wall jack so that it can do two things at once. Luckily, this is easy to do. You need to buy a *splitter* (the techy term is *modular duplex jack*), which is a little doohickey that you can buy for a couple of bucks just about anywhere — at an office supply store, one of those megastores, or even the supermarket. The splitter, shown in Figure 1-5, plugs into the wall jack to give you two places to plug in phone cables instead of just one. You plug the network cable into one connector and your tele-phone cable into the other connector. It doesn't matter which cable goes into which socket.

However, to avoid confusion, put some nail polish, a little sticky star, or some other add-on near the connector of your network connection cable so that you know which is which if you want to move the telephone.

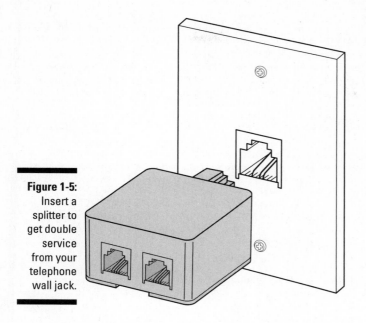

Figure 1-5:
Insert a
splitter to
get double
service
from your
telephone
wall jack.

For shared Internet access, only one computer on the network needs to have a modem. If the computer that's hosting the shared Internet access has an external modem, follow these steps:

1. **Plug the splitter into the telephone wall jack.**

2. **Plug the modem, not the telephone, into the second side of the splitter (the network line is on the other side).**

3. **Plug the telephone into the appropriate connector on the modem.**

   Now you have three devices on your telephone jack: a network connection, a modem, and a telephone.

If the computer that's hosting the shared Internet access has an internal modem, you need a *Y-connector,* which is an adapter that looks like the capital letter *Y.* The bottom of the connector, where the two sides of the Y meet, plugs into the wall jack (to join the network). The two ends of the Y plug into the modem and the NIC (it doesn't matter which connector goes into which device). (There's no room on this setup for a telephone.)

If you have multiple telephone lines in your house, all the computers on your network must be connected through the same telephone line (telephone number). Computers can't communicate across different telephone lines. (Your regular telephone service can't do this either. For example, if someone is talking on line 1, you can't pick up a telephone connected to line 2 and eavesdrop, er, I mean, join the conversation.)

Here are a couple of drawbacks to using telephone wiring:

✔ Every computer must be near a telephone jack. Very few households have a telephone jack in every room, so this may limit your choices for computer placement.

✔ The maximum distance between any two computers is about 1,000 feet, but unless you live in the White House, that shouldn't be a major problem.

Electrical wires

You can network your computers with electrical line connections that work by plugging the manufacturer's network adapter device into the power outlet on the wall. The device has an attached cable that connects to the computer. Today, most of the electrical-wire network-connection hardware is designed for a USB port. Electrical-wire networking operates at about 10 Mbps. Some network equipment manufacturers use the term *powerline* instead of electrical wire.

I'm not kidding when I say *wall outlet device.* Plugging the network adapter into a power strip doesn't work.

Here's the other stuff you need to know about powerline networking:

✔ **Um, where do you plug it in?** If your house is like most houses, only one wall outlet is near the computer, and you're already using both plugs: one for the computer and one for the monitor. Most manufacturers of electrical line networking hardware supply a special power strip into which you can plug your computer and monitor. You can plug that power strip into the plug on the wall outlet that the network device isn't using.

✔ **How friendly do you want to be with your neighbor?** I could get into all the gory details about hubs and transformers and radio waves, but I'll cut to the bottom line: If your neighbor has a home network that's connected through electrical wires, your neighbor may be able to access your network because you probably share the same transformer. That's

either terribly convenient or terribly scary, depending on your relationship with your neighbor. But, to resolve this problem, the network equipment manufacturers provide software to help guard your system against
unauthorized users. That software requires a separate installation and
configuration process, which must be repeated whenever you add a
computer to your network. It's quick and easy to install, so be sure to
use it!

Wireless connections for the cable-phobic

Generally, people choose wireless connections because they're willing to give
up the speed and reliability of Ethernet (or phone line or powerline) to avoid
dealing with cable. This attitude comes from one of two motivations (or, in
some cases, both of two motivations): They don't want to go through the
effort of pulling cable through the house, or they hate the sight of the cable
because it doesn't match their decorating scheme. When installing home networks, my experience has been that the man of the house loves the "fun" of
pulling cable through the building, and the woman of the house says "ugh,
ugly."

If you opt for wireless technology, you'll be working with *radio frequency (RF)*
communication technology. Some manufacturers offer *infrared (IR)* network
communication technology devices, but I don't recommend them. In fact,
except for the next section that explains why I don't recommend them, I
won't mention IR again in this book.

Infrared wireless connections

Infrared (IR) technology works by creating a direct signal, via a light beam,
between computers. Your TV remote control (the frequently used technical
jargon for that device is *clicker*) uses IR technology; you have a little red
square on the remote control device and a red square on the television set or
cable box. You point one little red square at the other square to use the
device. This means you can't select a channel using the remote control if
you're holding it while you're in the kitchen and the television set is in the
living room.

Computer IR networking works the same way. The infrared connectors must
"see" each other, which limits IR networks to those that have all the computers in the same room. Also, one computer can't make a straight-line connection with two other computers at the same time, so if your network has more
than two computers, you have to buy additional IR hardware devices that collect and bounce the IR signals around the room.

One problem I've encountered during my tests of IR connections is that bright sunlight interferes with the signal. You need opaque window coverings if you want to go with IR connections unless you plan to use your computers only at night. On top of all of those inconveniences, IR connections are slow.

'Nuff said.

Radio frequency wireless connections

Radio frequency (RF) technology isn't new; it has been around for a long time. I used it when I was a child (many eons ago) for walkie-talkie conversations with friends in the neighborhood. You probably use it today to open and close your garage door or to connect windows on upper floors to your household security system. I used to use it to unlock my car door, but I learned to hate the beeps, and I set off my car alarm system so often that I had the whole system disabled.

Here are some things to consider about RF network connections:

✔ They require a network adapter that's specific to RF technology, which means the adapter has to be equipped with the devices necessary to transmit and receive RF signals. Today, all network device manufacturers make RF devices, and the NICs are available for motherboards (you have to install them in the PCI slots inside the computer), USB ports, and PC Cards for laptops.

✔ The RF signals can usually travel about 150 feet, passing through walls, ceilings, and floors. This distance should be sufficient for most home network schemes, but the actual distance that you can achieve may vary from manufacturer to manufacturer. If you need greater distance, you can often extend the signal by placing a special box called an *access point* in a central location.

✔ The only things that can stop the RF signal dead in its tracks are metal and large bodies of water. Although you may think that only means you can't use RF technology in your castle with an iron drawbridge and moat, think again. Putting the computer (with its RF technology device attached) under a metal desk can interfere with transmission. A wall that has a lot of metal plumbing pipes can also keep computers from communicating. The only problem with large bodies of water I can think of are those that crop up if you've installed a pond or swimming pool in your den, or if you're trying to communicate between two submarines or from an underwater office in a Sea World type of amusement park.

When I was testing RF technology, several manufacturers assured me that the 150-foot limit applies only indoors and that most RF devices can achieve far greater distances with no walls or floors in their way. Uh huh, thanks. I'll appreciate that in the summer when I move all my computers onto my lawn or take them to a park. And, I've never seen an RF network that achieved anywhere near 150 feet of signal; you can count on about a third of that distance.

✔ You may experience interference from cell phones, pagers, home alarm systems, microwave ovens, and other wireless devices frequently found in your neighborhood. If those RF devices are properly shielded, however, you shouldn't have any problems. The newer RF devices, based on newer RF technical standards, eliminate a lot of the annoyances of interference.

✔ Technically, anyone with a computer equipped with RF technology can "join" your network without your knowledge. A neighbor or stranger could come within 150 feet of your house with a laptop, find the right frequency, and copy any files he finds. For security, some manufacturers of RF networking kits have built in a clever design feature that slows malevolent outsiders who are trying to grab your frequency and get into your system — the frequency changes periodically.

The RF signal that's sent and received across the network moves up and down within a given range (the technology is called *frequency hopping*), and this happens often enough to make it difficult to latch on to the current frequency — as soon as someone gets a bead on it, it moves.

By the way, the idea of frequency hopping for security comes from an invention and a patent that are credited to composer George Antheil and actress Hedy Lamarr. (Is anyone besides me old enough to remember her?)

Frequency hopping also acts as a performance enhancer. The speed is improved because you're effectively transmitting across a wider spectrum.

Saving Time, Trouble, and Money When You Buy Hardware

A slew of manufacturers make the equipment that you need to build your network, and you should make your purchasing decisions with an eye on both reliability and price.

Throughout the book, I mention some places to go for general research as you do your homework, as well as some places to buy equipment that I think provide good prices and service. None of these outlets knows that I'm telling you about this, so they aren't paying me any commission or giving me special treatment in exchange for telling you about them. I'm just one of those people who can't resist giving specific advice (which, as all parents know, doesn't work well with children, but I don't expect readers to respond with "Oh, Motherrrrr," and leave the room). You may discover resources that I don't mention here, and my omission isn't significant. It just means that I didn't know about (or knew about but didn't remember) that resource.

Doing your homework: Just like being in school

Making decisions about hardware, cable types, and other networking gizmos without first doing some homework is foolish. You're going to live with your decisions for a long time. In fact, everybody in the household will have to live with your decisions, so to avoid listening to gripes later, get everyone to help in the decision-making process. Home networking is a hot topic, and computer experts have been testing technologies and reporting their findings. Use their expertise to gain knowledge and then discuss your findings with the rest of the family. You can find reviews of the pros and cons of networking schemes in the following places:

- ✔ **Start with any friends, relatives, or neighbors who are computer geeks.** All computer geeks are used to this treatment; people ask us for free advice at dinner parties, while we're in line at the movie theater, and almost anywhere else. Do what most people do — call the geek and pretend it's a social call. Then, after you ask, "How are you?" and before the geek has a chance to answer that question, ask your technical questions. (This is how most people interact with their computer-savvy friends.)

- ✔ **Paw through newsstands, especially those in bookstores.** You can find an enormous array of computer magazines on the shelves. Look for magazines that fit your situation. For example, a computer magazine named *Programming Tricks for C++* is probably less suitable than *Home PC Magazine.* Look for *PC World, PC Magazine,* and other similar publications. If the current issue doesn't have an article on home networking, check the masthead (the page where all the editors are listed) to see where you can call or write to ask for specific issues.

- ✔ **Search the Internet for articles and advice.** Type **home networking** into any search box, and you'll probably find that the number of results is overwhelming. If that approach seems onerous, try some of these popular sites that surely have the information you're seeking: www. pcworld.com, www.zdnet.com, or www.cnet.com. These sites all have search features, so you can find information easily. They also have reviews, technical advice, and "best buy" lists.

Plunking down the money: Tips for buying

After you decide which type of hardware and cabling you want to use for your home network, you need to buy the stuff. You can buy kits or individual components, and many people buy both. Your cost should be less than $60 per computer to create your network.

Most manufacturers offer kits, which is a way to buy everything you need at once. Here are some things to keep in mind before you buy a kit:

✔ **Most kits are designed for a two-computer network.** If you have a third computer, just buy the additional components individually. Some manufacturers make four-computer and five-computer kits.

✔ **Kits aren't necessary if one of your computers has a built-in network adapter.** Most computer manufacturers sell computers that are already set up with network hardware (usually with an Ethernet NIC).

In Table 1-1, I list some reliable manufacturers of networking products.

Table 1-1	Network Connection Manufacturers
Manufacturer	*Web Site*
3Com	www.3com.com
Belkin	www.belkin.com
D-Link	www.dlink.com
Intel	www.intel.com
Intellon	www.intellon.com
Linksys	www.linksys.com
Netgear	www.netgear.com

Even if you buy a kit, you may also have to buy individual components. Perhaps you have three computers, or maybe one of the Ethernet cables in the kit isn't long enough to reach the computer on the second floor. After you measure the distances, figure out where the available ports are, and do all the rest of your research, you may find that buying individual components is the only approach you can take. A plan that doesn't match a kit isn't uncommon, and kits are really a convenience, not a money-saver. Most people find that buying individual components costs about the same as buying kits.

Every retail computer store sells hardware components for all types of network connections, and your city or town probably has many small independent computer stores in addition to major chains such as CompUSA. Most appliance retailers (Circuit City, Best Buy, and others) also carry computer networking equipment, and so do office-supply stores (Staples, Office Max, and others). Even some of the warehouse outlets carry networking equipment. On the Internet, visit www.cdw.com and www.buy.com to find good deals on networking hardware.

Be sure you know an online merchant's return policy before you purchase. And, be sure that the Web site is secure before you give out your credit card number. When you're on a secure Web site, the address bar displays https:// instead of http:// (the *s* is for *secure*). Furthermore, at the bottom of your browser window, you should see an icon that looks like a closed lock.

Chapter 2

Installing Network Adapters

● ●

In This Chapter

▶ Hooking up external network adapters

▶ Installing adapters on laptops

▶ Troubleshooting adapters

● ●

After you decide what type of connection to use (I'm rooting for Ethernet; I don't see any reason to compromise on speed and performance), you need to install the hardware that enables the network connection. This task must be performed on every computer on the network.

If your computer came with a network adapter, you don't have to install one as long as you're using the connection type that adapter is built for. For example, if your computer has an Ethernet adapter, but you want to have a wireless network, you have to bypass (ignore) the built-in adapter and install a wireless adapter.

It's Okay to Mix and Match NICs

Every computer on your network doesn't have to have the same type of network interface card (NIC) connection. Although you must use an Ethernet NIC for all the computers that are being connected with Ethernet cable, you can use a USB NIC on one computer and an internal NIC in another computer. To understand this, you have to understand the difference between network connection type and network device connection types:

✔ The *network connection type* is the network wiring type, as in Ethernet, phone line, wireless, and so on.

✔ The *network device connection type* is the way the NIC connects to the computer. Your choices are internal, USB, and PC Card (for laptops).

Adding USB Connectors — Easy as Pie

If you purchased a kit or an individual connector that is designed to work with a Universal Serial Bus (USB) port, installation is a snap. You don't even have to turn off the computer. Just push the USB end of the cable into your USB port (see Figure 2-1).

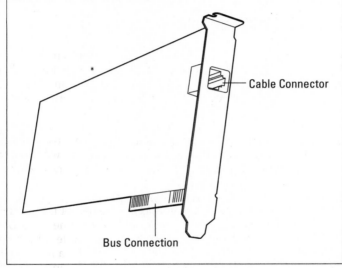

Cable Connector

Bus Connection

Figure 2-1:
Your USB network device has a cable connector for the USB port.

You may decide to add a USB hub to your USB port, especially if you attach (or intend to attach) several peripheral devices to a computer. *USB hubs* are hardware devices that enable you to add USB peripherals when you run out of USB ports. (Some users have more USB devices than their computers will support.) The hub holds additional USB ports.

Some hubs plug into an electrical outlet so they provide their own power instead of grabbing power from the computer, and this is important if your hub has printers, scanners, or other "power pig" devices. One end of the hub looks like the regular USB connector, and this end goes into the USB port on your computer. The other end of the hub is a set of USB connectors that are waiting to receive connections from USB devices.

If your computer is running when you connect the cable to the USB port, the operating system notices what you did and immediately displays a message offering to complete the software side of the installation of your network device. That means special driver files that control your use of the device are automatically set up in your computer (if Windows has built-in drivers for your device).

Consult the documentation that came with your USB adapter to see if Windows has the drivers — if not, the package has a CD that contains the drivers, and instructions for installing them are in the package, too.

Installing Laptop Adapters

Why should desktop computers have all the fun? Laptop network adapters let you add your laptop computer to your home network. Most laptops have USB ports, so if that's the method you want to use to connect your laptop to your network, follow the instructions in the previous section to attach the USB network adapter.

If your laptop doesn't have USB ports, or you're already using the USB ports for other things, you can use a PC Card network adapter, which is sometimes called a PCMCIA network adapter. (*PCMCIA* stands for Personal Computer Memory Card International Association.)

The PC Card is about the size of a credit card. One end of the card is the *external* side. That side has a device that provides a connection for the network, in the form of an RJ-45 connector for Ethernet cable. The other end of the card, the *internal* side, has a row of 68 tiny holes. By a fortunate coincidence, the back of the PC Card slot in the laptop has 68 tiny pins. An arrow on the card indicates which way to plug it into the PC Card slot so that the holes meet the pins inside the slot (see Figure 2-2).

Figure 2-2:
PC Cards
are clearly
marked so
that you
know how
to insert
them.

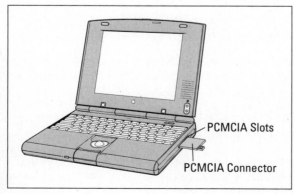

PCMCIA Slots

PCMCIA Connector

Push the card into the slot firmly. When the card is fully engaged, a little button next to the slot pops out — you press the button when you want to eject the card (the same way a floppy drive works). Your laptop probably has two PC Card slots, one on top of the other. The slots are usually on the side of the computer, hidden behind a flip-down cover that protects both slots.

Unless the documentation for your laptop has instructions to the contrary, it doesn't matter which slot you use for your adapter.

If you turned off your computer before you inserted the PC Card, when you restart the computer, Windows notices the new hardware device. Use the documentation that came with your network adapter as a reference and walk through the wizard that installs the driver for your PC Card. If you didn't turn off the computer, follow the directions in the documentation to install the drivers.

Troubleshooting Network Adapters

Sometimes adapters don't work properly (or at all). In this section, I go over the common adapter problems and their solutions. Some of these problems may not show up until after you've completed the configuration of your adapter (covered in Chapter 6). The problems and possible solutions presented here are for trouble that's specific to adapters, not general network communications problems. For example, a failure to communicate may be the result of incorrect network settings, not the result of a problem with the physical adapter.

No adapter icon on the taskbar

You can display an icon for your network adapter on the taskbar (on the right side, where the time appears, which is called the *notification area* of the taskbar). The icon is handy because you can click it to open the adapter's Properties dialog box (instead of using all the steps required to get to it through Control Panel). In addition, the taskbar icon displays error messages when a problem arises and displays reassuring messages when everything is fine ("Status: Connected").

Windows Vista permanently plants an icon for your adapter on the taskbar, but if you're running Windows XP, you may not see one. You can change that by opening the adapter's Properties dialog box and selecting the option to display the icon. Use the following steps to get to the Properties dialog box in Windows XP:

1. **Choose Start➪Control Panel➪Network and Internet Connections➪Network Connections.**

2. **Right-click the listing for Local Area Connection and choose Properties.**

   The Properties dialog box opens.

3. **Select both options at the bottom of the dialog box by clicking the check boxes to insert check marks (see Figure 2-3).**

   This action puts an icon on your taskbar and also tells Windows to display messages above the icon if something is amiss.

Figure 2-3:
Enable the
taskbar icon
so you can
keep an
eye on the
health
of your
network
connection.

4. **Click OK.**

Two adapter icons?

I get a great many calls and e-mail messages from people who say they have two adapters listed in Control Panel (and two icons on their taskbars).

If you're using Internet Connection Sharing (ICS) to share a DSL or cable modem that's attached to a computer (instead of using a router), the computer that has the modem is supposed to have two adapters. One adapter is connected to the modem with Ethernet cable, and the other adapter is connected to the network with the type of wiring you've chosen for your network.

If you're not using ICS, you don't need two adapters, but you probably have two adapters connected to your computer. This is common when your computer has a built-in adapter (usually Ethernet), and you installed an adapter for another type of connection (such as wireless). You can disable the unneeded connection and its icon:

✔ In Windows Vista, click the taskbar icon and choose Network and Sharing Center. In the Network and Sharing Center window, click the View Status button next to the connection you want to disable and then click Disable.

✔ In Windows XP, click the taskbar icon to open its Status dialog box and then click Disable.

If you use a PC Card on a laptop that's displaying two adapters, and you're absolutely sure there is no built-in adapter, the problem is that you don't use the same PC Card slot every time you insert your adapter.

Windows treats each PC Card slot as a unique device, with its own hardware identification, and it retains information on inserted devices even when they're no longer inserted. If you open Device Manager and examine the hardware properties of both adapters, you'll find that one adapter is displaying an error indicating that it's not connected (for a wired network) or indicating that no signal can be found (for a wireless network).

It's perfectly safe to ignore the duplicate connections because the PC Card that's inserted will work properly. If the situation bothers you, just remember to use the same PC Card slot every time you insert the adapter. Then disable or remove the other connection by using the directions earlier in this section.

Cable Unplugged error

Your adapter icon may display an error indicating that a network cable is unplugged. The error may be in a balloon over the taskbar icon (which probably has a red X on top of it), as shown in Figure 2-4, or in the status message that's displayed when you select the adapter in Control Panel.

Figure 2-4:
An unplugged cable means a problem.

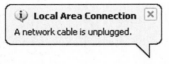

ⓘ **Local Area Connection** ✕
A network cable is unplugged.

Of course, the first thing to do is check the cable connection on the adapter. Even if the cable appears to be connected, give it a push to make sure it's plugged in properly. If that connection is good, check the connection at the concentrator (hub, switch, or router).

If the connections seem to be okay, move the connector to another port on the concentrator. Unplug a cable you know is working (because the computer it's connected to isn't displaying an error message), and plug the cable from the errant computer into that port. If that works, the port is bad on the concentrator. A bad port almost always means the concentrator is having a problem that will soon spread to the other ports (which translates to "you need a new concentrator").

If changing the port doesn't work, change the cable. Run another cable between the computer and the concentrator. If that works, toss the old cable in the trash.

If neither of those steps cures the problem, the adapter is probably bad and needs to be replaced. If your warranty is still in effect, contact the manufacturer for a replacement. Otherwise, disable the connection and buy a replacement NIC (make it a USB device so you don't have to open the computer to install it).

No Signal Can Be Found error

For a wireless adapter, the error No Signal Can Be Found is the equivalent of the Ethernet "Cable Unplugged" error. It means the adapter can't find the network.

Start by checking around the computer (and its adapter) for interference. Is the computer near metal (such as a file cabinet) or a cordless phone base unit? If so, move the computer to see if the adapter can find the signal.

The problem may be distance or interference you can't easily see (such as metal in the walls). To determine if this is your difficulty, try moving the computer into the same room as the access point or router (routers have access points built in). If the signal is restored, move back toward your original computer location in small increments. When you lose the signal, you know you're past the point of connectivity and you must relocate the computer.

If you can't get a signal anywhere, and you know the adapter's settings and your network configuration are correct, your adapter is probably bad. If it's under warranty, arrange for a replacement; otherwise, buy another one (the good news is that the replacement will be cheaper than the original adapter because computers and computer peripherals just keep getting cheaper).

Chapter 3

Installing Ethernet Cable

- -

- -

*I*nstalling Ethernet network interface cards (NICs) provides only half the connections needed for computer-to-computer communication. Now you need to let the NICs communicate with each other. You accomplish this connection via Ethernet cable. In this chapter, I tell you everything you need to know to connect NICs using Ethernet cable. When you're finished, you have the fastest, most reliable network connectivity available.

Ready, Set, Run

The way cable is strung through a building is called a *run,* and your plan for running the cable depends on how easily you can string the cable between the computers and the concentrator. Your run is actually a series of runs because each computer must be individually attached to the concentrator. (The *concentrator* is the device that holds all the connections and provides the conversation pit for your computers; it can be a hub, a switch, or a router.)

Ethernet cable has many aliases

Ethernet cable comes in many forms, but today's standard cable for home networks is CAT-5 or CAT-5e (the *e* stands for *Enhanced*). CAT-5 is short for *Category 5 twisted-pair cable*. (Categories run from CAT-1 through CAT-6.)

CAT-5 cable is also called *twisted-pair cable* because the cable's wires are twisted along the length of the cable (see Figure 3-1).

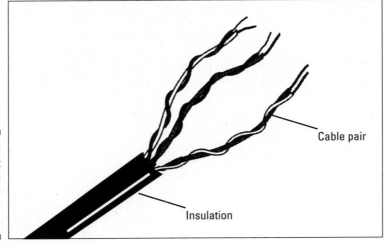

Cable pair

Insulation

Figure 3-1:
Ethernet
cable is
also called
twisted-
pair cable.

Other terminology used to describe Ethernet cable includes the names
10Base-T and *100Base-T, which* are derived as follows:

- ✔ **10 or 100:** This part of the name represents the speed of data transmission in megabits (a megabit is a million bits). Until a few years ago, 10Base-T was the standard, but today, 100Base-T is the lower standard, and 1000 Mbps (also called *gigabit*) is becoming popular (and requires CAT-5e to take advantage of the speed). The Ethernet hardware devices (NICs, hubs, and switches) are rated for speed; older devices support 10-megabit transmissions, while newer devices support 100-megabit or 1000-megabit transmissions. Most concentrators can auto-detect the speed of the other hardware on the network and adjust transmission speed so all the hardware can communicate.

- ✔ **Base:** This stands for *baseband signaling,* which means that only Ethernet signals are carried on the cable. Ethernet does not share its cable bandwidth the way telephone cable and electric cable do.

- ✔ **T:** This code identifies the physical medium that carries the signal as copper. 100Base-F, for example, is fiber optic cable.

CAT-5 and CAT-5e cable come in two types:

- ✔ Unshielded twisted-pair (UTP)
- ✔ Shielded twisted-pair (STP)

The difference between the two types is pretty obvious — shielded twisted-pair cable has a shield. The *shield* is made of metal and encases the wires, reducing the possibility of interference from other electrical devices (radar, radio waves, and so on).

I'm not aware of a great difference in performance between UTP and STP cable. UTP is less expensive, and almost all the CAT-5/5e cable in use is UTP. The only time I've ever installed STP is at client sites in towns that required STP for certain types of cable runs (for instance, if you're running cable through a ceiling that also contains other wiring). If you think the building codes in your town may require STP for the way you're planning to run your cable, check with the local authorities.

Both UTP and STP cable are available in fixed lengths, or *patches*. At either end of the cable is an *RJ-45 connector,* which you use to connect the computers in your network to the *concentrator,* or hub, of the home network.

Networking consultants buy big rolls of cable, cut each run to the appropriate length, and make their own connectors. That's more work than running precut cable lengths that already have connectors attached.

Concerning the concentrator

All the lengths of cable share the same home base, a concentrator, which is either a *hub* or a *switch* (routers have switches built in, so if you're using your router as a concentrator, you have a switch). Each cable run goes from the concentrator to a computer (or from a computer to the concentrator, depending on how you like to envision it).

At each end of a length of cable is a connector called an *RJ-45 connector.* One connector attaches to the concentrator, and the other connector attaches to the NIC in a computer.

When you purchase a concentrator, you have a choice between buying a hub or a switch. The difference between them is the way they send data to computers — the switch takes a more intelligent approach. When data is transmitted across the network, the ID of the target (receiving) computer is identified within the data packet. A hub ignores the computer ID and sends the data to all the computers on the network. The computers check the computer ID, and the computer that's supposed to receive the data accepts it; the other computers ignore it. However, the hub has to split up the bandwidth to send the data to all the computers, so the transmission speed to each individual computer is reduced. A switch notices which computer ID is the target of the data transmission and sends the data only to that computer, using all the available bandwidth for the transmission.

One of the ports on a hub or a switch may differ from the others, although it looks the same. That port is an *uplink port,* and you don't use it to connect a computer to the hub. Instead, this port has a special use (see the section "Curing Your Network's Growing Pains," later in this chapter). Look for an icon or label to identify the uplink port, or read the documentation that came with the hub so that you know which port to avoid.

The network arrangement shown in Figure 3-2 is called a *star topology*, although I'm not sure how that name was developed. Personally, I think the resemblance to a star is a little obscure. Perhaps *wheel spokes* is a more accurate description — which would explain the use of the word *hub* (as in the hub of a wheel).

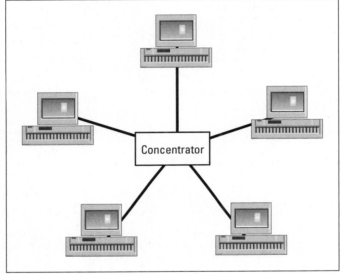

Figure 3-2:
Notice the multiple cable runs from the concentrator to each computer in an Ethernet network.

Deciding Where to Put the Concentrator

The concentrator is the core of the network; everything travels to it (and flows from it). You should place the concentrator in a location that reduces the amount of cable you need to schlep through the house. For example, a reasonably logical person can count on the following scenarios:

 ✔ If you have two computers on the second floor and one on the first floor, putting the concentrator on the second floor means you'll have only one long cable run.

 ✔ If all your computers are on one floor, the logical place for the concentrator is at a midpoint among all the computers.

 ✔ If the same number of computers are on the first floor as are on the second floor, find a location that's as close as possible to being equidistant from each computer.

Where you decide to locate the concentrator requires a couple of other important considerations, so logical thinking doesn't always work (much like applying logical thinking to politics or economic theories, or to guessing what "that look" on your spouse's face really means). The following sections help you work through the not-so-logical considerations you need to take into account.

Concentrators are environmentally fussy

Concentrators have some environmental requirements, and if you don't cater to them, your concentrator will probably get sick and may even die. To ensure that your concentrator is in the correct environment, do the following:

- **Provide good air quality.** After you connect the cables, you don't have to manage the concentrator — no baby-sitting is required. That means you can tuck it away somewhere, but you must provide a dry (not humid), dust-free environment.

- **Avoid covering the concentrator.** Don't place it in a drawer, and don't wrap it in plastic to avoid dust — it needs circulating air to prevent overheating.

- **Avoid excessive heat.** Keep the concentrator away from direct sunlight, radiators, heaters, and any other heat sources.

- **Avoid proximity to other electrical devices.** Don't put the concentrator next to fluorescent lights, radios, or transmitting equipment.

Concentrators are innately powerless

Ethernet concentrators require electrical power, so they must be located near an electrical outlet. Unless you want to do some fancy electrical work (or you don't mind the cable(s) keeping you from closing the closet door all the way), a closet — which otherwise would be a great location to hide a concentrator — won't work because there is usually no electrical outlet nearby.

Keep your concentrator plugged into a surge protector. Plug the surge protector into a wall outlet and then plug the concentrator into the surge protector. Surges travel rapidly through cable, and when they do, they zap everything in the cable's path. A good surge can take out every NIC on the network. A *really* strong surge can push the damage past the NIC and fry the computer's motherboard. (Remember, every NIC is connected to the cable, and every NIC is also connected to its motherboard.)

Distance Depends on What You Choose to Measure

Your cable run has to connect every computer to the concentrator, but you can only buy patch cable in specific lengths. The longer the cable, the more you pay. Ethernet networking kits have one piece of cable for each connector in the kit, and each piece of cable is the same length (usually 20 or 25 feet). Given these facts, the word *epicenter* becomes meaningless. For example, if the midpoint between two computers is a distance of 28 feet, and you have two 25-foot lengths of cable, put the concentrator within 25 feet of one computer so that you only have to buy one longer cable.

Cable doesn't run from the concentrator to a computer in a straight line. It runs along baseboards, through walls, across ceilings, and sometimes even runs along *all* of these conduits. You can't really measure the amount of cable you'll need between the concentrator and a computer with an "as the crow flies" mentality. The only way to measure properly (and therefore buy the right cable lengths) is to read the sections on running cable later in this chapter. Then, depending on the way you run your cable, you'll have an idea of the length of cable you'll need to connect each computer to the concentrator.

The maximum length of a single Ethernet cable run is 100 meters, which is about 328 feet. After that, the data transfer rate degrades or disappears.

You may have to account for traveling up walls as well as placing the cable across walls, ceilings, or floors. And of course, don't make your measurements too fine — you need to account for some slack. After all, why would you want the cable to come out of the wall in a straight line to the computer? You would have to leap over the cable to cross the room.

In the end, what you're looking for is a location for the concentrator that requires as few very long cable lengths as possible. Make these considerations:

- ✔ You're most likely to end up with a concentrator that is very near two computers while being very far from the third computer. In the long run (yeah, the pun was intended), you'll end up saving money, time, and hassle if you accept this fact right now.

- ✔ Find a way to position the concentrator near the conduit you're using for the cable run (you may decide to run cable through a wall or a ceiling, or along baseboards). If the cables from all your computers come out of a wall, put the concentrator very close to the wall to avoid the need for longer cables. Some concentrators come with devices that permit wall mounting so that the concentrator doesn't take up table or shelf space.

Handling Cable Correctly

Be careful about the way you handle cable as you run it through the chase. (A *chase* is the opening through which you place the cable, like inside a wall, in a hollow space above the ceiling, or along the baseboards of a room.) Keep the following tips in mind:

- **The bigger the hole (within reason), the better.** When you drill holes to run cable between rooms or floors, make the holes slightly larger than the connector at the end of the cable. Connectors are delicate, so you don't want to force-feed them through small openings.

- **Keep everything neat, just like your mother taught you.** When you run cable from the entry point in the room (the entrance hole) to the computer, snake the run along the baseboard or the top of the quarter round until you're close to the computer. Keeping the cable tucked off to the side helps to ensure that no one trips over the cable.

- **Be nice to the cable.** Avoid bending cable at a sharp angle. If you have to run the cable around a corner, don't pull it taut.

- **When in doubt, staple like a madman.** You can use cable staples, which are U-shaped nails that act like staples, to attach cable to a surface. Use cable staples that are large enough to surround the cable — do not insert them into the cable.

- **Use an artist's touch.** You can paint the cable to match your baseboard or wall, but don't paint the concentrator.

Connecting two patch cables

If you need a longer piece of cable, you can connect two pieces of patch cable with a coupler. A *coupler* is a small plastic device with two receptacles (one at each end) that accept RJ-45 connectors — you end a cable run in one receptacle and begin the next piece of cable in the other receptacle. This works just like the similar extension device for telephone lines.

Couplers don't have a terrific history of reliability. Frequently, when you encounter problems with computer-to-computer communication, the blame falls on these connections. Never put a coupler inside a wall or in any other location that's hard to reach because you need easy access to the coupler if you have to check or replace the connection. The best plan is to use a coupler as a temporary solution while you wait for delivery of a custom-made patch cable that's the correct length.

Even though couplers work similarly to telephone-extension devices, do not use a telephone coupler for your computer cable.

Making your own patch cables

If you know you have a big networking job ahead of you, you can save a lot of money by making your own patch cables. You can make your own by taking CAT-5/5e cable, cutting the right length, and attaching an RJ-45 connector to each end. This process is rather easy — I can barely change a light bulb, but I've been making my own cable connectors for years. To make your own patch cables, you need cable, RJ-45 connectors, a wire stripper, and a crimper to seat the connection properly.

You can buy bulk cable inexpensively — a 300-foot roll of cable costs about the same as two 50-foot patch cables. If you buy a larger roll of bulk cable, the price per foot is even lower (sell what you don't use to a neighbor who is installing a home network).

The RJ-45 connectors cost a few pennies each, but you'll probably have to buy at least a 20-pack — I've never seen them sold individually. Buying a crimper should set you back less than $100, and a wire stripper costs a few dollars.

Of course, you can make your investment in these supplies pay off by hiring yourself out to install cabled networks for your friends and neighbors.

To make a patch cable, follow these steps:

1. **Cut the length of cable you need.**

   Don't forget to account for climbing up or down walls, running along baseboards, and allowing slack.

2. **Use the stripper to remove about half an inch of insulation from the end of the cable.**

3. **Push the wires into the holes on the RJ-45 connector.**

   You'll find they slide in easily.

4. **Position the crimper where the wires meet the connector and press firmly.**

   Most crimpers come with instructions, including illustrations, to explain exactly how to crimp the connector. Most crimpers can handle a variety of connector sizes (for example, your crimper can also probably make regular telephone wire connectors, called *RJ-11* connectors), so make sure you use the position marked for RJ-45 connectors.

5. **Repeat Steps 2 through 4 for the other end of the cable.**

The Chase Is On: Running the Cable

The permutations and combinations of runs depend on the physical layout of your home, of course, but the ideal way to run cable in your home is to find a way to lay the cable in a straight line between the concentrator and each computer on the network. Sounds easy, doesn't it? Good luck! The opening through which you wind and wend the cable is called a *chase*. The chase may be inside a wall, in a hollow space above the ceiling, along the baseboards of a room, or in a combination of these opportunities. If you're lucky, you can find a straight-line chase between the concentrator and each computer.

Cabling within a room

If you put the concentrator in the same room as one of the computers (or if all the computers on your network are in the same room), you don't need to drill holes in walls or floors. Put the concentrator next to one computer. Connect the closest computer to the concentrator with a short length of cable. Then run a longer piece of cable from the concentrator to the other computer(s). Run the cable along the baseboard, not across the floor.

Cabling between adjacent rooms

Cabling your network is easy if your computers are located in adjacent rooms on the same floor because you only have to drill one hole between the rooms. Put the concentrator in one room and run one length of cable between the concentrator and the computer. Run another section of cable through the wall to the computer in the other room. You need to drill only one hole, as shown in Figure 3-3.

Cabling between nonadjacent rooms on the same floor

If your computers are on the same floor but aren't in adjacent rooms, you need to do a bit more work. The most direct and efficient cabling route is a chase along your home's beams. Most houses have beams between floors that run straight through the house, either from front to back, side to side, or both. You can usually expect a clear chase from one end to the other.

The logical way to access the chase is to drill a hole in the ceiling or floor (depending on whether the chase is above or below the level you're working on).

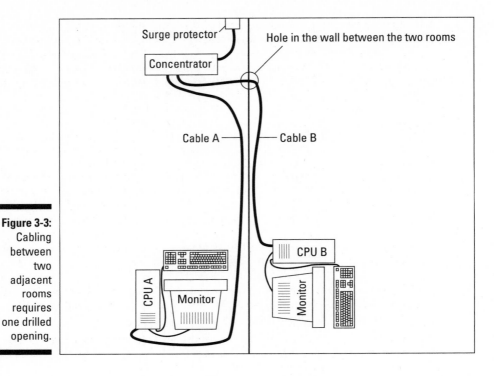

Figure 3-3:
Cabling
between
two
adjacent
rooms
requires
one drilled
opening.

I hate drilling holes in the ceiling because, to say the least, the blemish looks crummy. Even if I paint the cable to match the wall, I know it's there. Instead, I use closets or walls to get to the chase.

Keeping your drill holes in the closet

Wiring through closets is a great way to hide the side effects of cabling. If you have a closet in every room that holds a computer, you're in great shape. It's less important to clean up the hole and touch up the paint when you work in a closet, unless you're some kind of decorating fanatic. If every room doesn't have a closet, don't worry — you can still confine the cabling to the corners of the room.

Drill a hole in the closet ceiling or floor of each room that holds a computer (one room also holds the concentrator). Choose between the ceiling or the floor, depending on the location of the chase.

Bring the cable through the chase to each computer. You can use a *fish* (a tool specially designed for fishing cable that is sold in hardware stores) or a wire coat hanger you've untwisted (the hook at the end grabs the cable).

Of course, a portion of the cable has to run between the closet and the computer or concentrator. If you have enough clearance under the closet door, run the cable under the door and then attach it to the baseboard with U-shaped staples as it moves toward the computers. If you have no clearance under the closet door, drill a hole in the bottom of the doorjamb to bring the cable into the room.

Cable that's all walled up

For any room that lacks a closet, bring the cable into the room from the chase at a corner. If the cable enters the room through the ceiling from the chase above, bring the cable down the seam of the walls that create the corner (and paint the cable to match the wall). Then run the cable along the baseboard to the computer. If the cable enters the room through the floor from the chase below, run the cable along the baseboard to the computer.

Here are a couple of other schemes to consider if all your computers are on the same floor:

- ✔ If your computers are on the second floor, run the cable across the attic floor (or crawlspace above the second floor). Then you can drop the cable down a corner to each computer.

- ✔ If your computers are on the first floor, run the cable across the basement ceiling (or crawlspace). Then you can snake the cable up to each computer.

Cabling between Floors

If your computers are on different floors, you have more work to do. You need additional cable because your cable length measurement must include the height of the room in addition to the horizontal length required to reach the computer. Here are some tips on what to do if you have a multilevel home network on your hands:

- ✔ **Basement/second-floor room arrangement:** If you have one computer in the basement and another on the second floor, you need sufficient cable length to make the trip to the concentrator. Putting the concentrator on the first floor instead of next to one computer may be easier because you may have a problem finding cable that's long enough to span from the basement to the second floor.

- ✔ **Stacked room arrangement:** If the rooms are stacked one above the other, you can run the cable through the inside of the walls, near a corner. Use openings around accessible radiators and pipes, and use stacked closets when you can. If the stacked rooms occupy three levels, put the concentrator in the middle level. If you're moving between two floors, put the concentrator on either floor.

✔ **Kitty-corner room arrangement:** If the rooms are on opposite ends of the house, in addition to being on different floors (as far away from each other as humanly possible), you have to use both walls (or closets) and ceilings. For the vertical runs, use any openings around pipes that are available (houses with radiators usually have lots of space next to pipe runs). If no pipes are available, use the inside of the wall. For the horizontal runs, find a chase above or below the room.

Now, here are some bonus tips to help you run cable across multiple levels:

✔ **Use gravity to your advantage.** After you drill your holes and find the space in the wall or next to a pipe, work from the top down. Put a weight on the end of a sturdy piece of twine and drop it to the lower floor. Then tape the cable to the twine and haul the cable up. This way is much easier than pushing the cable up through the walls and using a fish to grab it from the top.

✔ **Use ducts if you can.** You can also use HVAC (heating, ventilation, and air conditioning) ducts, but you should be aware that many municipalities have strict rules about this choice. Some building codes forbid using HVAC ducts to run cable of any type; other building codes just set standards. The advantage of using HVAC ducts is that they go into every room, and they're usually rather wide. The disadvantage is that they rarely travel in a straight line, so you may have to run cable through several rooms to connect a computer to the concentrator. *Never* enter the duct system by drilling a hole. You must use existing entry and exit points, usually through the grate over the point at which the duct meets the wall.

✔ **Network everything.** Haul some electrical wire, regular telephone cable, and stereo speaker wire through the walls when you run your network cable. Later, if you want your electrician to add outlets for all the computer peripherals you'll probably accumulate, you want to add a phone jack, or you want to add speakers, most of the work is already done. In fact, if you bring several telephone wires along, you have a head start for installing a home security system or a home intercom system. If you think you'll be adding more computers in the future, haul extra lengths of Ethernet cable.

✔ **Consider getting more than one concentrator.** If you have a large amount of space to cover, you may actually save money on cable, not to mention saving yourself some trouble, if you use more than one concentrator. And you'll have a head start if you decide to add computers to your home network later. See the section, "Getting into the Zone," later in this chapter, for more information.

Beauty Is in the Eye of the Decorator

After you finish all the cabling, and the computers are connected to the concentrator, an interesting thing occurs in many households. The person in the household who cares most about the décor (usually Mom) walks around the house muttering sentences in which the word *ugly* frequently occurs. Teenage daughters look at the new high-tech system you installed and react with comments like "Gross!" (Teenage sons don't seem to notice.)

Somebody, perhaps a guest (if not a member of the family), eventually remarks, "We have a network at work, and we don't have holes in the wall that exude cable, and we don't have cable crawling along the floor or the baseboard."

Professional network installers use accessories to make the hardware decorator-friendly, and there's no reason you can't put the same finishing touches on your system. An added benefit is that some of the accessories also make the installation safer, removing cable from places that may cause someone to trip.

Adding cable faceplates

If you run cable through walls, you can end the cable run at the wall using an Ethernet socket that's attached to the wall with a faceplate, as shown in Figure 3-4. Then, you just need to run a small piece of cable from the computer to the faceplate. You can buy multi-outlet faceplates, which you'll need in the room that contains the concentrator.

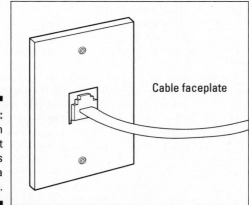

Cable faceplate

Figure 3-4:
You can
connect
computers
to a
faceplate.

To use a faceplate to create an Ethernet socket, pull the cable through the hole in the wall and use a cable stripper to remove about an inch of insulation from the cable. If the cable is a patch cable, cut off the connector first. Then insert the wires into the socket and push against the socket to seal the connection (these are similar to electrical connections that just snap into place). Attach the socket to the faceplate and attach the faceplate to the wall (pushing the wires back into the wall). A punch down tool helps solidify the connection between the line and the wall jack.

Using floor cable covers

In any networking situation, a certain amount of cable is exposed because you have to run cable between the wall and the NIC in the computer. The best way to hide as much cable as possible is to put the computer desk against the wall at the point where the cable exits the wall. If that solution isn't possible, cover the cable that runs between the wall and the computer. Floor cable covers can help make your network installation less ugly and can also provide safety by eliminating the chance of tripping over the cable.

Floor cable covers come in two models: covers that lie atop the cable and covers that hold the cable in a channel (see Figure 3-5). Both cover types provide several advantages over loose cable:

- **Cable covers hug the ground and don't move.** You can't accidentally nudge them up into the air as you walk and then trip over the loop you created (which is what frequently happens with Ethernet cable).

- **Cable covers are wide.** And the slope to the top of the cover is very gentle, which lessens the chance that you'll trip.

- **You can use cable covers under a rug.** Don't run cable under a rug without a cover, because the rubbing of the underside of the rug against the cable can weaken or break the cable's insulation jacket.

Most floor covers are made of plastic or rubber. You can paint the plastic covers, but I find that paint wears away quickly on rubber. If you're running the covers over a carpet, you can even glue carpet strips to the top of the cover, which may help hide the fact that your family room is crawling with cable.

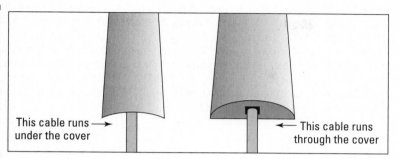

Figure 3-5:
Cable covers hide ugly cable and reduce the risk of someone tripping over the cable.

This cable runs → under the cover

← This cable runs through the cover

Curing Your Network's Growing Pains

You can be almost certain that your home network will grow — you'll add more computers. (Read how to run cable from the new computer to the concentrator in the section, "The Chase Is On: Running the Cable," earlier in this chapter.) But what happens if you run out of concentrator connections? If you start your home network with a kit built for two computers, where do you plug in additional computers?

You have two solutions:

✔ Buy a larger concentrator (and sell the original concentrator to a friend who's building a home network).

✔ Buy another small concentrator and link it to the first concentrator.

You shouldn't need any instructions for carrying out the first solution.

The second solution, however, requires a little bit of homework — you need to read the instructions that came with both concentrators to understand how to link them. Every concentrator has an uplink port, which is designed specifically to connect one concentrator to another concentrator, instead of connecting a computer to a concentrator. (Notice that a concentrator that's meant to accommodate four computers has five ports.) Before you use an uplink port, here's what you need to know:

✔ **Where the uplink port is:** The uplink port is always at the end of the row of ports (usually next to the place where the power cord goes).

✔ **What the uplink port looks like:** Notice that the uplink port is usually marked differently from the other ports, either with an icon (the other ports have no icons) or with the word *uplink.* (If nothing is visible, check the documentation that came with the hub.)

✔ **What kind of cable you need to hook up two hubs:** Sometimes you need to use a *crossover cable* when you connect two hubs through their uplink ports. You can buy this special cable from the same places that you can purchase regular Ethernet patch cable. Many concentrator manufacturers have a toggle switch to change between regular and crossed cable. Some manufacturers have uplink ports that automatically detect the type of cable and make internal adjustments to make sure that patch cable works the same as a crossover cable. Read the documentation that came with your concentrator.

Run cable from the new computer(s) to the new concentrator and connect the old concentrator to the new one via the uplink port (or the other way around). Read the documentation for both concentrators to see whether you need to use a crossover cable and also to see whether the connection from the uplink port goes into a regular port or into the other uplink port. Figure 3-6 illustrates a network with two concentrators.

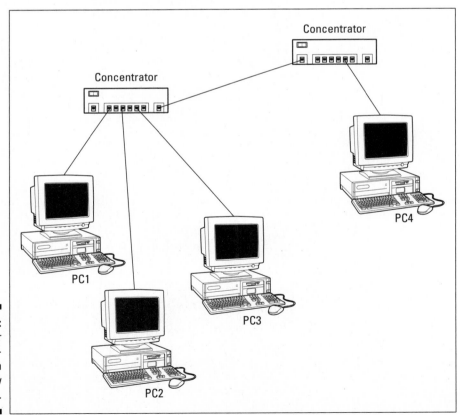

Figure 3-6:
Add another concentrator when you outgrow the first one.

Don't add another router

If one of your concentrators is a router, when you outgrow the number of ports, don't buy another router; instead, buy a switch. Use one of the router's ports to connect the switch using Ethernet cable. Remember that one of the router's ports is dedicated to the connection to your broadband modem, so don't touch the cable in that port.

If your computers aren't widely separated and the fact that you've outgrown your concentrator is the result of adding more computers than the router has ports, buy a large switch (such as an 8-port or 16-port switch). Connect all of the computers to the switch and then connect the switch to the router. You can use the extra ports on the switch in the future to add more computers, or to add one of those nifty Network Storage Drives (very large hard drives that connect directly to a switch as if they were another computer on the network). These are handy devices for storing backups or media files.

Getting into the Zone

You can gain advantages from linked concentrators, even if one concentrator has enough ports for all the computers on your network. The concept is called *zoning,* and you can zone your network to make cabling easier.

For example, consider that you have two widely separated computers on the first floor. One computer is in the family room at the front of the house, and the other computer is in the kitchen at the back of the house. You have two computers on the second floor, also at opposite ends of the house.

You can place a single concentrator in the family room and run cable across the first floor to the kitchen computer. Then you can run cable through the wall to the computer on the second floor at the front of the house. Finally, you can run cable through the wall and across the house to the computer on the second floor at the back of the house, but doesn't that seem like a lot of cable?

Instead, create zones for your network. For example, you can put two concentrators in the basement or in the attic. Place one near the front of the house and one near the back of the house. Drop the cables from two computers to each concentrator. Then link the concentrators to each other. Because you're using the attic or basement (where beauty doesn't count as much), you can string the cable across rafters, using hooks or duct tape. As you can see in Figure 3-7, zoning is logical and easy and provides for network growth.

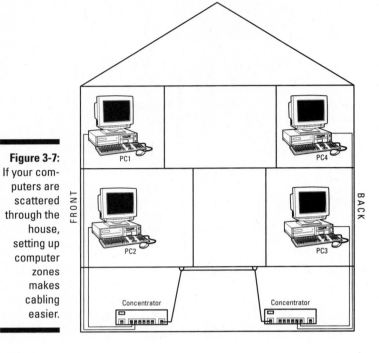

Figure 3-7:
If your computers are scattered through the house, setting up computer zones makes cabling easier.

Chapter 4

Using Wires That Are Already There

In This Chapter

▶ Installing a phoneline network

▶ Using your power lines to create a network

Suppose you don't want to drill holes, climb into the attic, or slither through the crawlspace to drag Ethernet cable through the house. Or suppose you do, but the chief decorator in your house objects strongly. What can you do to get the reliability and easy setup of hard-wired computer networks?

I have the answer. (Of course I do. What author would pose a question if she didn't already know the answer?) You can set up your home networking wiring with wires that already exist in your home — phone and power lines. This chapter covers the instructions that you need to connect all your computers by using the existing cable in your home.

One Standard, Indivisible, with Liberty and Networking for All

Technical standards are usually developed by groups of manufacturers who come together to form an association for the specific reason of setting standards. Eventually, if enough manufacturers adopt the standards, all the other manufacturers have no choice but to use the new standards. It usually doesn't take long for standards to become universal, global, and totally accepted. At that point, most of the nonstandard stuff disappears from store shelves, and you can feel safe when you shop. (The most dramatic evidence of this is the history of videotape equipment for home use — although you may not be old enough to know people who rushed out to buy Beta equipment and movies on Beta tapes. Beta was introduced first, but VHS won the standards battle.)

If you buy networking equipment that meets standards, no matter what manufacturer's networking hardware you buy, it's going to work with anything else you buy. To check on the manufacturers of the equipment that you need to buy, you need to know about the following standards:

- Telephone line technology (called *phoneline* networking) has been standardized by the Home Phoneline Networking Alliance (www.home pna.org).

- The HomePlug Powerline Alliance (www.homeplug.org) sets standards for network devices that use household electrical wires.

Manufacturers that are members of these organizations usually have a statement to that effect on their equipment boxes. Their Web sites state that they are members of, or subscribe to the standards developed by, these organizations. Don't buy equipment that doesn't reference these organizations.

Tapping into Phone Lines to Connect a Network

If you've chosen to install a phoneline network, you have some easy homework tasks. You need to make sure you get the fastest possible speed for transmitting data across the network. The first version of phoneline equipment, dubbed HomePNA Version 1.0, transferred data at the rate of 1 megabit per second (1 Mbps). Then, phoneline equipment designed for HomePNA Version 2.0 became available, operating at about 10 Mbps. As I write this, manufacturers have begun making plans for equipment based on the standards for HomePNA Version 3.0, which transfers data at the rate of 128 Mbps.

For phoneline networking, adapters are available in the form of Universal Serial Bus (USB) network adapters, as well as PC Card network adapters for laptops. At this point, you should already have installed the phoneline network adapters on the computers. If you haven't, page back to Chapter 2 for installation instructions.

Whose line is it, anyway?

The telephone lines that run through your walls have a great deal more power than you need for *POTS,* which is the technical jargon for *plain old telephone service.* The multiple wires that are inside telephone cables don't all use the same frequency. The wires that provide POTS have one frequency, but other wires use other frequencies. The technical terminology for this is *Frequency Division Multiplexing (FDM).* The different frequencies are described as follows:

✔ The POTS frequency services telephones, fax machines, and modems. Because all of these devices share the same frequency, you can't receive telephone calls when you're connected to the Internet via a modem.

✔ A different frequency is available for special devices that provide high-speed Internet access, such as digital subscriber line (DSL) and Integrated Services Digital Network

(ISDN) devices, enabling you to use a high-speed device and a POTS device simultaneously.

✔ The hardware in your telephone line network uses *still another* frequency to communicate among all the computers on your network. POTS and high-speed Internet connection devices continue to operate on their own frequencies and are therefore available to you.

You don't have to worry about which frequency any service or device is using; the network devices and telephone wires automatically know which frequency to use. The only thing you have to do to ensure that your home network operates properly is to connect all the computers to the same telephone number (which isn't a problem unless you have two or more telephone numbers in your home).

The phone jacks that you use to create your network must all be on the same telephone line. If you have multiple phone numbers in your house, be careful to use only the jacks that are connected to the same phone number. If your house is wired for a second telephone line, but you haven't had the telephone company activate the line with a telephone number (or you cancelled that telephone line in favor of cell phones, but the wiring still exists), you can use the jacks that are attached to this inactive line for home networking. That's because all you need for home networking is the copper wire, and the absence of dial tone is totally irrelevant.

Now it's time to connect the computers so that they can "talk" to each other. To create your phoneline network, just put one end of a regular telephone cable into the network adapter on the computer and put the other end of the telephone cable into the wall jack.

Okay, you're done. You now have a network. Well, you have to install the software drivers (the documentation that came with your adapters has instructions, and Chapter 6 of this book discusses installation of drivers), but the hardware stuff is done.

Where do I plug in phones?

Hello? What? It's not that simple in your house? Oh, I see; you actually want to use a telephone in at least one of the rooms that has a computer. And you want to use a modem and a fax machine?

Don't worry. Your phone line can handle as many devices as it has frequencies. What you have to do is to *gang,* or join, multiple devices so that each device is individually accessible. Each device has to be connected to the telephone line, and I go through the options in the following sections.

Ganging the network and the telephone

Your phoneline network adapter has two jacks; one is labeled *line* (meaning the wall jack) and the other is labeled *phone.* The labels may use slightly different wording or may use icons instead of text, but it's not difficult to figure out which jack is for which purpose.

Use the line jack on the phoneline network adapter to connect the computer to the wall jack using standard telephone cable (which was probably included in the package that contained your phoneline network adapter). Then, plug a telephone into the other jack on the network adapter. Incidentally, on occasion, I've inadvertently put the connections in the other way around, connecting the phone jack to the wall and the line jack to the telephone — and it all worked! I suspect the wiring is identical in both jacks, but as these devices get more powerful (and more complicated), some day you may have a network adapter in which the labels on the jacks *do* matter.

You could instead use your wall jack for two devices at the same time by plugging a *modular duplex jack* (commonly called a *splitter*) into the wall receptacle. The splitter, which you can buy at the supermarket or at an office-supply store, has a standard RJ-11 plug at the front, just like telephone cable. The back end has two RJ-11 receptacles, into which you can plug two devices. Use one receptacle for cable coming from the telephone and the other for cable coming from the phoneline network adapter on your computer.

Ganging the network, the telephone, and an external modem

If you have an external modem and you also want to have a telephone near the computer that's using the wall jack for network communications, you can easily gang the three devices. All external modems have two RJ-11 receptacles. One receptacle is for the cable that goes from the modem to the wall jack, and one receptacle accepts cable from the telephone. The receptacles are marked, usually with icons (one icon looks like a wall jack, and the other looks like a telephone). If your modem doesn't have icons, it has labels — *line* and *phone.*

Follow these steps to gang the network, telephone, and an external modem:

1. **Plug a splitter into the wall jack.**

2. **Insert the cable from your computer NIC into one side of the splitter.**

3. **Insert the cable from the external modem's line receptacle into the other side of the splitter.**

4. **Plug the cable from the telephone into the telephone receptacle on the modem.**

You probably figured out that this gang arrangement means that the external modem and the telephone don't have their own individual access to the wall jack. A gang arrangement isn't just sharing; it's a highly exclusive, fickle marriage. The modem and telephone are both POTS devices that can't operate simultaneously anyway. (I explain POTS in the sidebar, "Whose line is it, anyway?," earlier in this chapter).

You can't use the modem and the phone line at the same time (and that's true even if you weren't using your telephone lines for networking). If you pick up the telephone while you're using the modem, you don't hear a dial tone. Instead, you hear a lot of strange whistling and beeping noises called *white noise.* (In addition, picking up the phone disrupts the modem communication, so hopefully you aren't downloading an important file at that moment.) Anyone calling your house hears a busy signal, so you won't hear the phone ring when you're online, either. When you're not using the modem, you can use the telephone normally, even though it isn't plugged directly into the wall. The modem's connection to the wall jack provides a pass-through connection to the telephone line.

Ganging the network, the telephone, and an internal modem

If your computer has an internal modem, the part of the modem that you access at the back of your computer probably includes two receptacles — one for the telephone line and one for a telephone (just like an external modem). Follow the instructions for ganging the network, the telephone, and an external modem in the preceding section.

However, if your internal modem doesn't have a receptacle for the telephone, or if you're using a PC Card modem on a laptop, you must arrange the gang a bit differently. In fact, you have some choices about how all the devices get to the wall jack. Follow these steps:

1. **Put a splitter in the wall jack and insert the cable from the telephone into one receptacle.**

2. **Join the cables coming out of the NIC and the internal modem.**

   You can choose one of the following methods, which also are shown in Figure 4-1:

   A. Use a Y-connector (conveniently, it looks like a capital *Y*), which accepts both of the RJ-11 connectors (one from the modem and one from the NIC) on one end. Insert the RJ-11 connector (at the other end of the Y-connector) into the empty side of the splitter.

   B. Use a splitter to accept both RJ-11 connections, and then plug the splitter into the empty side of the splitter that's in the wall jack.

   C. Use a splitter to accept both RJ-11 connections, and then plug the splitter into a length of telephone cable that has a receptacle at one end and an RJ-11 connection at the other end.

   D. Use a splitter to accept both RJ-11 connections and then plug the splitter into a connector that has a receptacle at each end. Then run cable between the connector and the splitter in the wall jack.

If you're using a USB or PC Card network adapter, the principle is the same — just substitute your adapter for the NIC shown in Figure 4-1.

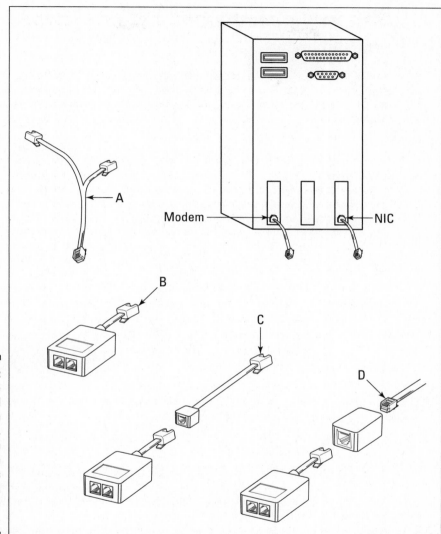

Figure 4-1:
Gang the internal modem and the NIC, and then send both devices to the wall jack as one connection.

Too many computers, not enough phone jacks?

Perhaps you have two computers in the same room, but the room has only one phone jack. Maybe you have two computers, each one in its own room, but one of those rooms lacks a phone jack. Relax; it's easy to solve these problems.

If two computers are in the same room, connect one computer to the wall jack and connect the other computer to the second jack in the first computer's network adapter. This is called a *daisy chain,* and it puts both computers on the network. If the computers are in separate rooms, you have to run telephone cable between them. This is easier to do if the rooms are adjacent, but you can buy very long lengths of telephone cable, which means that you can probably connect two computers that are 50 feet apart or more. If you want to hide the cable or connect two computers on separate floors, Chapter 3 (which is all about cabling a house for an Ethernet network) is filled with information and tips about getting cable from one place to another in your home.

In fact, you can use the daisy chain approach to attach your whole network to one wall jack, connecting the first computer to the wall jack, connecting the second computer to the other jack in the first computer's network adapter, connecting the third computer to the other jack in the second computer's network adapter, and so on. This frees all the other wall jacks in your house for telephones, modems, and fax machines. A phoneline daisy chain can accommodate up to 25 computers. However, no two computers on the chain can be more than 1,000 feet apart (which shouldn't be a problem, even if you're living in a mansion).

Phoneline networks and DSL service

You can use your phoneline network even if you've chosen to use a digital subscriber line (DSL) modem for Internet access, as long as the DSL service is residential and not business class. Residential DSL is also called *asynchronous* DSL (ADSL), while business-class DSL service is *synchronous* (SDSL). The difference between the two classes of service is the upload speed. ADSL offers fast download speed (when you open a Web page or collect your e-mail, you're downloading) and slower upload speed (when you send files to a server on the Internet or send e-mail, you're uploading). Businesses that need to maintain Web sites use SDSL because they can upload new files and graphics quickly and because SDSL comes with specific IP addresses for their Web servers. In addition, ADSL runs on your existing telephone lines, while SDSL requires the telephone company to bring a separate line into your house.

Even though ADSL uses a different frequency from POTS and computer networking, most DSL providers tell you to put a filtering device on your telephone line to avoid the possibility of interference. These devices are variously referred to as *filters, microfilters,* or *microsplitters,* and they are plugged into a wall jack. Do *not* plug the cable from your network adapter into a filter. Remove the filter, plug in the cable, and then attach the telephone to the second jack on your network adapter. You can use the filter on any wall jack that only has a POTS connection (telephone, fax, or answering machine).

Incidentally, the filter doesn't protect your POTS connections from problems introduced by the DSL connection — it's the other way around. Phoneline technology for POTS is primitive compared to the way technology has learned to use the wires in phone lines in recent years. The filters protect your DSL signal so the less advanced POTS communications can't interfere with your Internet access.

Sharing an Internet connection on a phoneline network

Chapter 7 describes the steps required for setting up your Internet connection so that all the computers on the network can share the connection. However, for each networking connection type (Ethernet, phoneline, powerline, or wireless), you must bear in mind, and contend with, specific considerations. In this section, I present an overview of those considerations for phoneline networks.

For any connection type, the technical challenge is to connect the network to the Internet device. If the Internet device uses the same type of wiring, there's no problem. If the Internet device uses a different type of wiring, you have to get from here (your network) to there (the Internet device).

If your Internet device is a telephone modem that's attached to one of the computers on your network, then, by default, your Internet device is using the same type of wiring as your network. Read Chapter 7 to find out how to set up Internet Connection Sharing.

If your Internet device is a DSL/cable modem that is using an Ethernet connection, you get from here (phoneline) to there (Ethernet) by using a bridge. Because bridges cross chasms, that's an apt name for the device, isn't it? A network *bridge* is a device that sits in the middle between two topologies. The bridge has at least one connector that matches the network wiring (let's call it the on ramp) and at least one connector (the off ramp) that matches the wiring of the Internet connection device.

Phoneline bridges have multiple connectors (ports), and the number of connectors varies by manufacturer. All the connectors look the same, so you have to pay attention to the labels.

At least one port is an RJ-11 (telephone line) port that lets the bridge connect to your network. The port may be labeled *phoneline, wall,* or *HPNA.* Connect telephone cable (which is probably included with the bridge) from this port to a wall jack or to the second jack on any network adapter. This connects your bridge to your network. If a second RJ-11 port exists, it's probably labeled *phone,* and you can use that to connect a telephone, modem, or fax machine to the network.

To connect the bridge to your Ethernet modem, look for a port labeled *LAN, Uplink,* or *Ethernet.* This is an RJ-45 connector. Connect that port to your modem using Ethernet CAT-5/5e cable (which is probably included with the bridge). If there's a second RJ-45 port on the bridge, it's to connect the bridge to an Ethernet hub, bridging two networks (one phoneline and one Ethernet). You need this port only if you're connecting two disparate networks in your home. For instance, the computers on the first floor may be connected by Ethernet, but when you added a computer or multiple computers to the second floor, you decided not to run Ethernet cable upstairs. Run one length of cable from the first floor to the bridge, and the two networks are connected!

If your Internet connection device is DSL, there's good news. Recently, because of the rising popularity of phoneline networks, manufacturers began offering phoneline DSL modems in addition to the standard Ethernet DSL modems. Your DSL provider may have a kit that you can buy. The kit contains all the equipment you need to create the network and share the Internet connection with all the computers on the network. In fact, some of these devices offer tons of features in addition to home networking and shared Internet access. Those features take advantage of all the nifty things you can do using telephone lines, such as setting up intercom systems and room-to-room dialing, forwarding calls from one extension to another, and lots more.

Troubleshooting phoneline networks

If your telephone lines generate a lot of static, the problem not only affects regular telephone communication, but it also affects your network communication. For voice services, static is annoying, but it doesn't prevent you from using the telephone. For network communication, static can have a more serious effect. Static can prevent computers from communicating, or it can corrupt the data that's being exchanged across the network.

Static is almost always the telephone company's fault because its source is almost always the telephone lines entering your house. Telephone cable doesn't age well because the insulation that protects the cable erodes over time. If the insulation isn't doing its job, the wires can touch each other or be affected by moisture. If your telephone cables are underground, water can be in the duct. If your telephone cables are above ground, the problem with eroding insulation is often compounded by squirrels and other varmints who love to chew on the insulation.

It has been my experience that phone companies aren't terribly cooperative about replacing telephone lines that are deteriorating and causing static. First of all, when you call to complain about static, the technician usually takes the approach that the problem is in the wiring that's inside your house (which most telephone companies won't work on without charging you) or in the telephone you're using. If you have static regardless of the extension you use, and if you've checked with neighbors who report occasional (or constant) static problems, you can be insistent that the problem is in the telephone company's wires, not in your house wiring.

Even when the telephone company admits that its wires are causing the problem, it often replaces one section of wire (perhaps the direct connection between your home and the nearest junction box), but not the wires that run from the junction box back to another box on the system. If static continues, or returns after a short time, you may have to fight to get insulated telephone cable delivered to your house. Your state has a public utilities commission that regulates and oversees public utilities such as the telephone company, and the commission has procedures for customers who want to force utility companies to "do it right."

One clue that your telephone lines have static is that telephone modems operate at speeds well below their rating, and even occasionally lose the connection. You can also hear static by picking up the phone, pressing one digit, and listening to the "silence" for a moment — at least it's supposed to be silence.

If your phone lines and phone service are fine, but one or more computers can't communicate with the network, check your phoneline network adapters (and bridge, if you're using one). Read the documentation that came with your phoneline hardware to see which indicator lights should be working and what color the light(s) should be. For example, most phoneline devices have an indicator labeled *link* that displays a green light when the device is working properly. If the green light isn't glowing on one of the network adapters, you need to figure out whether the adapter is broken or whether something is interfering with its ability to function.

To see if the adapter is faulty, change its connection. The best test is to move this adapter to a computer that has a working adapter — just switch the two adapters. If none of the other tests are conclusive, this is the only way to tell whether the adapter is bad or a connection to your phone line isn't working properly.

Another test is to move the connection point for that adapter. For example, if the adapter is plugged into a wall jack, move it to another wall jack or to the second port on a working adapter (you may have to use a longer telephone cord). If this works, the wall jack may have a problem. If the adapter is plugged into a splitter on a wall jack, remove the splitter and plug the telephone cable directly into the wall. If this works, the splitter is bad. If the adapter is on a USB port, plug another USB device into the port (you may have to borrow one if you don't have any other USB devices). If the new device doesn't work properly, the problem is with your USB port. If the new device works, you can eliminate the USB port as the source of your problem. If you have an internal phoneline NIC, try moving the NIC to another PCI bus.

If none of these tests are conclusive, read the troubleshooting directions in the documentation, check the support pages on the manufacturer's Web site, or call the manufacturer's technical support department.

Powering Up Your Network with the Electric Company

If you choose your home's power lines for your network, you don't need to run cable through the walls, the floors, or anywhere. Each network adapter plugs into the power outlet on the wall. The manufacturers that make network devices for electrical lines refer to their products (and the topology) as *powerline* devices.

The more I've worked with powerline networks, the more I appreciate this technology. It offers the portability of wireless networks without the annoying hassles that wireless technology introduces. You can put a computer anywhere in the house (or, for that matter, on the porch or the deck), just as wireless users can. The speed of powerline communications is more consistent (it doesn't suffer serious degradation as you move computers farther apart the way wireless does). Nothing interferes with the signal, so you don't have to worry about locating your computer away from anything metal or operating on the same frequency. And, with powerline networking, you escape the annoying "tweaking" of the antennas and computer locations.

In fact (and I shouldn't admit this because I spend so much time extolling the virtues of Ethernet), I put a powerline network into my own home. Now, before you call me a hypocrite, I hasten to explain that I have a very large three-story home (plus a big basement), and it's a very old home without many straight chases either horizontally or vertically. When I put computers on the third floor so my grandchildren could use computers when they visit, I couldn't face the chore involved with wiring Ethernet for computers that aren't used all that frequently. So I set up powerline adapters on those computers, then came down to the first floor and plugged a bridge into a wall outlet near my router, and connected the bridge to the router. The whole exercise took less than 15 minutes, and my third-floor network works wonderfully well (although it's not as fast at transferring large files as my 100Mb Ethernet network).

Using USB powerline adapters

Powerline network adapters are USB devices, which makes installing them a piece of cake. Merely plug the USB connector into the USB port on your computer and then plug the network adapter into the wall outlet. You're done. (Some manufacturers require the installation of software before you connect the adapter, but that usually takes only a minute.)

Because Windows automatically sees a USB device when you connect it, the operating system launches the process of installing drivers automatically. Walk through the wizard, referring to the documentation that came with your powerline adapter. If your version of Windows doesn't have drivers for your adapter, use the driver(s) on the disk that came with the adapter. Details on performing these tasks are available in Chapter 6.

Using your built-in Ethernet adapter

Because almost all computers come with a built-in Ethernet adapter, some manufacturers of powerline equipment have come up with a nifty way to use that adapter for powerline networking. You can buy a powerline adapter that connects to your existing adapter. This means you can spare a USB port for other USB devices (such as printers and scanners).

Essentially, these powerline adapters are bridges; they connect your Ethernet adapter to the powerline adapter with a short Ethernet cable (which comes with the device). The powerline adapter also has a standard plug, which connects to the wall outlet.

Powerline networks and Internet Connection Sharing

If your Internet device is a telephone modem that's attached to one of the computers on your network, then, by default, your Internet device is using the same type of wiring as your network. All the computers reach the modem over the network, accessing the computer that has the modem, and there's no separate wiring for the modem. Read Chapter 6 to find out how to set up Internet Connection Sharing.

If your Internet connection is a DSL or cable modem, those are Ethernet devices, and you need to connect your powerline network to the Ethernet connection on the modem. The hardware device that accomplishes this trick is a *bridge*. See the discussion about phoneline bridges earlier in this chapter to understand how bridges work and how to make the connections. The only difference is that for powerline networks, you need to connect one end of the bridge to a wall outlet (near the modem) and the other end of the bridge to your DSL or cable modem using Ethernet cable (which often comes with the bridge).

DSL powerline kits

In addition to powerline adapters and bridges, you can buy powerline devices that combine routers and modems. One device, connected to your DSL telephone line, hooks the entire powerline network into the Internet.

Powerline security

A potential security problem exists with powerline networking: a neighbor who is also running a powerline network could access your computers and files. Your immediate neighbors probably share the same transformer that your house uses and may even share some of the same physical wires. This means that network communication within your house could travel to your neighbor's house. The solution to this potential security breach is to create a network password and to encrypt all transmissions between computers on the same network.

Your powerline network adapter has a software CD that contains a security application that takes care of the potential security problems. Install the software on every computer on your network.

When you install your first powerline adapter software, create a network password by changing the default password (most manufacturers use *HomePlug* as the default password). Enter the new password using any combination of letters, numbers, and capitalization (passwords are case sensitive). Write the password down and don't lose the piece of paper. When you install the other powerline adapters, enter the same password in the security dialog box.

After the software is installed on all the network computers, the computers find each other (because they all have the same password), and all communication across the network is encrypted.

Troubleshooting powerline communications

I've installed many powerline networks, and they generally run smoothly. However, I've received a couple of troubleshooting calls from families who report that one computer cannot find the network. The same problem existed with each call: the powerline adapters were plugged into surge protectors.

Always plug powerline adapters into the wall outlet (unless you purchase a special power strip from your adapter's manufacturer). Use the surge protector for the computer and monitor. Power strips that have surge protection features don't work properly with powerline network adapters because the technology that provides surge protection can interrupt the flow of data.

Most powerline adapters have built-in surge protection — check the specifications before you buy.

Chapter 5

Look Ma, No Wires

In This Chapter

▶ Understanding wireless technology

▶ Positioning computers

▶ Wireless network security issues

▶ Finding wireless hotspots for public use

*I*f you opt to use wireless technology, you don't have any cables to run through the walls or the floors, or even from the computer to an outlet. All you have to do is install the wireless network adapters and their attendant software files (covered in Chapter 6), and you have a network. Of course, you have to perform all the other tasks required to enable file, printer, and Internet sharing, but this book deals with all of that and makes it all easy to accomplish.

Sounds cool, doesn't it? Well, it is, most of the time — but not all networks perform well with wireless topology. In this chapter, I explain what you need to know, and also what you need to think about, as you plan and install your own wireless network.

Please bear in mind that wireless technology is changing so fast that new and marvelous stuff appears frequently, and new types of products may be available when you read this. I can, of course, only talk about the products, technologies, and specifications I'm using as I write this. If you didn't purchase this book minutes after it appeared on the shelves of your favorite bookstore, you're probably going to find more wireless product types than I mention here. However, the basic technology doesn't change, so the contents of this chapter should be useful as you plan and build your *WLAN (wireless local area network)*.

Translating the Geek-Speak of Wireless Technology

To set up a wireless network that works, you have to understand how *radio frequency (RF)* communications work, and you also have to gain some understanding of the variety of wireless communication standards. Purchasing hardware without this knowledge puts you at risk for incompatible nodes on your network.

Radio frequency: Hello, den? Kitchen here

The computers on the network communicate via radio waves sent through the air. Attached to the network adapter you installed on each computer is a device called a *transceiver*. It's a thin antenna that pokes out from the adapter. As its name implies, a transceiver both transmits and receives radio waves. The distance the transceiver signal is certified to traverse varies depending on the wireless technology you've adapted. Check the manufacturer's documentation to find out how far apart you can place computers.

The transceiver that's included with wireless network adapters sends radio waves in a wide arc; it isn't point-and-shoot technology. Each computer is unaware of the location of the other computer(s), and each computer spins its radio waves up, down, and around in the hope of finding a soul mate to talk to.

Wireless standards — alphabet soup

Wireless network standards are changing faster than any other set of standards in the network communications market. This phenomenon is the result of the growing popularity of wireless network communications. For example, corporate network administrators want to be able to let mobile warriors log on to the main network (cabled with Ethernet) when they show up at the office, without having to provide Ethernet equipment hookups for them. Corporate workers want to be able to amble over to the company's mail server and pick up their e-mail on their handheld devices. The use of wireless technology will result in more (and cleverer) applications for this convenient connection method.

The Institute of Electrical and Electronics Engineers (IEEE) is responsible for setting the standards for wireless local area networks, and the family of specifications is contained in the standards known as 802.11. Currently, the 802.11 family contains four sets of standards for you to choose from: 802.11a, 802.11b, 802.11g, and 802.11n.

802.11a

The 802.11a standard is fast, but it often requires more complicated devices and is sometimes more difficult to configure (depending on the type of hardware devices you use on your network). It's most often found in large corporate networks, where it serves its wireless purpose in the midst of wired Ethernet enterprises. Technically, 802.11a can transmit data at a speed of 54 Mbps ("technically" means that speed is rarely achieved in the real world). It uses the 5 GHz band, which is less likely to run into other devices that cause interference problems.

802.11b

The 802.11b standard was originally called *Wi-Fi* (which stands for *wireless fidelity*, but almost nobody who uses the term Wi-Fi knows that because Wi-Fi has become a term that means "network wireless"). Wi-Fi hardware devices are widely available, and they're all reasonably priced. All manufacturers of network devices make Wi-Fi products.

This standard can technically communicate at a speed of 11 Mbps, but I would be surprised if you achieved that speed consistently. One thing I did notice, however, is that 802.11b devices tend to maintain their speed (even if it's less than 11 Mbps) better over long distances than do 802.11a devices.

The 802.11b devices operate on the 2.4 GHz band, which is also used by other radio frequency devices. This could give you a problem with interference. See the section, "Detouring around obstructions," later in this chapter, for information about interference.

You may also see devices that are marked as 802.11b+. This is a slightly faster version of 802.11b, but I've read about some problems with compatibility between the two "b" standards if you use equipment from different manufacturers.

To make sure you can purchase Wi-Fi products from multiple manufacturers that can "talk" to each other, a group exists to certify compatibility. WECA (Wireless Ethernet Compatibility Alliance) was formed in 1999 to certify interoperability of wireless local area network products that are built on the IEEE 802.11b specifications. Look for the Wi-Fi certification logo when you buy hardware. However, keep in mind that while hardware compatibility ensures communication, different manufacturers may implement security measures differently (and that's not covered by Wi-Fi certification).

802.11g

Until recently, the 802.11g standard was the standard for wireless networks. Manufacturers of 802.11g devices advertise communication rates of 54 Mbps using the same 2.4 GHz band that 802.11b uses.

Some 802.11g devices are marked G+B. This means that they automatically recognize and communicate with both 802.11b devices and 802.11g devices. The term used to describe these devices is *dual-band*. Dual-band devices provide a way to expand your existing wireless network without starting all over. (G+A devices are also available for corporate users.) When a G+B device communicates with a device using 802.11g, communication is established at the higher speed possible with 802.11g. However, when a G+B device communicates with a device using 802.11b, the speed drops to that of the 802.11b device.

802.11n

At the time I write this, the 802.11n standard is still waiting for final approval, but consumer demand has encouraged manufacturers to release 802.11n products before final certification and final sets of standards. If you're purchasing 802.11n products before final standards are approved, buy all your products from the same manufacturer to ensure compatibility.

This new standard is much faster than any previous wireless networking product because 802.11n devices transmit multiple streams of data called "spatial streams." The higher the number of spatial streams, the higher the throughput, which means the speed at which data moves from point A to point B is radically improved over previous standards. Manufacturers claim speeds up to 600 Mbps.

Remember that wireless "speed" is an iffy proposition unless your entire network is set up outdoors, with no walls, furniture that has metal components, and so on. It would be unusual if you managed to get the speed that the device is capable of producing.

Positioning Computers

You have two issues to consider when deciding where to place computers on a wireless network: the distance between the computers and the need to avoid potential sources of interference with the wireless radio signals.

How far can you go?

Distance is a serious problem for wireless home networks. Most manufacturers rate the range of wireless adapters at a couple hundred feet indoors and over a thousand feet in open spaces. But those are technical possibilities, and it's unlikely you'll be able to count on those numbers as you decide on placement for your computers. In fact, many home wireless networks don't achieve half those distances, and some don't achieve a third of them. The distance problem is aggravated (or mitigated, depending on how you look at it) by whether the computers are in a "line of sight" with each other.

If you've planned a nifty wireless network that covers several floors of your home, you'll probably have to redo your plan. You can usually extend the distance of the signals with a hardware device, either a router or an access point. (See the section, "Empower Your Network with Hardware Doohickeys," later in this chapter.)

You don't have to move your entire network onto your front lawn to achieve maximum distance because "open space" just means that computers aren't separated by solid structures. For example, if you have a computer in the kitchen and a computer in the family room, and you have one of those "designed for open living space" houses, it's probably fine that the computers are 100 feet or more apart. The separations between the rooms are probably not much more than archways, or even furniture, instead of a solid wall (containing pipes and ducts) with a small doorway.

The farther an RF signal has to travel, the slower it moves. So, you need to decide whether distance or speed is more important to you.

Detouring around obstructions

Radio waves travel freely in the air until they run up against metal or water. Both elements stop radio waves in their tracks. The water problem probably isn't something to worry about in your house unless you plan to store your computer under a waterbed. However, the metal problem can be serious. Solid thermal glass panels that are well sealed can also interfere with RF signals.

Plaster walls with metal lath and walls that hold cast-iron plumbing pipes frequently interfere with the ability to run a wireless network in a home. Of course, you could replace all the plaster with drywall and replace the drainpipes with PVC pipes, but that seems like a bit much just to have a wireless network. Some people have reported that the metal ductwork for heating and air-conditioning systems also interferes with wireless communications.

The problem of metal isn't restricted to what's in your walls. You also can't put your computer under a metal desk or in a place where a metal file cabinet or bookcase stands between the computers that need to talk to each other.

Another (actually, more common) obstruction that your wireless network may encounter is radio-signal interference. For example, the 2.4 GHz frequency that's used by 802.11b and 802.11g devices is also used by most cordless telephones. In fact, you should always avoid putting a computer near the phone's base station (which is an extremely active transceiver). Microwave ovens also "broadcast" in the 2.4 GHz band, so keep your computers away. In addition, you can experience interference from fluorescent lights.

Incidentally, it's not necessarily only the network communications that bear the brunt of interference; the other device (such as the phone) frequently shares the problem. I have friends with wireless networks who send me rather loud, and extremely annoying, clicking noises when they talk to me on their cordless telephones. They usually don't hear the loud clicks; the clicks only sound like a little bit of static on their end. On my end, the loud clicks drive me crazy. The network problems drive *them* crazy because a file transfer can suddenly fail because the connection was interfered with.

A less disastrous form of interference comes from any dense obstruction that might be in the path of your wireless signal. By less disastrous, I mean that communications aren't stopped dead, but they're slower and travel only a short distance. For example, a pile of books near the antenna can mess up your wireless signal.

Regardless of the jokes or rumors you may have heard about your electric garage door unexpectedly opening when you transfer files across your wireless network, interference isn't a problem. Garage doors operate in the 433 MHz range, far away from the ranges used by computer network devices.

Empower Your Network with Hardware Doohickeys

Suppose that you want to share a digital subscriber line (DSL) or cable modem with all the computers on your wireless network. Suppose that you have two computers on the first floor, and you're dying to do work on your wireless-equipped laptop while you relax in your bed (on the second floor), but the signal doesn't reach. Don't worry; manufacturers have come up with some clever devices to overcome your problems. In this section, I give you an overview of some of these doohickeys.

Wireless routers

By definition, a *router* transfers data between multiple networks. In home networks, you can use a router to move data from one network (your home network) to another network (the Internet). This is how you share a DSL or cable modem Internet connection with all the computers on the network.

A *wireless router* (frequently called a wireless local area network (WLAN) router) has an antenna that captures the signals from all the computers on your wireless network, effectively acting like a hub or a switch.

The router also has ports for Ethernet connections. For most wireless home networks, the Ethernet port connects the DSL or cable modem to the router. However, you can also use those ports as a hub for an Ethernet network, essentially combining three networks: the wireless network, an Ethernet network, and the Internet.

A router also provides IP addresses to the computers on the local network. Because it does so, it's acting as a Dynamic Host Configuration Protocol (DHCP) server. The router provides a single point of communication with your DSL or cable Internet service provider (ISP). (The ISP sees only the router, not the individual computers that are on the network.) Some routers even come with built-in firewall capabilities.

WLAN routers are easy to install and configure. You must physically connect the unit to a DSL or cable modem using Ethernet cable. The port is usually labeled *WAN* (for wide area network) or *Ethernet.* The manufacturer's instructions can help you make the connections.

Access points

An *access point* is a device that connects the computers on a wireless network to each other (like a hub on an Ethernet network) and to a single access point on an Ethernet network. You can connect an access point to a router, to a hub or switch that connects an Ethernet network, or to a computer Ethernet adapter that is connected to a DSL or cable modem. (You use Internet Connection Sharing (ICS) to share the connection). The access point antenna is more powerful than the antennas on your wireless network adapters and provides a way to extend and speed wireless communications.

It's unusual to find an access point in wireless home networks because a router usually serves your purposes better (wireless routers have built-in access points). It's certainly more efficient to share a broadband Internet connection through a router rather than to set up ICS. The computer that holds the Ethernet adapter that connects the modem also has to have a wireless adapter to connect to the network, so you have to install and configure two adapters.

Signal boosters

Some manufacturers offer devices called *signal boosters,* which are specifically designed to enhance the wireless signals on your network. Boosters make your transmissions faster or let them travel farther.

However, signal boosters have to be plugged into an access point; they can't stand alone. Manufacturers also offer wireless bridges, which must also be plugged into an access point. These devices aren't generally useful for a home network; they are used in corporate environments that maintain multiple topologies.

Understanding Wireless Network Security

In a cabled or wired network, you have a built-in method for preventing unwanted visitors from joining your network. All you have to do is keep your eyes open. To join your wired network, a user has to come into your home and plug a computer into one of your network ports. That port may be an RJ-45 connector on an Ethernet hub, a telephone jack, or an electric plug. If somebody came into your house and plugged a computer into a network device, you'd certainly notice.

Your wireless network, however, uses radio waves that can move through walls, ceilings, and doors to receive and transmit data. As a result, any wireless-equipped computer within transmitting distance may be able to join your network. Unless a user yells "Hi, I'm plugging in," you won't know a new node has been added to your network. If your next-door neighbor decides to work on her front lawn on a nice day, her wireless-equipped laptop could inadvertently become a node on your network. A more sinister laptop user could deliberately lurk nearby to grab information from your network computers. At best, the interloper becomes a parasite, getting Internet access from your shared Internet connection. At worst, he gets to the files on your network or plants viruses on your network computers.

Lacking a direct-port requirement for plugging into your network, you have to find another way to secure your network and the data it holds.

In small networks (home networks and small business peer-to-peer networks), wireless security is enabled by using two security components: Service Set Identifiers (SSIDs) and data encryption.

The steps required to install and set up these security features are covered in Chapter 6, but in the following sections, I give you an overview of the wireless security issues and components. My explanations are simplified, in fact over-simplified (this subject is the basis of very thick books), but they should help you understand what your options are as you configure your wireless network components.

SSIDs

SSIDs are required before your wireless network adapter can talk to other computers on your network. If you're using Windows XP, configuring the SSID is automatic. If you're using an earlier version of Windows, you must go through a configuration process. The configuration steps depend on your version of Windows and the network hardware you purchased, so check the documentation that came with the hardware.

OS X for Macintosh computers also natively supports wireless networks and installs an SSID.

SSIDs are nothing more than an imitation of the requirement for naming your workgroup — all the wireless computers have to have the same SSID to communicate with each other. Because it's possible for an interloper to configure a computer with the SSID you're using, this doesn't really qualify as a great security measure, but it can prevent accidental intrusions.

If you use the default SSID that's built into your network hardware, anybody can join your wireless network. (In a wired network, if an intruder wanted to join your network by configuring his computer with the same name you applied to your workgroup, he would still have to plug his computer into a port within your home — and that's something you'd notice.) To make it difficult for unseen intruders to join your network, you must create a unique SSID for your network and configure every computer to look for that SSID during startup.

As an experiment (well, to be honest, to win a bet I made with a colleague), I once took a wireless laptop computer configured with the default SSID around a neighborhood. As I wandered across the front lawn of several houses, my laptop found, and joined, the wireless network installed in each house. None of those households had changed the default SSID. I was able to see every shared drive, and I could have opened any document in any shared folder. I also could have transferred any file from my computer to the network (including a virus).

If you want some extra income as a computer consultant, perform the same experiment and then knock on each door, explain that you know how to secure wireless networks (because you've read this book), and sign up each household as a client. The extra income will provide a really nice vacation, or even a new car.

Broadcasting across the airwaves

Most access points (including the access points contained within wireless routers) have a configuration option that lets you determine whether your router broadcasts your SSID. By default, all access points send out a broadcast signal, announcing the network name (the SSID). This makes it easy to find the network when you're attaching a new computer to the network.

However, broadcasting also makes it easy for anyone else within RF range to learn the name of your network, eliminating one of the steps needed to invade your network. For example, I recently set up a wireless network at a friend's house. Immediately after installing a wireless network adapter on one of the computers, the dialog box shown in Figure 5-1 appeared.

None of the network SSIDs displayed in the dialog box matched our network (we had turned off broadcasting). My friend examined the names and told me these were his neighbors. Notice that two of his neighbors were not only broadcasting their SSIDs, but were running unsecured networks. With a click of the mouse, I could have joined those networks, giving me access to files and the opportunity to wreak havoc. To invade the neighbor with the secured network, I would have to know the password. Unlike malicious computer users, I don't have password-breaking software on my computer, so I was basically locked out of that network. (Password breakers and other hacking tools are easy to find on the Internet.)

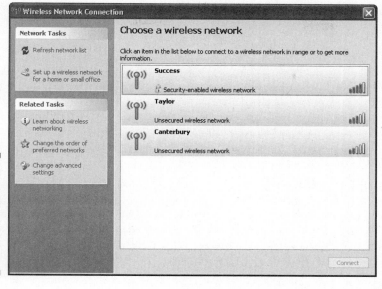

Figure 5-1:
Look at all
the wireless
networks
available
to this
computer!

Of course, the down side is that when you add a new computer to your network, you have to type in the network SSID to configure the computer for the network. Big deal! How hard is that?

Turning off broadcasting doesn't turn off the process of sending a broadcast signal every few seconds. Instead, it tells the access point to turn off the display of the SSID during the broadcast. The signal continues to pulse so that you can connect computers to the network.

Data encryption

You can encrypt data as it passes among the computers on your wireless network. Only the computers you configure as members of your own network can decrypt the data transmissions. The theory is that anyone glomming on to your wireless network won't be able to capture the data that's moving through the network (but the theory is fallible — read on). Two encryption schemes are available for wireless home network equipment: Wired Equivalent Privacy (WEP), and Wi-Fi Protected Access (WPA).

WEP

WEP is designed to encrypt data as it travels among the computers on your network. To make sure that the computers are entitled to get encrypted data, WEP uses features that verify a computer's participation in the network, such as the SSID or the specific hardware ID of a network adapter (all computer hardware has a built-in unique ID). Those features are usually called *encryption management functions*.

The network computers can encrypt and decrypt data because the sending and receiving computers have been assigned encryption verification keys (called *shared keys*) during configuration.

Unfortunately, the transmission of the management data, such as the shared keys, the SSID, and even the workgroup name, isn't encrypted — it's clear text that any eavesdropping computer can read (assuming the user has the software required to eavesdrop). When an eavesdropper has the authentication information, it's a simple task to configure a computer to participate in data exchanges.

WEP doesn't provide a serious, strong identification challenge for a computer or user that's attempting to receive data. The IDs and the keys are set up during configuration of the network adapters and access points, and they don't change (unless you go to the trouble of changing them manually on every computer). This makes it easy for interlopers to pretend to be authenticated members of the network.

Now that I've disparaged WEP as an encryption device, I urge you to use it if you don't have any way to use WPA, which is stronger (and is covered next). I'm not retracting my opinion, but for home networks, WEP is certainly a feasible and useful security device. It's unlikely that network interlopers are trying to gain your shared keys or determine the hardware IDs of your adapters because it's unlikely that you have data on your computers that makes it worth all that effort. WEP prevents casual or inadvertent eavesdropping.

An attacker has to be rather dogged in his efforts if he wants to break WEP security. Of course, if you're in charge of the wireless network at the Pentagon, or at some corporation that is developing a secret formula for making everyone thin without dieting, you should move to WPA. After all, for the kind of information available on your network, interlopers would make the effort to eavesdrop on your network data exchanges. It's unlikely they would do all that work to get into a home network.

WPA

Wi-Fi Protected Access (WPA), which is approved by the Wi-Fi Alliance, provides more security than WEP.

WPA also works with authentication and keys, but it eliminates many of the security soft spots that WEP contains. All transmissions, including the exchange of management data, are encrypted.

In a corporate network, WPA works with central authentication features, which strengthens the security even more. In a small peer-to-peer network (such as a home network), where no central authentication servers are available for storing keys and other authentication functions, WPA runs in *home mode*. Home mode is also called *pre-shared key (PSK)* mode, and it uses manually entered keys or passwords that are easy to set up. You set up your keys when you configure your network devices (the steps are covered in Chapter 6).

All you need to do is enter a password (also called a *master key*) for each of your network nodes (computers, access points, and router). WPA runs your security from that point on. The master key allows only devices with a matching master key to join the network, which keeps out eavesdroppers and other unauthorized users. Then, WPA uses encryption algorithms that are more powerful than those provided in WEP.

However, WPA presents a small problem for people who have already installed Wi-Fi hardware — either WEP or WPA security is built into the hardware chips, but not both. If your network hardware doesn't support WPA, most manufacturers offer what's called a *firmware update* to move existing wireless hardware to the new security standard. A firmware update is a small program that applies itself to the chipset (the process is called *burning*). If you have older WEP equipment, you should be able to download the update from the manufacturer at no cost.

Firmware updates are specific to manufacturer and model. You cannot update your model number with a "similar" model number. Installing the wrong firmware turns your hardware into a useless piece of metal. If your model has been discontinued, don't use the firmware for the replacement model. Instead, contact the manufacturer to see if firmware is available for your hardware. If not, continue to use WEP or buy a new device.

Mix and match WEP and WPA

If some of your network devices support WEP, and other (newer or updated) devices support WPA, you can mix those devices on your network. However, your network security drops to the level of the weakest security feature, which is WEP. If running WEP makes you nervous or just "un-geeky," eventually you should update your network hardware to gain WPA support.

Experts claim that WPA isn't a total security solution; it's just better than WEP. Security for wireless networks is an emerging technology, and as more wireless devices become popular, security will continue to improve.

A real problem with these security features is the way they're applied — some manufacturers apply higher-level security measures only in access points (or in routers, which have built-in access points) instead of applying security features in network adapters. If you're not using an access point, check with your manufacturer to see if you can apply security with your network adapters.

Wireless Hotspots for Public Use

Throughout the world, companies are setting up public-use wireless networks, called *hotspots,* enabling anyone with a wireless network adapter on a laptop to get to the Internet. You'll find hotspots at airports, chain stores (especially coffee shop chains), and all sorts of other locations. Today, a number of cities are providing wireless access on a city-wide basis.

An up-to-date list of hotspots is available at www.wi-fihotspotlist.com. You can search by country, state, or city to find a hotspot near you.

Hotspots are either commercial (you pay a fee to use the network) or public (free). Free hotspots are often available from nonprofit organizations that are committed to eliminating the digital divide that exists between economic levels.

Some corporations provide membership in commercial hotspots to let their mobile warriors join the company network while they're on the road. (Goodness, we wouldn't want an employee to have an hour's free time in an airport when she could be working!) Two popular commercial hotspot companies are Boingo (www.boingo.com) and T-Mobile (www.tmobile.com). These companies offer thousands of hotspot locations, and you can enroll online (or start your own hotspot branch as a franchise business).

To use a hotspot, your laptop must have a wireless adapter as well as software that can join the hotspot network. Windows XP and Windows Vista both discover the network automatically and ask you if you want to join it. If you do, the operating system automatically finds the technical information it needs and configures your adapter.

Some hotspots don't broadcast the SSID, so you have to find out what it is. Some public hotspots post the SSID on a sign, but if you don't see a sign, you have to ask someone. In an airport, no one may be available (or the person "minding the store" hasn't the vaguest idea what an SSID is). Don't assume that an employee of the coffee-shop whose hotspot you're using knows the SSID either (trust me).

To join the hotspot network, you need to fill out a logon dialog box (just as you do with your own home network). If you have a membership with the hotspot operator, you just fill in your logon name and password. If you don't have a membership, you're asked to fill in credit card information. (Free hotspots tell you the logon name and password to use.) You use your browser to log on, and specific instructions are available from the hotspot provider.

Here are some guidelines for using hotspots:

✔ You must be using an 802.11b, 802.11g, or 802.11n adapter — I know of no hotspots that support 802.11a.

✔ Some hotspots don't use encryption, so you may have to reconfigure your adapter to turn off encryption. However, more and more hotspots are using WPA.

✔ Don't use a hotspot that doesn't apply encryption unless you're running a firewall on the computer.

✔ Even if you're running a firewall, don't send sensitive data through a hotspot because the firewall can't protect data during transmission.

✔ Be sure to log off when you're done because the clock that's watching your session and determining the fee you'll pay doesn't shut off until a log off closes your session record.

Part II

Configuring Computers for Networking

"I guess you could say this is the hub of our network."

In this part . . .

After you've installed all the hardware and connected all the computers, you have to perform a few software-based chores. You can put away your tools because you do the rest of the setup stuff at the computer. The only tools you need are keyboards and mice.

The chapters in this part of the book walk you through the tasks required for setting up the software side of networking. None of the tasks are complicated, and many of them are automated or semi-automated — the computer does most of the work for you, which is what computers are supposed to do.

Some of the stuff you have to do is routine technical stuff, like installing *drivers* (software files that control network hardware devices). You also have to set up each computer so it's willing to share some of its contents with the rest of the network.

The information in the chapters in this part goes beyond simple networking procedures: You also learn how to share your Internet connection among all the computers on your network. Installing shared Internet access probably cures more family problems than an expensive therapist. You don't have to set rules about time limits, and you'll no longer hear the whines and yells that echoed through the house when somebody stayed online too long.

Chapter 6

Putting It All Together

- -

- -

Simply connecting cable (or antennas) to your home computers doesn't create a network. It's like attaching a VCR to your TV set: After the cable is connected, you still have to set up the system before you can do anything with it. On a computer network, you have to set up everything by installing the software that controls the communication features. This chapter shows you how to do this.

Throughout this chapter, I use standard techie terminology, and to avoid confusion, you must understand that the piece of hardware that connects each computer to a network is called a *network adapter*. It's the device that connects to cable (for cabled networks) or provides an antenna (for wireless networks). Back in the days when adapters were available only for cable and had to be installed manually inside the computer, they were known as Network Interface Cards or Network Interface Connections and commonly referred to as NICs (pronounced "nicks").

When you see the word *NIC,* it also means network adapter, and when you see the term *network adapter,* it also means NIC. If you get used to both terms, you can easily discuss your network (or get help from techies for problems) because techies tend to use the word *NIC.*

Prep Your Network Devices

Technically, the Windows network setup processes are designed to configure all the computers on your network to communicate with each other by using a connection device such as a hub or a switch. That's the "meeting place" where the computers gather together so they can converse with each other. In addition to the computers, other network devices (routers, modems, and so on) have to meet so the computers can talk to the devices and vice versa.

Installing drivers for network adapters

Your network connectors are hardware devices, and every hardware device on a computer needs a *driver*. Drivers are files that the operating system uses to communicate with the hardware, telling the hardware what to do, when to do it, and how to do it.

If your NIC is built into your computer's system board (sometimes called a *motherboard*), the drivers exist in Windows and are loaded when you boot the computer.

If you're adding a NIC, it's almost certainly connected to a USB port, and Windows discovers USB devices as soon as you connect them (you don't have to turn off your computer to connect a device to a USB port). Automatic detection of devices is a feature called *Plug and Play.*

The Plug and Play feature is like a little elf that looks at all the hardware in your computer during startup, and when a new Plug and Play hardware component is detected, he notifies Windows. As soon as Windows hears about the new hardware, it wants to begin installing the software drivers immediately.

If your network connector is a USB device, and you installed it while your computer was running, the Windows Plug and Play elf was watching and offered to install the software as soon as you plugged in the connector — you didn't have to restart the computer. This ability to install a device without shutting down the computer is called a *hot installation,* and it's one of the coolest things about USB devices (yes, that's a pun).

Windows sends a message to your screen to tell you that it has found the new hardware you added and then checks its own driver files to see if a driver exists. If Windows doesn't have a driver for your network connector, the Add Network Wizard appears so you can install the driver manually (covered later in this chapter in the section "Manually Setting Up the Network").

Preparing other network hardware

Most networks have hardware devices in addition to the NICs on the computers. There may be a router that acts as a concentrator to connect the computers as well as enable those computers to share a high-speed Internet connection. There may even be a telephone modem that all the network computers share to reach the Internet.

Some networks may have bridges, which are devices used to mesh two different types of network technology. For instance, a wireless network isn't totally wireless if it shares an Internet connection because there's cable between the router and the DSL/cable modem.

Or, you may have a mixed network, in which a couple of wireless computers meet one or more Ethernet-cabled computers, and they all join together with a wireless access point or a wireless router, or even a wired router.

Perhaps you have a powerline or phoneline network that shares an Internet connection via a router, which means you have a powerline or phoneline bridge device to bridge the gap between your topology and the Ethernet topology the router uses.

If your network is totally connected with Ethernet, you can prep the additional devices either before or after you configure the computers for networking. But if you take care of setting up the additional devices first, you won't have to interrupt the network configuration process when you want to set up a shared Internet connection.

The important thing to know is that all of these doohickeys (wireless routers, access points, and bridges) can only be configured by Ethernet, so you have to connect the device to a computer with an Ethernet cable to perform the prep. After the devices are running properly, you can remove the cable and let them run in their native mode.

Wireless Ad-hoc mode versus infrastructure mode

Wireless networks can be established in two ways: in Ad-hoc mode or in infrastructure mode. *Ad-hoc mode* is used when you just want two or more wireless computers to find each other. This is useful if all you want to do is access the other wireless computers (for exchanging files). *Infrastructure mode* means you've installed an access point or a router (or both) so that you can take advantage of security features (such as assigning an SSID and encrypting communication, as explained in Chapter 5) and can share an Internet connection. Throughout all my discussions of wireless networks in this book, I assume you're using infrastructure mode.

The only network device that doesn't require a setup configuration process is a concentrator (a hub or a switch). Just plug it in and attach the computers and other network devices with Ethernet cable.

Connecting wireless doohickeys to an Ethernet adapter

Here's the dilemma — to install and configure a wireless router or an access point, you must connect a computer to the device with Ethernet cable. The router/access point is not a totally wireless device; it has a wireless side and an Ethernet side. The Ethernet side is used to connect to a router or to a concentrator that is connected to a router. After the device is set up, you can disconnect the Ethernet connection to the computer you used to set up the device and let the device perform its tasks wirelessly (although a wireless router continues to use a wired connection to other devices such as modems). Your router or access point has an Ethernet cable in the box, along with a software disc and instructions.

If you're connecting wireless computers to an existing Ethernet network, just plug the access point into your concentrator. You can access the device from any computer on the network that's attached to the concentrator.

Most computers come with an Ethernet adapter built in, and if one of your computers has one, you can connect the router/access point to it. Check the back of your computer to see if you have one. Don't confuse an Ethernet adapter with a telephone modem (also built in to many computers). Here are some clues to telling which is which:

✔ The documentation that came with your computer should have information about the devices installed in the computer.

✔ A telephone modem adapter usually has two connectors — one for the modem and one for a telephone.

✔ The Ethernet connector at the end of the cable is an RJ-45 connector, which is slightly larger than the RJ-11 connector for telephone wire. A telephone wire connector falls out of an RJ-45 port, and an Ethernet cable connector doesn't slide into an RJ-11 port easily.

✔ The Device Manager dialog box includes an Ethernet adapter in the list of devices if you have one. (Chapter 14 has information about using the Device Manager.) Here's how you get to the Device Manager:

   • In Windows XP, click Start, right-click My Computer, and choose Properties. Move to the Hardware tab and click Device Manager.

   • In Windows Vista, click Start, right-click Computer, and choose Manage. Select Device Manager in the left pane of the Management Console.

If you have no Ethernet adapters on any computers on your network, take the router/access point to a friend who has a computer with an Ethernet adapter. Set up the device and bring it back home.

Configuring routers

To reach the router configuration window, you must access the router through a browser (using a computer attached to the router). Each manufacturer has a unique configuration tool, along with documentation and instructions for configuring your network. To enter the configuration tool, you must open your browser and enter the router's IP address in the address bar. Here are the IP addresses of the popular routers:

✔ Belkin: 192.168.2.1

✔ D-Link: 192.168.0.1

✔ Linksys: 192.168.1.1

✔ Netgear: 192.168.0.1

All router configuration tools are configured to make you enter a username or a password or both. If you haven't changed the default username and password, use the entries provided in Table 6-1 to fill out the user name and password fields when the login screen appears. Then, secure the router's configuration tool by creating your own login name and password.

Table 6-1	Login Names and Passwords for Popular Routers	
Manufacturer	*Login Name*	*Password*
Belkin	(Field does not exist)	(Do not fill in)
D-Link	admin (lowercase)	(Do not fill in)
Linksys	(Do not fill in)	admin (lowercase)
Netgear	admin (lowercase)	password (lowercase)

Read the instructions from the router's manufacturer and from your ISP to configure the router. You can set basic LAN configuration options or, if necessary, more exotic (and complicated) options.

Don't mess with advanced settings on your router unless you do so under the guidance of a trained professional.

For routers, you must use the settings provided by your ISP, including (but not necessarily limited to)

- ✔ The subnet mask
- ✔ The IP address of the ISP's gateway
- ✔ The IP address of the ISP's DNS server (or multiple DNS servers)

The documentation for the device provides information for the router's settings, including (but not necessarily limited to)

- ✔ Entering a new password to replace the default password
- ✔ Setting up DHCP services
- ✔ Setting security values
- ✔ Setting firewall options (if the router includes a firewall)

If your router is wireless, after you finish the setup processes, you can disconnect the Ethernet cable and let the antenna connect to the wireless adapters on the computers.

Configuring access points

Connect your wireless access point to a computer via Ethernet cable and insert the CD that came with the device. Most manufacturers' installation CDs automatically launch a setup and configuration wizard that's easy to use. If your access point software is not wizard-based, read the installation guide that came with the device (some installation guides are on the CD).

Manually Setting Up the Network

In both Windows XP and Windows Vista, you can perform the individual tasks required to connect your network computers and share an Internet connection. The steps aren't difficult, but if you think you may be totally technically deficient (and you don't have a thirteen-year-old in the house — they seem to know all this techie stuff instinctively), you should take the wizard route (covered in the section "Using the Windows Home Networking Wizards," later in this chapter). The Windows home networking wizards approach all the tasks in the right order and can automatically find some of the data you're required to enter when you configure your network.

If you want to take the do-it-yourself route you have to specify configuration data so the computer can join the network. For the NIC, the settings are for both the network and the shared Internet connection (and are supplied by your ISP).

Welcome the computer to your network

You have to give your network a name, which is called a *workgroup* name. Actually, Microsoft has already named your workgroup, but since almost everyone in the world knows those names, it's dangerous to leave the default name in place.

- Windows XP names your workgroup MSHOME.
- Windows Vista names your workgroup WORKGROUP.

To name your network and add a computer to the network, use the appropriate steps for your version of Windows, as described next.

Joining a network in Windows XP

To add a computer running Windows XP to a network, use the following steps:

1. **Click Start and right-click My Computer.**

2. **Choose Properties from the menu that appears.**

   The System Properties dialog box appears.

3. **Move to the Computer Name tab (see Figure 6-1).**

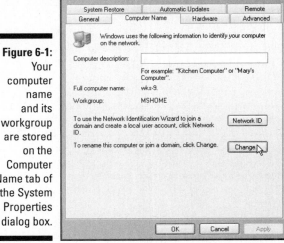

Figure 6-1: Your computer name and its workgroup are stored on the Computer Name tab of the System Properties dialog box.

4. **Click the Change button.**

   The Computer Name Changes dialog box appears.

5. **Enter your network name in the Workgroup field and click OK.**

   Windows welcomes you to your own network (see Figure 6-2).

Figure 6-2: Welcome home!

6. **Click OK and follow the prompts to save the network name and restart your computer.**

The Internet: From your house to the world and back

The Internet works by using communication hardware to move data from server to server all over the world. A hierarchy of computers accomplishes this massive feat. For you, sending and receiving data starts and ends with your hardware, which is responsible for moving data between your computer and all the other computers on the Internet.

You're not hooked up directly with the Internet computer you want to communicate with (such as Microsoft's Web sites) — your data moves through a bunch of computers to get to your target. The hierarchy of computers that runs the Internet starts (or ends, depending on how you look at it) with a group of computers called the *backbone*. Backbone servers are strategically placed throughout the world, and they communicate with the next layer of servers, all of which communicate with the next layer, and so on.

You use your hardware to communicate with an ISP, which is a company you connect to in order to move through the Internet. The ISP uses its hardware to communicate with the next layer of servers, and each layer moves data to the next until the packet of information reaches the target server (the Web page you want to see or the mailbox of the recipient of your e-mail message). Each time a server moves data to another server, it's called a *hop.* If you want to see how many hops it takes to get from your computer to a particular place on the Internet, check out the sidebar "Tracing the route to a Web site."

Joining a network in Windows Vista

To add a computer running Windows Vista to a network, use the following steps:

1. **Click Start and right-click Computer.**

2. **Choose Properties from the menu that appears.**

   The System Properties window appears.

3. **Click Change Settings.**

   The Computer Name tab of the System Properties dialog box appears.

4. **Click the Change button.**

   The Computer Name Changes dialog box appears.

5. **Enter your network name in the Workgroup field and click OK.**

   Windows welcomes you to your network.

6. **Click OK and follow the prompts to save the network name and restart your computer.**

Tracing the route to a Web site

Windows has a nifty utility that lets you trace the route from your computer to a Web site, and you can use it while you're connected to the Internet. It's a command-line utility, so you need to open a command window by choosing Start⇨All Programs⇨Accessories⇨Command Prompt.

In the command window, type **tracert *WebSite*** (substitute the name of the Web site you want to track down for *WebSite*) and press Enter. (Tracert stands for *trace route*.) The tracert utility tracks the hops between your computer and the target server. For example, I wanted to see the number of hops involved in communicating with one of my own Web sites from my office. Here's what appeared on my screen after I entered **tracert ivens.com**:

```
Tracing route to ivens.com [64.226.173.212]
over a maximum of 30 hops:
 1  10 ms  10 ms  10 ms  dsl092-230-065.phl1.dsl.speakeasy.net
       [66.92.230.65]
 2  10 ms  10 ms  10 ms  dsl092-239-001.phl1.dsl.speakeasy.net
       [66.92.239.1]
 3  10 ms  10 ms  10 ms  border1.fe5-14.speakeasy-
       27.ext1.phi.pnap.net [216.52.67.91]
 4  10 ms  10 ms  10 ms  core1.fe0-1-bbnet2.phi.pnap.net
       [216.52.64.65]
 5  10 ms  10 ms  10 ms  p3-3.phlapa1-cr1.bbnplanet.net
       [4.25.93.33]
 6  10 ms  10 ms  10 ms  p4-0.phlapa1-br1.bbnplanet.net
       [4.24.11.82]
 7  10 ms  10 ms  10 ms  p15-0.phlapa1-br2.bbnplanet.net
       [4.24.10.90]
 8  10 ms  20 ms  10 ms  so-0-0-0.washdc3-nbr2.bbnplanet.net
       [4.24.10.185]
 9  10 ms  20 ms  10 ms  so-7-0-0.washdc3-nbr1.bbnplanet.net
       [4.24.10.29]
10  30 ms  30 ms  30 ms  so-0-0-0.atlnga1-br1.bbnplanet.net
       [4.24.10.14]
11  30 ms  30 ms  30 ms  so-0-0-0.atlnga1-hcr9.bbnplanet.net
       [4.0.1.250]
12  30 ms  30 ms  30 ms
       gigabitethernet0.nethostat1gig.bbnplanet.net [4.0.36.14]
13  30 ms  30 ms  30 ms  64.224.0.67
14  30 ms  30 ms  30 ms  64.226.173.212
Trace complete.
```

The trace started with my ISP, Speakeasy.net, and then Speakeasy moved me through the Internet to the servers of the company that hosts my Web site. Note the time lapses displayed on the screen, which are calculated in milliseconds (ms). I'm using a high-speed Internet device — a digital subscriber line (DSL) — and if you try this with a telephone modem, you'll probably see much higher numbers, indicating slower communication rates.

For both Windows XP and Windows Vista, if the computer you're setting up is using a wireless connection, Windows also prompts you to join the wireless network (which you named when you set up your router or access point) by entering the SSID. The SSID does not replace the network name, it's an additional name to provide the additional security required for wireless networks — in effect, wireless networks have two network names.

Sharing a connection with a router

Assuming you set up your router according to your ISP's instructions, as discussed earlier in this chapter, your computers should automatically find the router and be trolling the 'Net immediately.

If you have a problem accessing the Internet, check the ISP's instructions and the setup guide that came with your router to see if you have to add the router's address to each NIC. If so, use the following steps:

1. **Open the NIC's Properties dialog box, select TCP/IP, and click Properties.**

2. **Click the Advanced button.**

3. **Enter the router's IP address in the Gateway field.**

Sharing a telephone modem

If you're using a telephone modem to connect to the Internet, you need two things:

✓ **An account with an ISP:** To find an ISP that you can trust, ask friends or check reviews in computer magazines.

✓ **A software connection to the ISP:** The software connection to the ISP is part of the dial-up networking (DUN) feature that's built into Windows.

Install a DUN connection on the computer that has the modem. Before you start, be sure you have the following information at your fingertips (it's all provided by your ISP):

✓ The local phone number that you dial to log on to your ISP.

✓ Your online account username.

  ✔ Your online account password. (Some ISPs give you a password. Others let you choose the password yourself, and you must give it to the ISP when you sign up.)

  ✔ The TCP/IP settings needed to communicate with your ISP's server.

In both Windows XP and Windows Vista, use the Network Connection feature in the Network and Internet section of Control Panel. The Properties dialog of your network connection (the modem) lists the options you need to configure, following the instructions from your ISP. When you select the option to share the connection, Windows automatically sets up the Internet Connection Sharing (ICS) feature. The TCP/IP settings for your ICS configuration must be duplicated in each NIC on each computer in the network.

You can also use ICS to share a cable/DSL modem that's attached directly to a computer, but that's a waste of power and speed. Buy a router and connect the modem to it so the computers on the network don't have to depend on the host computer to access the Internet. (If you don't want to use a router, the setup of ICS is similar to the telephone modem setup discussed in the previous paragraph, so just duplicate the TCP/IP settings on every computer.)

Using the Windows Home Networking Wizards

Windows XP provides two networking wizards: one for cabled networks and one for wireless networks. When Windows XP encounters a network cabled with powerline adapters or phoneline adapters, it thinks it's looking at Ethernet cable, which is fine and dandy because both of these network cabling types act like Ethernet (well, a slower form of Ethernet).

Windows Vista has a wizard that walks you through the process of setting up a wireless network. If you have a cabled network, Windows Vista discovers it automatically, and you only have to fine tune the settings.

I cover these wizards in the following sections.

Windows XP Network Setup Wizard

The Windows XP Network Setup Wizard walks you through the steps you need to complete to have your computer join a wired network.

To launch the Windows XP Network Setup Wizard, follow these steps:

1. **Choose Start⇨Control Panel.**

   The Control Panel window opens.

2. **Click Network and Internet Connections.**

   The Network and Internet Connections window opens.

3. **Click Network Setup Wizard.**

You can also get to the Network Wizard through the Start menu, but that requires more mouse clicks, and I always take the easiest way.

The first wizard window is a welcoming message that requires no action on your part except clicking Next to see a window that tells you to check a list of tasks before running the wizard. The text in the window also explains that the wizard will search for a shared Internet connection device on your network.

The tasks referred to are the installation of your network hardware and the installation of the hardware's drivers. Because you've done that (unless you didn't pay any attention to all the stuff I wrote earlier in this chapter), click Next to get started. In the following paragraphs, I discuss the options and actions you face in the remaining wizard windows.

Select a connection method

The next wizard window (see Figure 6-3) asks you to select a connection method, which means it's setting up your Internet connection in addition to creating your network.

Figure 6-3:
The wizard
offers
multiple
choices to
describe the
way this
computer
connects to
the Internet.

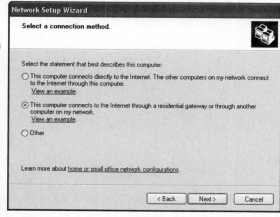

Direct connection to a modem

The first option is labeled "This computer connects directly to the Internet. The other computers on my network connect to the Internet through this computer." Select this option if the computer you're currently working on has a modem (either a dial-up modem or a DSL/cable modem) attached directly to the computer with cable, and you plan to share the connection. To share a connection via a modem connected to a computer, you must use the Windows Internet Connection Sharing (ICS) feature (discussed earlier in this chapter).

If you're using ICS to share a connection with a modem that's attached directly to a computer, make that computer the first one you set up.

Direct connection to a router or to a computer with a modem

The second option is labeled "This computer connects to the Internet through a residential gateway or through another computer on my network." Select this option if either of the following circumstances applies:

- You are connected to a router (Windows uses the term *residential gateway* for router) by Ethernet cable running between the computer and the router (you are using the router instead of a hub or a switch to connect the computer to the network).

- Another computer, which you already set up, has a cable connection to a router, and this computer will share that connection, and both computers will be plugged into a concentrator in order to talk to each other.

The Other option

The third option is labeled "Other," which you should select if any of the scenarios described in the following paragraphs fit your situation. After selecting the "Other" option, click Next to see the wizard window shown in Figure 6-4.

Figure 6-4:
More options are available if the first wizard window didn't describe your setup.

In the Other Internet Connection Methods wizard window, you have the following three options:

✔ **Direct connection to a concentrator or a modem that won't be shared:** The first option is labeled "This computer connects to the Internet directly or through a network hub. Other computers on my network also connect to the Internet directly or through a hub." Select this option if the computer is connected to a concentrator (a hub or a switch), as are the other computers on the network, and the concentrator is connected to a router (which is, in turn, connected to a modem). All the computers on the concentrator share the Internet connection via the router.

If you ignore the text in the option that refers to connecting to the Internet directly, this is a common configuration for networks. Your computers meet at the concentrator, which in turn connects to a router to let all the computers share a connection.

If you don't ignore the text about a direct connection to the Internet, it's because this computer is attached to its own modem, which won't be shared with other computers. The other computers could be sharing a different modem via a connection to a router or to a concentrator that is attached to a router. Or, the other computers also have their own modems (which means you have to have a phoneline, DSL, or cable connection for each individual modem connection — highly unlikely).

✔ **Set up only an Internet connection:** The second option on the Other Internet Connection Methods wizard window is for setting up an Internet connection, via a modem that's attached to this computer, when you have no interest in setting up a network. The option is labeled "This computer connects directly to the Internet. I do not have a network yet."

I have no idea why anyone who is not setting up a network would launch the Network Setup Wizard. I've tried to figure out why this option is presented, but I can't read the minds of the Microsoft programmers who included this option. You can set up an Internet connection on a single (non-networked) computer through the Internet Connection options in Control Panel.

✔ **No Internet connection available:** The last option on the Other Internet Connection Methods wizard window is labeled "This computer belongs to a network that does not have an Internet connection." Select this option if you're just setting up a network for file and printer sharing and you don't have a modem in the house. While this option hardly ever applies to a home network, it's used in many corporate businesses to create a small network that must be absolutely secure but also must be able to share files. For example, the accounting department, especially the payroll department, of a corporation stores files with sensitive information such as social security numbers, bank account numbers, and so on. The risk of information being stolen from the computers is reduced by eliminating Internet access.

Name the computer

In the next window, the wizard asks you to enter a description of the computer and to give the computer a name. The description is optional, but the computer name isn't. Each computer on the network must have a unique name. Click Next after you've named the computer.

Name your network

In the next window, you must name your network. By default, the wizard selects the name MSHOME, but you can change it to any name you want (many people use the family name). The network name must be the same on every computer in the network. Click Next to continue.

Enable file and printer sharing

In the next window, you can enable file and printer sharing. The wizard explains the consequences of each choice in the text displayed in the window (see Figure 6-5).

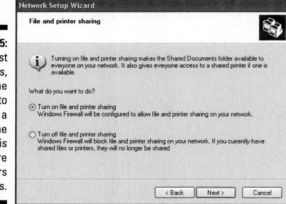

Figure 6-5:
In most families, one of the reasons to install a home network is to share printers and files.

You may see a warning that enabling file and printer sharing is dangerous if you have a direct connection to the Internet. If you've paid attention to firewalls and other security devices described in this book, it's safe to enable file and printer sharing.

Confirm the settings

The wizard shows you the network settings it's going to apply to the computer (see Figure 6-6), your NIC, the network software, and even the firewall, which saves you a whole bunch of manual steps. When you click Next, it applies the settings, which takes a few minutes.

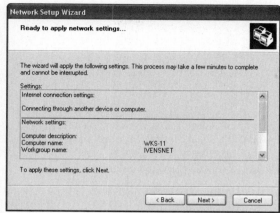

Figure 6-6:
The
Network
Setup
Wizard
ready to
apply your
network
configu-
ration
settings.

After the settings are applied, the wizard offers a variety of ways to set up computers that are not running Windows XP. However, you can *not* use any of these methods for a computer running Windows Vista (which has its own network wizard). If you have any computers running a version of Windows earlier than Windows XP, you can use any of the methods described in the wizard window.

Run the wizard on all the computers on your network to finish building your network.

Windows XP Wireless Network Setup Wizard

If you're setting up a wireless network, you have a network setup wizard designed specifically for you. To launch it, use the following steps:

1. **Choose Start➪Control Panel.**

   The Control Panel window opens.

2. **Click Network and Internet Connections.**

   The Network and Internet Connections window opens.

3. **Click Wireless Network Setup Wizard.**

The wireless network setup was introduced in Service Pack 2 of Windows XP. If you haven't downloaded and installed SP2, do that before you set up your wireless network. The Windows Update center (its icon is on the right side of your taskbar) has the selections you need to accomplish this.

The Wireless Network Setup Wizard assumes you're setting up your network in infrastructure mode (see the sidebar, "Wireless Ad-hoc mode versus infrastructure mode," earlier in this chapter). The wizard provides the basic configuration options for security — to set up file and printer sharing, you must run the "regular" network wizard or set up each adapter manually.

Set basic wireless configuration options

Walk through the wizard windows, starting with the window that asks you to create an SSID for your wireless network, and select an encryption option (see Figure 6-7). For more about SSIDs and encryption, read Chapter 5.

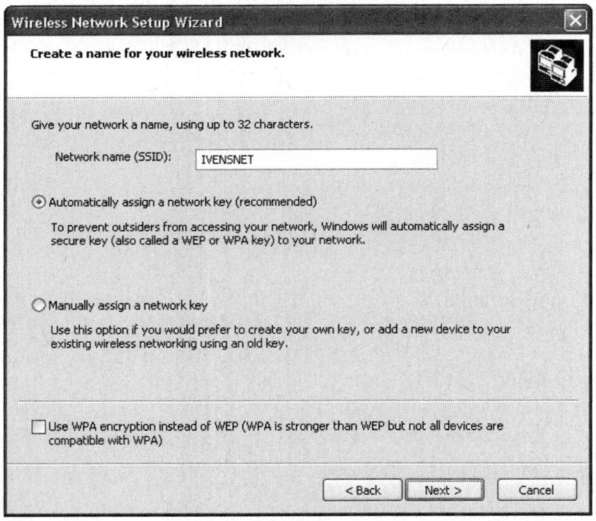

Figure 6-7:
Setting up your wireless network is easier with a wizard that's designed specifically for this purpose.

> **Wireless Network Setup Wizard**
>
> **Create a name for your wireless network.**
>
> Give your network a name, using up to 32 characters.
>
> Network name (SSID): IVENSNET
>
> ⦿ Automatically assign a network key (recommended)
>
>   To prevent outsiders from accessing your network, Windows will automatically assign a secure key (also called a WEP or WPA key) to your network.
>
> ○ Manually assign a network key
>
>   Use this option if you would prefer to create your own key, or add a new device to your existing wireless networking using an old key.
>
> ☐ Use WPA encryption instead of WEP (WPA is stronger than WEP but not all devices are compatible with WPA)
>
>   [< Back] [Next >] [Cancel]

In the following paragraphs, I assume you selected the option to assign a network key (the encrypted password) automatically. If you prefer to assign a key manually, see "Setting up network keys manually," later in this chapter.

Saving the settings

The security settings (SSID and encrypted password) must be the same on every wireless computer on the network. The wizard offers you two ways to save the settings the wizard creates so you can use them on all the computers: Save the settings to a USB flash drive or set up the other computers manually.

For this step (saving settings), the wizard only saves the settings; it doesn't apply the settings to this computer. That step occurs after you've saved the settings because the wizard uses the saved data for this computer as well as for the other computers.

Saving the settings for automatic transfer to the other wireless computers on the network is much better than manually matching the security settings on the other computers. These settings are much more complicated than those required on a wired network.

A USB flash drive is a cute little storage device that is sometimes called a keychain drive (because you can hang it on a keychain) or a stick drive. You plug the device into a USB port and have instant access to the drive. You can save files or copy files from the drive to a computer. Flash drives come in a variety of sizes from 256MB to several gigabytes.

If you don't have a flash drive, the wizard offers the option to print all the settings so you can use the printed document to enter data in the other computers.

For those of you who are flash drive impaired, there's another option, which I came up with when I realized I didn't want to type in those long, arcane settings. (The first time I set up a wireless network, I didn't have a flash drive, although now I couldn't live without one on every computer.) Here's a typical printout, and I'll bet you don't want to type all this stuff in, either:

```
Network Name (SSID): Ivensnet
Network Key (WEP/WPA Key):
75101c23af79474ab9ad12165b2591cb6f04824b139c4480199b91cd87
        a1e
Key Provided Automatically (802.1x): 0
Network Authentication Type: WPAPSK
Data Encryption Type: TKIP
Connection Type: ESS
```

To be able to copy and paste this stuff into the wireless setup for the other computers, I created a plain text printer file. To accomplish this, I had to install a plain text printer that was configured to print to a file. Then, when the wizard printed the document, I selected that printer. This gave me a text file that can be opened in Notepad on any computer, and it fits on a floppy disk so I could take it to the other wireless computers.

To install a text printer on your computer, open the Printers folder and start the Add Printer Wizard. Install the printer using the following configuration options:

- ✔ Specify a local printer.
- ✔ Deselect the option Automatically detect and install my Plug and Play printer (there's no text printer plugged into any port).
- ✔ Select FILE (Print to File) as the port.
- ✔ In the Manufacturer list, select Generic.
- ✔ In the Printers list, select Generic/Text Only.
- ✔ Use the default printer name (Generic/Text Only).
- ✔ Don't make this printer the default printer.
- ✔ Don't share the printer.
- ✔ Don't print a test page.

When it's time to have the wizard print the wireless network settings, select the Generic/Text Only printer in the Print dialog box. You don't have to select the option Print to File because the printer is already configured to print to a file. Just click the Print button. When the Print to File dialog box opens, enter a filename and add the extension .txt to the filename (so it automatically opens in Notepad). Copy the file to a floppy disk, insert the floppy disk in the disk drive of the next computer you set up, double-click the file to open it, and copy and paste the information into the wireless network wizard on the other computer.

If any computer on your network lacks a floppy drive (they're becoming extinct faster than some endangered animal species), stop now, go to your favorite office supply store, and buy a USB flash drive. You really don't want to enter all these settings manually — not only is it tiresome and time-consuming, the risk of making a typo is very high.

Applying the settings

When the settings exist on a USB drive, the wizard displays the window shown in Figure 6-8. If you selected the option to save the settings to a print-out (which you might have saved as a text file), the wizard walks you through all the individual settings so you can enter data in every field of every wizard window. I'm assuming that you preferred the option to save to a USB drive.

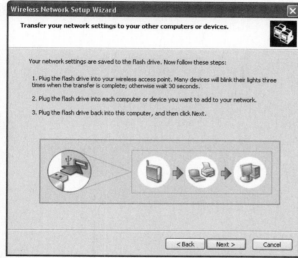

Figure 6-8:
Apply the settings to every wireless computer on the network.

Follow the prompts to transfer the settings to the computer. When all the computers are configured, the last wizard window offers an option to remove the settings from the USB drive. This is a good idea because USB flash drives tend to be carried around, and you don't want to leave the drive somewhere that permits an outsider to use the settings to gain access to your computer.

On the other hand, it's good to have the settings available for the next wireless computer you purchase. The solution is to copy the settings to a CD and put the CD away in a safe place.

The settings on the USB drive are saved in a folder named SMRTNTKY, which contains a subfolder for device information and files for the settings.

Setting up network keys manually

If you choose not to automatically assign a network key (encrypted password), in the wizard window for naming the network, select the option Manually Assign a Network Key and click Next. The window that appears differs depending on whether you selected the option to use WPA encryption (explained in Chapter 5).

If you deselected the WPA option and are using WEP (because the devices you purchased don't support WPA), the next wizard window looks like Figure 6-9.

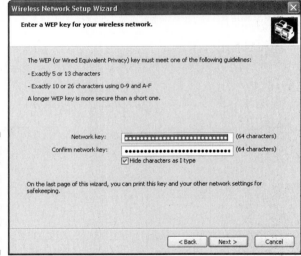

Figure 6-9:
The rules for WEP keys are spelled out in the wizard window.

If you selected the WPA option, the next wizard window looks similar to the WEP window, but the rules are different (the minimum number of characters is 8 instead of 6, the maximum is 63, and the mixed alphanumeric character key must be exactly 64 characters long).

If you accept the default entries, you'll have to print out the data because you certainly can't read what's entered in the wizard window. Because you've opted to do this manually, make it a true manual task. To enter a password of your own making, deselect the Hide Characters As I Type option and enter a phrase or series of characters that you'll remember when you set up the other computers.

Windows Vista Wireless Network Setup Wizard

Windows Vista only supplies a wizard for configuring wireless networks because setting up wired networks is completely automated by the operating system. After you use the steps described earlier in this chapter to change the name of the network in the Computer Name tab of the System Properties dialog box, Windows Vista creates your network.

For your wireless Windows Vista computers, use the following steps to set up your network with the Windows Vista Wireless Network Setup Wizard:

1. **Choose Start⬦Network.**

   The Network folder opens.

2. **Click the Network and Sharing button on the Network folder toolbar.**

   The Network and Sharing window opens.

3. **In the left pane, choose Set Up a Connection or Network.**

4. **In the next window, click Set Up a Wireless Router or Access Point (see Figure 6-10) and click Next.**

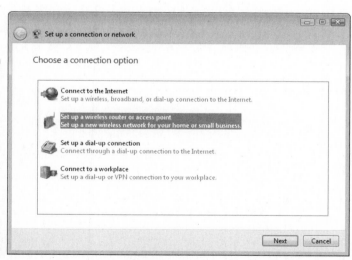

Figure 6-10:
Selecting the option to set up a wireless router or access point is also the option to set up a wireless network.

The next window explains the processes the wizard performs to set up your network.

5. **Click Next to continue.**

6. **Continue to click Next to move through the wizard windows. When you finish the wizard, your network is set up and configured.**

For your other Windows Vista wireless-equipped computers, follow the first two steps and then choose Connect to a Network from the task list in the left pane. Follow the prompts to join the additional wireless computers to the network.

Macintosh Can Join the Family, Too

If you have a Macintosh in the house, you can add it to your network, but the process is no cakewalk. It won't work unless you've chosen an Ethernet solution for your home network.

New Macs (and some older Macs) have built-in Ethernet adapters. You can buy NICs for the older Macs that lack adapters.

If you installed a NIC, use the installation CD that came with the NIC to install drivers. When all the software is transferred to the Mac, you need to restart the computer.

AppleTalk and EtherTalk (the protocol that runs AppleTalk over an Ethernet network) are preinstalled on most Macs. Make sure that AppleTalk is active — check the Active radio button in Appleshare. Also, make sure that the right network connection is selected. In the Apple menu, select Control Panels and select the Network or AppleTalk option. Then select the Ethernet or EtherTalk option (the default in OS X) and close the window.

MacTalk is the default networking mechanism for Mac OS machines. Unfortunately, MacTalk doesn't know about Windows; PCs don't speak MacTalk. Your challenge is to convince the Mac to communicate using Windows-compatible networking protocols. You can meet the challenge by using TCP/IP as the network protocol. In a way, you're creating an environment in which the Mac interacts with the PC as if both of them were communicating over the Internet.

 If you're running OS X, the ability to connect to Windows computers is built in. If you're running an earlier OS and you've purchased software to assist your efforts to join a peer-to-peer network that includes Windows machines, follow the instructions to complete the installation of networking protocols provided by that software.

Set the TCP/IP configuration in the TCP/IP Control Panel, entering a TCP/IP address for the Mac. In addition, the Mac must be configured for sharing, which is like selecting File and Printer Sharing in the PC:

1. **Open the Apple menu and select Control Panels.**

2. **Double-click the Sharing Setup option.**

3. **Enter your name, a password, and the name of the computer.**

   In the File Sharing section, check out the label on the File Sharing button.

4. **If the File Sharing label is Start, click the button to activate file shar-ing. If the label is Stop, the service is already running.**

Chapter 7

Configuring Computer Sharing

In This Chapter

▶ Creating shares on each computer

▶ Hiding files with hidden shares

---

*A*fter you install the network hardware, install the cable to connect the computers, and set up the operating system to recognize and use those items, your computers are members of the network. Each computer can *see* the other computers on your network. You can view the computers that are connected to your network by opening the network folder, which is My Network Places in Windows XP and Network in Windows Vista. Figure 7-1 shows the My Network Places folder for a home network.

Figure 7-1:
The computers on the network are displayed in the network folder.

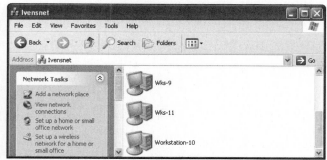

The list of computers you see includes the computer you're using, which of course you don't access through the network folder because you're already there.

Seeing a computer in the network folder means that the computer is up and running and is physically connected to the network. It doesn't mean that you can look inside the computer to see the files that are contained within it or that you can copy files from one computer to another. Computers don't share any resources until you configure them for sharing. I cover how to do that in this chapter.

The word *share* is used a lot in network computing:

✔ As a verb, *share* means configuring a resource on one computer so that people working on other computers can use it.

✔ As a noun, a *share* is a resource that's configured for access by users on other computers. If you configure your C drive for sharing, that drive is known as a share.

✔ Because you name a share when you create it, the term *sharename* describes the name you assigned the share, and the *sharename* is what network users see when they view shares in the network folder.

You have to create the shared resources that you want to offer to remote users. The most common shares are folders because those are the containers for files. However, you can also share drives and peripheral devices, such as a printer, CD-ROM, and USB flash drive. (Sharing printers is covered in Chapter 9, and the other types of shares are discussed in this chapter.)

Every share you create on a particular computer shows up in the network folder when you open (double-click) that computer's icon.

Understanding Hierarchy: Shares Have Parents and Children

Shares have a pecking order. Shares are made up of *parent shares* and *child shares*. This matches the hierarchy for drives, folders, and subfolders on your computer.

In the normal hierarchy you see in Windows Explorer, a parent is any container that can contain another container. A drive is the parent container for a folder, and a folder is a child of a drive. A folder can be a parent of a subfolder, and a subfolder is a child of its parent folder (and, by extension, I guess it's also a grandchild of a drive).

Having trouble? Think of the way the filing cabinet in your home office holds all your tax files or a manila envelope in your filing cabinet holds all the tax information for last year — both the filing cabinet and the manila envelope are parents because they both have something contained within them. The bottom line is that parents exist at every level of the hierarchy. You can remember this pretty easily if you figure that the youngest generation is the one that's least likely to have children of its own.

Figure 7-2 demonstrates the order in which containers and contained items are stored on your computer. This ordered pattern is called the *hierarchy*. Drives are the top of your computer's hierarchy and may contain folders or files or both. Folders can contain other folders or files or both.

(C:) This parent contains folders and subfolders

Parent container (Folder)   File

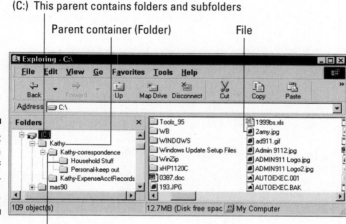

Figure 7-2:
The hierarchy of computer components.

Child containers (Subfolders)

When it comes to shares, however, the parent-child relationship begins on the level at which you create a share. For example, consider that you want to allow all the users in your home network to be able to share a drive. The drive that's being shared is a parent share. The same goes if you decide not to share a drive, but instead share specific folders. When you share a folder, that folder is a parent share, and any subfolder is a child share.

Memorize this rule because it's important to the way you maintain control over shares: *Every child in a parent share is automatically shared.*

The hard drive is also called the *root,* and the folders and files that are displayed when you look at the drive in Windows Explorer or My Computer are said to be located on the root.

Sharing a Hard Drive

Home networks commonly share all the folders and files on the hard drives of every computer. Sharing a drive is a convenient way to make sure that you can find and use files, no matter where they are on a computer. You don't automatically see the contents of a hard drive on another computer. First, you have to configure the hard drive for sharing.

Sharing a hard drive on a computer that's running Windows XP or Windows Vista requires a small skirmish with the operating system, which doesn't like the idea of sharing a drive.

Sharing a hard drive in Windows XP

Use the following steps to share a drive if you're using Windows XP:

1. **On the computer you're sharing, open My Computer.**

2. **Right-click the hard drive you want to share and choose Sharing and Security from the shortcut menu that appears.**

   The Sharing tab appears, and it may display a message that warns you that sharing a drive isn't a good idea. Beneath the message is a link you can click to indicate that you understand the risk but want to share the drive anyway.

3. **Click the link to share the drive.**

   The Sharing tab changes to reveal the options that allow you to share the drive.

4. **Select the Share This Folder on the Network option.**

5. **Enter a name for the share.**

6. **Select the Allow Network Users to Change My Files option.**

   If you don't select this option, network users can view files but can't create new files or modify existing files. Because you're a network user, you want to be able to work on a file on this computer from a different computer, so there's not much point in restricting what network users can do.

7. **Click OK.**

Sharing a hard drive in Windows Vista

To share a hard drive in Windows Vista, take the following steps:

1. **On the computer you're sharing, open Computer.**

2. **Right-click the hard drive you want to share and choose Share from the shortcut menu that appears.**

   The Sharing tab, shown in Figure 7-3, appears, with the Share button disabled (grayed out). Windows Vista disables the button as a hint about its attitude toward sharing drives.

Figure 7-3:
The Share button isn't available, but you *can* share a drive in Windows Vista.

3. **Click Advanced Sharing.**

   If you've enabled the User Access Control feature, Windows asks you to confirm the fact that you want to make this change.

4. **Click Continue.**

   The Advanced Sharing dialog box opens.

5. **Select the Share This Folder option and name the share.**

   By default, Windows names the share to match the drive letter, but you can change the name if you wish.

6. **Click Permissions.**

   The Permissions dialog box opens so you can assign rights to network users who access this shared drive. The group named Everyone is the only group listed in the dialog box, and the default permission level, Read, has been applied (see Figure 7-4).

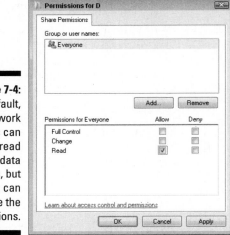

Figure 7-4:
By default, network users can only read (open) data files, but you can change the permissions.

7. **Select the Allow checkbox for Full Control to give network users the ability to create, modify, and delete files in this share.**

8. **Click OK twice to return to the drive's Properties dialog box, and then click Close to save your new settings.**

Sharing Removable Drives

You use the same steps that you used to share a hard drive when you want to share a peripheral (removable) drive. Peripheral drives are considered external to your computer (your hard drive is internal), such as a CD-ROM drive, a Zip drive, or a USB flash drive.

However, the results of sharing are a bit different because all your peripheral drives are also removable drives — therefore the contents change depending on which disk is currently inserted in the drive.

When you share a removable drive, you're actually sharing the bay, the empty drive. After it's shared, the share applies to any disk you place in the bay. This makes it a bit more difficult to decide about access controls. Some disks may have contents that you think everybody can use, and other disks may have contents that you prefer that nobody change.

CD-ROM drives are read-only. However, if you have a CD-R (CD-recordable) drive, never attempt to *burn,* or write to, a CD from a remote machine. It doesn't work properly. Burn CDs only from the machine that holds the CD-R drive.

Trying to set access controls for peripheral drives is foolish because you'd have to spend a lot of time changing the controls, depending on the disk that's inserted at any given time. The solution is to give full access to peripheral drives and then hide any disks that you don't want other users to access in a locked drawer.

Sharing Folders

If you've decided not to share the hard drives on your network computers, you need to share the folders that hold the files that you and other users need to access when you're working at a remote computer.

But, suppose you've shared the hard drive of your computer, and you understand the parent-child hierarchy, which essentially means that every folder on the shared drive is automatically shared. All a remote user has to do is access the shared drive, expand it to see all the folders, and then find the file she needs. In that case, why bother to share folders?

The reason to create shared folders, even if you've shared a drive, is to make it easier to get to shared folders from the other computers on the network. Remember, when you open the network folder and double-click a computer icon, all the shares on that computer are displayed. If the only share is the hard drive, it's going to take a lot of mouse clicks to navigate through the drive to get to a specific folder.

In addition, remote users (including you) may want to map a shared folder to a drive letter so that they can open the folder from My Computer (or Computer in Windows Vista) or Windows Explorer, instead of opening the network folder and drilling down through the shares. A folder must be shared to be mapped. Chapter 10 explains drive mapping and the convenience it offers.

You can create as many folder shares on your computer as you please, using the same steps you use to share a drive. However, instead of right-clicking the drive icon in My Computer (or Computer in Windows Vista) or Windows Explorer, right-click the icon for the folder you want to share.

You cannot share the Documents and Settings, Program Files, or Windows folders.

Windows XP Sharing Security — Sorting Out the Confusion

The problem with protecting or offering shares on a computer running Windows XP is that the situation changes depending on the file system being used on the computer. The following combinations are available, and each presents its own set of rules (and steps) for sharing resources:

- ✔ Windows XP Home Edition with FAT file system
- ✔ Windows XP Home Edition with NTFS file system
- ✔ Windows XP Professional with FAT file system
- ✔ Windows XP Professional with NTFS file system

All versions of Windows XP pay as much attention to sharing folders with other users of the same computer as with users who access the computer across a network. The options aren't always clear, nor are they always logical. Depending on your computer's configuration, different steps are required to configure shares. For example, your Windows XP Home Edition computer may not offer security options when you're working normally, but if you boot into Safe Mode, you see the configuration choices for setting security.

Windows XP includes a feature called *simplified file sharing* (sometimes called *simple file sharing*). It's not so darn simple, and it's very rigid. In my opinion, it takes away choices you should be able to make if you want to, but then I always have an attitude problem when I'm told, "this is for your own good, we know what's best for you, and we don't think you should be able to make your own decisions." You cannot turn off simplified file sharing in Windows XP Home Edition. You *can* turn it off in Windows XP Professional if you're running NTFS.

Depending on your combination of Windows XP version and file system, you may or may not be able to share your documents if you keep them in the standard My Documents folder. Because all Windows software automatically stores your data in your My Documents folder, this can be a real pain! (See the next section, "Sharing the Pre-shared Documents Folder," for a workaround.)

Going over all the permutations and combinations would fill several chapters, and you should be able to tell what your options are by the dialog boxes you see on the screen as you set up shared drives and folders. You can get more information on these details by reading *Windows XP For Dummies,* 2nd Edition, by Andy Rathbone (Wiley Publishing, Inc.).

Sharing the Pre-shared Documents Folder

Both Windows XP and Windows Vista install a shared documents folder on the computer. The files in this folder are automatically shared with other users of the computer, but not automatically shared with users on other computers on the network.

- ✔ In Windows XP, the folder is named Shared Documents
- ✔ In Windows Vista, the folder is named Public Documents

You can share this folder with network users instead of sharing the drive or folders on the drive. If this is the only shared folder on the computer, you have to copy all the files you want to share to this folder, which is not the most convenient way to work on a network. Remember that you yourself may be a network user if you created a document on one computer and want to work on the document later from another computer (maybe because your daughter is in the middle of something important on the original computer).

To make this work, you have to remember to copy any document you create (which is almost certainly saved in your own, private documents folder) to the pre-shared folder before you leave the computer. Then, if you work on the file at the same computer, the file changes, and you have to remember to copy it to the pre-shared folder again in order to let other network users (including you) access the file.

Few people find this paradigm efficient or even desirable. However, if your home network comprises Windows XP Home Edition computers running the FAT file system, this is your only option for sharing files across the network.

If you want to (or have to) share the pre-shared documents folder across the network, use the appropriate steps for your version of Windows, as described here.

Sharing the Shared Documents folder in Windows XP

To share the built-in Shared Documents folder across the network in Windows XP, use the following steps:

1. **Right-click the Shard Documents folder and choose Sharing and Security.**

   The Sharing dialog box appears.

2. **Select the options labeled Share This Folder on the Network and Allow Network Users to Change My Files (see Figure 7-5).**

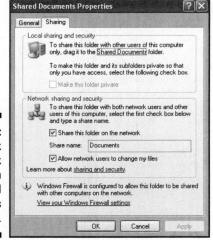

Figure 7-5:
Let network users work with files in the Shared Documents folder.

3. **Click OK to save the new configuration.**

Sharing the Public Documents folder in Windows Vista

To share the built-in Public Documents folder for Windows Vista across the network, take the following steps:

1. **Choose Start⇨Network.**

   The Network folder opens.

2. **Click the Network and Sharing Center icon on the toolbar.**

   The Network and Sharing Center window opens.

3. **Click the arrow to the right of Public Folder Sharing.**

   The sharing options for the Public Documents folder appear.

4. **Select the Turn On Sharing So Anyone with Network Access Can Open, Change, and Create Files option (see Figure 7-6).**

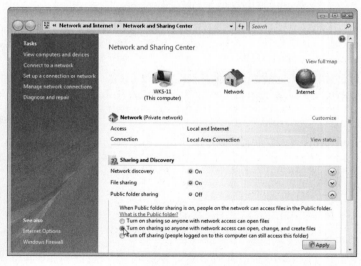

Figure 7-6:
Make the public folder public on the network as well as on the computer.

5. **Click Apply.**

   If User Access Controls are enabled, you must click Continue to proceed.

   The Public folder sharing listing now displays On.

6. **Close both folders.**

Both Windows XP and Windows Vista provide additional security settings to help you narrow the list of users who can access files or who can change files they're allowed to access. It's beyond the scope of this book to go into creating users and groups, but you can find out how to do this by reading *Windows XP For Dummies,* 2nd Edition, or *Windows Vista For Dummies,* both by Andy Rathbone (Wiley Publishing, Inc.).

Using Hidden Shares

You can hide a shared folder from the network. The cool thing about a hidden share is that you can get to it if you know it exists and if you know the trick for accessing it. (I provide the trick in this section.)

A hidden share can be a useful location for documents you don't want other network users to see when you can't easily set security options for the computer that holds those documents.

A hidden share works only if you keep in mind the basic rules about shares:

- **Shares are for remote users, and they're irrelevant when somebody is using your computer.** The folder you hide isn't hidden from anyone who is using your computer.

- **If you want to hide even one folder on a drive, you cannot share the drive, because as soon as you do, every folder in the drive can be seen.** Folders are children of drives, and when you share a parent, you share all its children.

- **A hidden share must be a parent share, because if it's a child of a share, it's visible in the network folder as soon as a remote user expands the parent share.**

The best way to hide a folder from everyone (users who work at the computer and users who access the computer across the network) is to make it a subfolder of a folder you're not sharing on a drive you're not sharing.

Create a parent folder for the express purpose of creating a subfolder that you want to hide. Give the parent folder an innocuous name so that nobody who uses your computer would be curious enough to expand the folder in the Computer folder and find your secret. For example, create a folder on your drive and name it *Tools* or *Maintenance.* Then create a subfolder and name it *Logfiles* or another name that seems equally boring or technical. In Logfiles, you can keep all your naughty and nice lists, and no one will suspect a thing, Machiavelli. Heh, heh, heh.

Creating a hidden share

To hide a folder's share, follow the steps to create a folder share that I describe in the previous section. However, when you give the share a name, make the last character of the share name a dollar sign ($). That's it, the share is hidden. Easy, huh?

Getting to your hidden share from a remote computer

When you work at a different computer and you want to get to a file that's in your hidden share, follow these steps:

1. **Choose Start⇨Run.**

   The Run dialog box opens.

   If you haven't moved the Run command to the start menu in Windows Vista, choose Start⇨All Programs⇨Accessories⇨Run.

2. **Type ***ComputerName******ShareName* **in the Open text box, substituting the real names of the computer and the share.**

   For example, if you're trying to get to a hidden share named Logs$ on a computer named Den, type **\\\\den\\logs$**. A window opens to display the contents of your hidden share.

Keeping the secret a secret

When you use the Run command, Windows saves the command. The next time you open the Run command, the last command that you typed appears. Just click OK to run the command again. Very convenient, eh? Uh, not if you share the computer with other users.

The way to prevent your command from being visible to another user is to make sure that you log off when you leave the computer you were using. This ensures that nobody else can sit at the computer using your logon name and settings — instead, they have to log on with their own username. The Run commands are saved on a user-by-user basis, so when a user named Mom is logged on, only commands issued by Mom are visible in the list.

Chapter 8

Setting Up Users

- -

- -

*U*nless you've bought a computer for every member of the family (rather unlikely), people share computers in your home network. One of the nifty features that you can take advantage of when users share the same computer is to provide each user with his or her own profile.

A *profile* enables each user to personalize the computer environment, and then, every time that user logs on to the computer, the same environment automatically appears. This means you don't have to live with (or constantly correct) the configuration settings that were created by other people who use the computer.

A user profile loads when a user logs on to a computer (using the *logon name* attached to the user account) and enters the password attached to that logon name.

If you didn't have a network, you wouldn't really need a password because Windows keeps track of your customized settings without one. A password keeps others from logging on to the computer using your name. If another user logs on with your name and changes the configuration, you have to live with those changes (or take the trouble to reset everything). The password is just a way to prevent someone else from pretending that he or she is you.

The technical term for no password is *null password.*

When you have a network with computers running Windows XP and/or Windows Vista, the operating system gets fussy about security and wants you to prove you are the person you say you are when you want to access another computer on the network, and part of that proof is the correct entry of your password.

In this chapter, I cover the user setup options and provide an overview of the tasks you have to perform to manage users.

Managing Users and Profiles in Windows XP

Windows XP uses logon accounts to control security, and security is tighter in Windows XP than it was in earlier versions of Windows (such as Windows 98 and Windows ME).

During the installation of Windows XP Home Edition, the system creates an Owner account and a Guest account. (Users who access the computer across the network use the Guest account.)

Windows XP Pro Edition automatically creates an Administrator account when you install the operating system.

Windows XP stores user profiles in a set of subfolders in the Documents and Settings folder on drive C.

Creating users in Windows XP

To set up a new user in Windows XP, follow these steps:

1. **Choose Start⇨Control Panel⇨User Accounts.**

   The User Accounts window opens, displaying a list of tasks.

2. **Click Create a New Account.**

3. **Enter a name for the account and click Next.**

   The name you enter is used to log on to the computer, so it's called a *logon name*.

4. **Select an account type for this user.**

   The account types are Computer Administrator (with permissions to perform all tasks on the computer) and Limited (with permissions to make changes to the user's own settings only). The first account you create must be a Computer Administrator (and is probably your own account). Then, using this account, you can create and manage additional users for this computer.

5. Click Create Account.

You are returned to the User Accounts window, where the new user is listed.

In a home network, you should make all adult users (and all pre-teen or teenage children who understand computers) Administrators so everyone can access settings and files. The only exception to this rule I can think of is creating a limited user account for your cousin who's affectionately known as "creepy sneak," who visits occasionally and wants to use the computer while he's visiting.

Completing this process only creates the account; you still have to set up the user's password. To do so, click the new user's listing and then choose Create a Password.

In the resulting window (see Figure 8-1), enter the password, and then enter it again to confirm it. You can optionally enter a password hint, which is a word or phrase that reminds the user of the password. This should forestall the problems that arise when a user forgets his password (notice I said *should;* I'm not guaranteeing anything!).

Figure 8-1:
Setting and
confirming
your
password
and
providing a
password
hint.

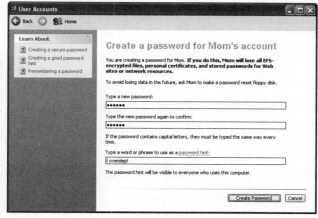

The password hint is visible to anyone who tries to log on as this user. Therefore, don't use a password "123main" with a hint "our address" or a password "spot" with a hint "dog's name." Make the hint something that's a bit obscure to anyone except the user. For example, if the password is "stupidclock," the hint may be "I overslept." That's a memory jog, not a description of the password, and a memory jog is the best type of password hint.

Changing passwords in Windows XP

Every user can change his or her own password and create a new password hint. Therefore, when you create new users, you can invent any password you wish, tell the user what that password is, and after the user logs on for the first time, he or she can change the password.

In fact, you can omit the password when you create a new user and tell that person to log on with a null password and then create a password.

When you view the listings in the User Accounts window, each username is listed, and under the name you see the text *Password Protected* if a password exists for that account. The text is missing for an account that lacks a password, and that user should log on to the computer and add a password.

Adding a password in Windows XP

To add a password to your user account, take the following steps:

1. **Choose Start➪Control Panel➪User Accounts.**

   The User Accounts window opens, displaying a list of tasks.

2. **Click the icon for your account.**

   A window opens for your account, with a list of tasks you can perform on the account (see Figure 8-2).

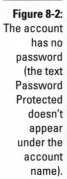

Figure 8-2:
The account
has no
password
(the text
Password
Protected
doesn't
appear
under the
account
name).

3. **Click Create a Password.**

    The Create a Password dialog box opens.

4. **Enter the password (twice) and optionally enter a password hint.**

5. **Click Create Password.**

    The password is saved.

Changing a password in Windows XP

To change an existing password in Windows XP, follow the steps in the previous section to open the User Accounts window and select the icon for your account.

In the window that opens, click Change My Password to display the Change Your Password dialog box seen in Figure 8-3. Enter the current password (to prove you are who you say you are) and then enter the new password twice. Optionally, enter a password hint.

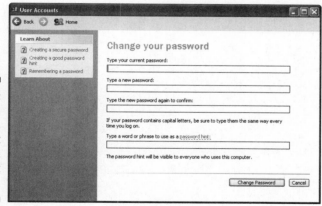

Figure 8-3: To change a password, you must know the current password.

Windows XP is designed to be friendly to computers that have multiple users. Among the features you'll love and rely on are a Welcome window that makes it easier to log on, the ability to switch to a new user without requiring the current user to log off (called *Fast User Switching*), pictures for each user's listing in the Welcome window, and other cool features. It's beyond the scope of this book (which concentrates on networking issues) to provide detailed instructions for enabling these features. Read *Windows XP For Dummies,* 2nd Edition, by Andy Rathbone (Wiley Publishing, Inc.) for more information.

Managing Windows XP user profiles

In Windows XP, each user has a folder tree (a parent folder and a group of child folders) that holds information about the user's profile. Every user's folder tree exists under `C:\Documents and Settings`.

For example, Figure 8-4 displays the folder tree for the user named Amy. You can see there are quite a few subfolders under Amy's folder, and many of those subfolders contain additional subfolders.

Figure 8-4:
Windows XP maintains profile settings for each user.

If you examine the contents of the folders, you can see the user's settings. For instance, a user's Desktop folder displays the icons that a user has placed on the Desktop. (On my home network, you can count on seeing an icon that's a shortcut to the Freecell game.)

As you create new users, you can save those users the trouble of creating a Desktop shortcut to a favorite application (which involves dragging a menu listing to the Desktop) by opening the Desktop folder of a user that already has the shortcut and copying the shortcut to other users' Desktop folders.

A user's My Documents folder is the *real* My Documents folder for this user. The My Documents folder that appears in My Computer, Windows Explorer, or on the Desktop is a shortcut to the real My Documents folder (to let the user avoid all the steps required to drill down through the profile folder tree to open My Documents). To determine the real location of My Documents, right-click any My Documents icon and choose Properties. The Properties dialog box (shown in Figure 8-5) displays the actual location of the folder.

Figure 8-5:
The real
folder
for My
Documents
exists in the
user's
Profile
folder tree.

It's important to understand the Profile folder tree as the source of real information because if you don't, you could copy, move, or even delete folders and files incorrectly.

Backup software that's configured to back up the My Documents icon at the top of My Computer or Windows Explorer will back up the shortcut, not the documents. (See Chapter 13 for more about using the real My Documents folder when you design your backup schemes.)

Managing Users and Profiles in Windows Vista

Windows Vista takes a similar approach to creating and configuring users and maintaining user profiles as Windows XP. However, the names of folders and windows are different (and I've never figured out why, except to guess that Microsoft just wanted Vista to look different and didn't care that many of us had finally memorized all the folder names in Windows XP).

Creating users in Windows Vista

To set up a new user in Windows Vista, follow these steps:

1. **Choose Start➪Control Panel➪Add or Remove User Accounts (under the User Accounts and Family Safety listing).**

   The Manage Accounts window opens.

2. **Click Create a New Account.**

   The Create New Account window opens (see Figure 8-6).

Figure 8-6:
All the tasks
for setting
up a new
account are
performed
in a single
window in
Windows
Vista.

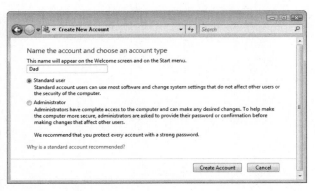

3. **Enter a name for the account.**

   The name you enter is used to log on to the computer, so it's called a *logon name*.

4. **Select an account type for this user.**

   The account types are Administrator (with permissions to perform all tasks on the computer) and Standard (with permissions to make changes to the user's own settings only). The first account you create must be a Computer Administrator (and is probably your own account). Then, using this account, you can create and manage additional users for this computer.

5. **Click Create Account.**

   You are returned to the User Accounts window, where the new user is listed.

Changing passwords in Windows Vista

As with Windows XP, any logged-on user can change his or her password at will by using the following steps:

1. **Choose Start➪Control Panel➪ User Accounts and Family Safety.**

   The User Accounts and Family Safety window appears.

2. **Click Change Your Windows Password.**

   The Make Changes to Your User Account window opens.

3. **Click Change Your Password.**

   The Change Your Password window appears (see Figure 8-7).

Figure 8-7: Change your password and optionally provide a password hint for yourself.

4. **Enter the current password and then enter a new password twice. Optionally, create a password hint.**

5. **Click Change Password to save the new settings.**

Managing Windows Vista user profiles

Windows Vista keeps user profile information in a folder tree under the folder named Users. If you have an Administrator account, you can expand user profile folders in the same manner explained earlier in this chapter for viewing Windows XP.

Each user's preferences are saved in his or her profile and loaded when that user logs on. This means, for example, that a user who doesn't want to use the Windows Vista Sidebar can eliminate it permanently or can use the Sidebar with different utilities than another user might choose.

The number of folders, and some of the folder names, in each user's folder tree are slightly different from Windows XP, but the general idea is the same. For example, Figure 8-8 shows a user's profile tree with the Desktop folder selected.

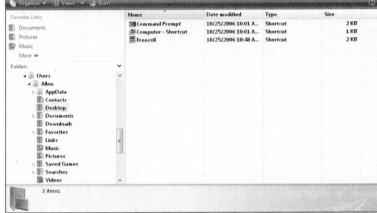

Figure 8-8: Everybody on my network has a Desktop shortcut for Freecell.

As explained earlier in this chapter for Windows XP, you can copy Desktop items and other types of items from one user's profile to another user's profile.

To learn more about the way profiles work and how you can manipulate the contents of profile folders, read *Windows Vista For Dummies* by Andy Rathbone (Wiley Publishing, Inc.).

Duplicating Users on Remote Computers

Because both Windows XP and Windows Vista are designed to enhance security, accessing remote computers is easier if you, as a user, exist as a user in the remote computers.

When you access a remote computer on the network, Windows checks to see if you exist on the remote computer. If you exist, you must exist with the same logon name and password you use to log on to the local computer.

If you have a matching account on the remote computer, you're automatically logged on using the logon name and password you used when you logged on to the computer you're using. The remote computer opens a window to show you its shared resources and lets you access the resources.

If you don't exist on the remote computer, you must log on using the name and password of an existing user on that remote computer. Windows displays a Connect To logon dialog box similar to the one shown in Figure 8-9.

Figure 8-9:
This user is
trying to
access
another
computer,
but his
local logon
name and
password
don't exist
on that
remote
computer.

To make sure everyone can access every computer, duplicate the steps enumerated in this chapter to create every user on every computer. Use the same logon name and the same password on every computer.

Part III

Communicating Across the Network

The 5th Wave   By Rich Tennant

In this part . . .

Now for the fun stuff — actually using your network for communicating from computer to computer, printing, exchanging files, and generally getting all the benefits of network computing.

In this part of the book, I walk you through the tasks required for setting up shared printing. You find out how to install and use printers that are attached to your own computer and to the other network computers.

You also find out how to get files from any computer on the network and how to send files from your computer to another computer. And, for real convenience, I explain how to open software and work on a file that's on another computer.

Chapter 9

Printing Across the Network

· ·

In This Chapter

▶ Setting up printers for sharing

▶ Installing a network printer

▶ Tricks and tips for printing

▶ Troubleshooting network printing

· ·

A terrific side effect of installing a computer network in your home is the ability to share a printer. Households without networks face some difficulties when it comes to printing. Network-deficient households (that seems to be a politically correct term, don't you think?) have had to rely on some less-than-perfect solutions.

One solution is to buy a printer every time you buy a computer. I can think of lots of other ways to spend that money, and I bet you can, too.

Another solution is to buy one printer and attach the printer to only one of the computers in your home network. Anyone who uses a computer that doesn't have a printer has to copy files to a floppy disk, go to the computer that has a printer, load the same software that created the files (the same software has to be installed on both computers), open each file from the floppy disk, and print. I guess all this walking comes under the heading of "healthy exercise," especially if the computers are on different floors of the house, but this setup isn't exactly a model of efficiency.

Neither of these scenarios is acceptable after you understand how easy it is to share printers over a network.

Setting Up Shared Printers

If you want all the computers on your network to be able to access a single printer, you have to set up the Windows printer-sharing feature. Then you have to set up the printer for sharing. You perform these tasks at the computer to which the printer is connected.

The most difficult part of setting up network printing is deciding which computer gets the printer. Here are some common guidelines you can follow:

- ✔ **Location.** If you have room for a table at one computer location (and storage space for paper), that's the computer to choose.

- ✔ **Usage patterns.** If one computer on the network is used far more often than any other computer, that's the computer to select.

Some households have more than one printer. You may have a black-and-white printer as well as a color printer. When you enable printer sharing, each user can choose a printer every time he or she wants to print.

You can attach two printers to one computer if that's more convenient, as long as the computer has sufficient ports. If one printer uses the parallel port (also called a *printer port*), and the other printer connects to the USB port, just plug them in. If both printers use USB connections, you probably have a second (or third or fourth) USB port. If you don't have any empty USB ports (what with all those cameras, scanners, and other doodads you like), you can buy a USB hub (which adds ports) for under $25.

Enabling printer sharing

The first thing you have to do is tell Windows that the printer attached to the computer should be eligible for sharing with other computers on the network. If you didn't set up printer sharing when you originally set up your network, you have to take care of that detail now.

Sharing printers in Windows XP

In Windows XP, printer sharing is a service that you enable in the Properties dialog for your network connection. If an icon for your Local Area Connection is available on the taskbar, click it, and then click the Properties button.

If you don't have an icon for your connection on the taskbar, use the following steps to enable printer sharing:

1. **Choose Start⇨Control Panel and click Network and Internet Connections.**

2. **Click Network Connections, right-click the Local Area Connection icon, and choose Properties.**

   The Local Area Connection Properties dialog box opens.

3. **Enable file and printer sharing.**

   Click the File and Printer Sharing for Microsoft Networks check box to select it (see Figure 9-1). Then click OK. You do not have to restart the computer.

Figure 9-1:
In Windows XP, enable File and Printer Sharing in the Properties dialog box of your Local Area Connection.

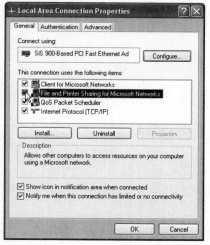

While the Properties dialog box is in front of you, select the option to display an icon for the connection in the notification area (the right side of the taskbar). Also select the option to display a message when the connection has a problem.

Sharing printers in Windows Vista

To enable printer sharing in Windows Vista, use the following steps:

1. **Choose Start⇨Control Panel and then click Set Up File Sharing (under the Network and Internet heading).**

   The Network and Sharing Center window opens.

2. **Click the arrow in the rightmost column for the Printer sharing listing to display the options for sharing printers.**

3. **Select Turn On Printer Sharing (see Figure 9-2).**

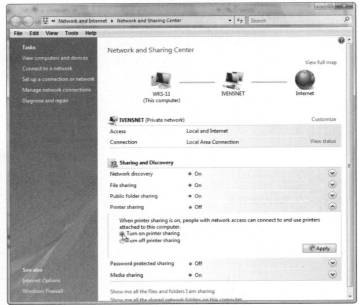

Figure 9-2:
Enable the
printer
sharing
feature in
the Network
and Sharing
Center
window.

Sharing the printers

Now that Windows is configured to permit you to share the printers that are connected to various computers, you have to set up each printer as a shared resource. Use the following steps to accomplish this:

1. **Open the Printers folder.**

   - In Windows XP choose Start➪Printers and Faxes.

   - In Windows Vista, choose Start➪Printers.

   An icon for the printer you installed on this computer is in the folder window.

2. **Right-click the icon for the printer you want to share and then choose Sharing from the shortcut menu that appears.**

   The printer's Properties dialog box opens, and the Sharing tab appears in the foreground (see Figure 9-3).

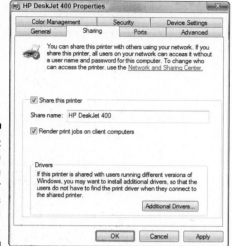

Figure 9-3:
Share the printer with the other computers on the network.

3. **Select the Share This Printer option.**

4. **Type a name for the printer share in the Share Name text box.**

   Printers are shared with a share name (the name you give the share). You can accept the name that Windows automatically enters, which is usually a shortened form of the printer model name, or you can use a name of your own choice.

5. **Click OK.**

   You are returned to the Printers folder, and your printer icon has a sharing symbol under it, indicating that this printer is a shared resource. This computer is now a print server.

The sharing symbol for Windows XP is a hand under an icon; for Windows Vista, the sharing symbol is two heads.

Providing printer drivers

Both Windows XP and Windows Vista include an Additional Drivers button in the Sharing tab to support printing for other versions of Windows. This means that you can store printer driver files on one computer that other computers, using different versions of Windows, can access when they use the printer.

In order to use this feature, you have to insert the original CD for the other versions of Windows (for example, insert the CD for Windows XP in the computer running Windows Vista) to install those drivers. If both versions of Windows have a driver for this printer, you don't have to provide drivers for Windows XP on your Vista computer, or vice-versa.

Some printers don't have drivers pre-installed in Windows. Those printers come with drivers for multiple versions of Windows on a CD because the manufacturer knows that the drivers aren't pre-loaded in Windows. If that's the case, you can use the manufacturer's CD to install all the drivers for all Windows versions on the computer that's connected to the printer, or you can install the appropriate drivers on the other computers that will use this printer.

Installing a Remote Printer

Put on your running shoes! After you configure a printer for sharing, it's time to run to the other computers on the network and install that same printer.

Of course, you're not going to perform a physical installation; the printer is staying right where it is. Installing a printer on a computer that has no physically attached printer means that you're installing a *network printer*.

The computer that holds the printer is the *print server;* the computer that uses the printer is the *print client.* All the computers on your network can be both servers and clients because it's possible to use a printer that's attached to the computer you're using and also, from the same computer, use a printer on another computer.

Choosing an installation method

Two approaches are available to you for installing a network printer:

  ✔ Find the printer in the Network folder by double-clicking the icon for the computer that has the printer. All the shared resources (folders and printers) for that computer are displayed. Right-click the printer icon and choose Connect from the shortcut menu that appears.

  ✔ Use the Add a Printer Wizard in the Printers folder, walking through all the wizard's windows to install the printer.

The first method is quick and easy, and the second method is time consuming (to say nothing of the fact that you have to tell the wizard the name of the printer, which you may not know or may have forgotten). I'm not even going to cover that method because there's no reason to use it.

If the printer you want to install came with drivers (because the drivers aren't installed in Windows), you need to have the CD from the printer manufacturer available as you install the printer on each computer on your network.

Running the installation procedure

For this example, I use the option to select the printer from the Network folder because it's faster and more efficient:

1. **Open the Network folder.**

   - In Windows XP, choose Start➪My Network Places or double-click the Desktop icon for My Network Places.

   - In Windows Vista, choose Start➪Network.

2. **Double-click the computer that has the printer you want to use.**

   All the shared resources on that computer (printers and folders) are displayed.

3. **Right-click the icon for the printer and choose Connect.**

   Windows XP and Windows Vista both copy many printer drivers to the hard drive when you install the operating system. Most of the time, those drivers are used when you select the Connect command.

4. **Follow the prompts to install the printer.**

   Similar to the installation of a printer attached to the computer (described earlier in this chapter), Windows installs the driver from its own drivers folder, or the manufacturer's drivers from a source that you specify if no Windows driver exists.

   The printer driver files are installed on your hard drive. Windows doesn't issue a success message, so open your Printers folder to see the remote printer listed. The printer is also available in the drop-down list you see whenever you select the Print command when you're working in software.

For convenience, you can keep the driver files (especially if you downloaded them from the manufacturer's Web site) on a network share that is easily accessible. Also, it may be easier if the drivers are on a CD (either a Windows CD or manufacturer CD) to share the CD-ROM drive on a single PC and then simply access that drive over the network as well. After all, that's why you have a network.

Creating a default printer

You can make the remote printer the default printer. (If there's no printer attached to the computer you're using, the default printer has to be a remote printer, of course.) Right-click the printer's listing in the Printers folder and choose Set as Default Printer. Windows puts a check mark next to the printer's icon to indicate that this printer is the default printer for the computer.

Renaming network printers

After you install a remote printer (a printer that's not connected to the computer you're working on), you can change its name to something that reminds you where it is or what it does. Doing so changes the printer name only on your computer; it doesn't change anything on the computer to which the printer is attached. Follow these steps to give the network printer a personalized name:

1. **Open the Printers folder.**

2. **Right-click the icon for the network printer and choose Rename from the shortcut menu that appears (or select the icon and press F2).**

   The icon title is selected (highlighted), which means you're in edit mode.

3. **Type a new name and press Enter.**

   Choose a name that describes the printer for you. For example, *HP-Den* is a good descriptive name and is easier to remember than *Printer Numero Uno* or *Clive*.

Using both local and network printers

If you have two printers in the house, you can attach them to separate computers. Just follow the steps that were explained earlier in this chapter for installing local printers, and then follow the steps to install each printer as a remote printer.

You can switch between printers when you want to print by using the Print feature of your Windows software. All Windows software works in the same fashion, so you can count on being able to use the following steps to switch printers:

1. **Choose File⇨Print from the menu bar of your software program.**

   The Print dialog box opens. The appearance of this dialog box differs depending on the particular software you're using, but the essential features are the same.

2. **Select a printer.**

   A list of installed printers (both local and network) appears in the Print dialog box, as shown in Figure 9-4.

3. **Click Print to print your document on the selected printer.**

Figure 9-4:
The Print dialog box in a Windows program displays a list of all the printers you've installed, whether they are local or network.

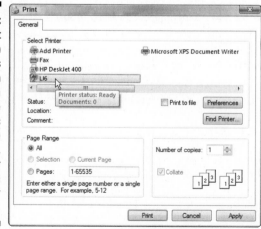

If you click the Print button on the toolbar or Ribbon of your Windows software or if you print from Notepad, the currently selected printer (usually the printer you marked as the default printer) receives the print job. No dialog box opens to afford you the chance to choose a different printer.

Devising schemes for using multiple printers

You can design all sorts of arrangements to take advantage of having multiple printers on your network, with each printer attached to a different computer. When you devise a method to manage your printers, your decisions should be based on the types of printers you own. Consider the following suggestions:

- **Make the local printer the default printer.** This option works well if all the printers are the same. With this scheme, you don't need the remote printer unless something happens to the local printer.

  If the local printer stops working or the cartridge goes dry and you don't have a spare one handy (or you're in a hurry and decide to worry about replacing the cartridge later), you can switch to the network printer quickly. Using the local printer for most print jobs saves you the annoyance of getting up and walking to the network printer every time you print. (If you need the exercise, you can always reverse the scheme.)

- **Configure the printers for different features.** If your printers can hold different paper sizes, you can make one of them the letter-size printer and make the other the legal-size printer. Or, you can put inexpensive paper in one printer and good bond in the other. Then just use the appropriate printer for each printing project. See the section, "Creating printer clones for specific features," later in this chapter.

- **Use each printer for its best feature.** For example, if one printer is an inkjet and one is a laser printer, use the laser for multiple-page print jobs (lasers usually print faster) or for print jobs with a lot of graphics (most laser printers have more memory than most inkjet printers).

Some of these printer setup schemes are important for more than convenience; they lower the cost of using printers. The business term for getting the most out of your printers (or any other piece of machinery) is *TCO* (total cost of ownership), and it's a significant consideration when you buy and use any type of equipment.

Managing Network Printing

Keeping the printing process on an error-free, even keel is slightly more complicated with network printing than it is for a one-computer, one-printer environment. However, it's not overly complex, and printer problems aren't all that common.

Understanding the spooler

When you send a file to a printer, Windows does some work on the file with the help of those drivers you copied to your hard drive when you installed the printer. Windows checks the file to make sure that everything is sent to the printer in a format that the printer understands. The work that Windows performs is saved in a file called a *spool file*. This process is called *spooling,* and it happens, unbeknownst to you, in the background. In addition to the spool file, Windows creates a second file, called a *shadow file,* which contains the name of the user who sent the job to the printer, the data format type of the print job, and other technical information.

The two files sit in the spooler, waiting for their turn at the printer. Documents are sent to the printer in a first-come, first-served order (unless you interrupt that order by using a process that I discuss in the next section, "Manipulating print jobs"). This lineup of documents waiting to go to the printer is called the *queue*. After the print job is done, the spool files are deleted automatically.

Manipulating print jobs

You can control individual print jobs that are sent to the printer, but you have to move fast, because everything happens very rapidly.

Printing controls are available in the printer's dialog box, which you can open with the following steps:

1. **Open the Printers folder.**

2. **Double-click the icon for the printer.**

   The printer's dialog box opens, displaying any print jobs that are currently in the queue.

You can pause, delete, and move the print jobs that are in the queue, but which print jobs you see depends on the following factors:

- If you open the dialog box for a remote printer, you see the jobs that you sent to that printer. Jobs sent from other remote users aren't visible and can't be manipulated.

- If you open the dialog box for a local printer, you see a list of all the jobs that the local and remote users have sent to that printer.

You can manipulate each job, or the printer itself, with the commands that are available in this dialog box. You can change the way that documents print in the following ways:

- **Pause a print job.** Right-click the listing for the print job and choose Pause Printing from the shortcut menu that appears.

  A check mark appears next to the Pause Printing command to indicate that the job status has changed to Paused. The print job is temporarily stopped, and the next job in line starts printing.

  Pausing a print job is a quick way to let an important print job jump ahead of the job that's in front of it.

- **Resume a print job.** Right-click a paused print job and choose Pause Printing again from the shortcut menu that appears to remove the check mark.

  The job status changes to Printing.

- **Pause the printer.** Choose Printer⇨Pause Printing from the menu bar in the Printer dialog box.

  All the print jobs are paused. Most of the time, you use this command to clear a paper jam in the printer or to change paper. To use this command on a Windows 2000/XP printer, you must have administrative rights (controlling the printer, rather than the print job, is an administrative task).

- **Cancel a print job.** Right-click a print job listing and choose Cancel Printing from the shortcut menu that appears.

  The document disappears from the queue and does not print.

- **Cancel all the print jobs.** Choose Printer⇨Purge Print Documents from the menu bar of the printer's dialog box. Because this is a command to the printer, not the print job, this requires administrative rights.

When you pause or cancel a print job, the printer usually keeps printing. That's because data that has been sent to the printer is in the printer's memory and continues to print.

You can also drag print jobs around to change the order of printing (you must have administrative rights on the computer that holds the printer). Select the job you want to move and drag it up in the queue if it's important or down in the queue if it's less important. However, dragging print jobs has two restrictions:

- ✔ You can't move any print job ahead of the job that is currently printing.
- ✔ You can't move the job that is currently printing — it's too late.

Printing Tricks and Tips

The printing processes in Windows run smoothly and automatically most of the time, even across a network. However, knowing a few tricks makes network printing easier for all the users on your network.

In the following sections, I present some clever, efficient, and money-saving schemes that home network users apply to network printing.

Using a printer shortcut on the Desktop

Most of the time, you print from a software program. You create a document, and then you print it. But sometimes you just need a printed copy of an existing document, and you don't want to open the software, open the document, and use the commands that are required to print the document.

If you put a shortcut to the printer on your Desktop, you can drag documents to the shortcut icon to print them effortlessly. Follow these steps to create a printer shortcut on your Desktop:

1. **Choose Start⇨Printers and Faxes in Windows XP or Start⇨Control Panel and click the Printers link in the Hardware and Sound section of Control Panel in Windows Vista.**

   The Printers folder opens. Make sure the folder isn't full-screen because you want to be able to see (and get to) the Desktop.

2. **Right-drag the printer icon to the Desktop.**

   When you release the right mouse button, a shortcut menu appears.

3. **Choose Create Shortcut(s) Here from the shortcut menu.**

   A printer shortcut appears on your Desktop.

A good place to put the printer shortcut is on the Quick Launch toolbar. That way, an open window can't hide it.

Using the printer shortcut is easy and timesaving. You can use it whenever you have any folder or window open (such as My Documents) that contains document files. Just drag a document file to the printer shortcut on the Desktop. That's all you have to do — Windows does the rest. You can leave the room or sit and watch as the following events take place:

1. The software that was used to create the file opens.

2. The file opens in the software window.

3. The software sends the file to the printer.

4. The software closes.

   Cool!

If you right-click a document file instead of dragging it to a Desktop shortcut, you can choose Print from the shortcut menu that appears. The same automatic printing events occur.

Using separator pages to identify users

If everyone in your household uses the printers, you are likely to experience a lot of printer traffic. Not everyone's going to run immediately to the printer to pick up his or her print jobs. What you have after a day or so is a nice jumbled pile of papers — and no one willing to claim them. Or worse, one user may wander over to the printer to pick up his print jobs and notice that several other print jobs are in the tray. This user may pick up the first piece of paper and read it — it isn't his print job, so he tosses it aside (invariably, it lands on the floor instead of on a tabletop). The user will probably continue to shuffle through the papers, taking his own documents and tossing the others helter-skelter.

It's less messy if each job comes out of the printer with a form that displays the name of the owner. Luckily, such a form exists in Windows, and it's called a separator page. A *separator page* (sometimes called a *banner*) automatically prints ahead of the first page of each document.

The downside of separator pages is that they can be a huge waste of paper. They work best if most of your print jobs are made up of multiple pages. You may end up spending the money you save on ink purchasing ream after ream of paper. Also, if your household is filled with people who don't believe that "neatness counts," you'll just have one extra piece of paper per print job to get shuffled around in a big ugly pile.

To turn on separator pages, use the following steps:

1. **Open the Printers folder.**

2. **Right-click the appropriate printer icon and choose Properties from the shortcut menu that appears.**

   The printer Properties dialog box opens, with the General tab in the foreground.

3. **Move to the Advanced tab.**

4. **Click the Separator Page button.**

   The Separator Page dialog box appears.

5. **Click Browse to select a separator file.**

   Separator files have the `.sep` extension. Choose `Sysprint.sep` for PostScript printers or `Pcl.sep` for non-PostScript printers.

6. **Click OK twice to close the dialog box.**

Creating printer clones for specific features

Many, if not most, home networks include at least one color printer, usually an inkjet printer. Cartridges are expensive and a pain to replace (all that alignment stuff in addition to physically removing the old cartridge and installing the new one properly).

Many times (in fact most of the time), the documents that are sent to the printer don't have to be printed in color, it's just that the printer automatically prints what the software sends, which is often a printout that contains color.

It's possible to change the options for all color printers on a job-by-job basis, to reset the printer's mode to monochrome (black and white), but it's rare that anyone takes the trouble to do this ("Oops, sorry Dad, I forgot").

Change the options yourself, and offer the printer in two modes: color and monochrome. Just install the same printer twice, creating duplicate printers. Then configure one for color and one for monochrome. It only takes a few steps to save money on color cartridges.

To accomplish this, you must know the port the existing printer is using because the duplicate printer must be assigned to the same port. Here's how to check the port:

1. **Choose Start⇨Printers (or Printers and Faxes).**

   The Printers folder opens, displaying the printer you want to duplicate.

2. **Right-click the icon for the printer you're duplicating and choose Properties.**

3. **Move to the Ports tab and make a note of the port the printer occupies.**

4. **Click Cancel to close the Properties dialog box.**

Creating a printer clone

Now you're ready to create your money-saving clone by using the following steps:

1. **Choose Start⇨Printers (or Printers and Faxes).**

   The Printers folder opens.

2. **Click the Add a Printer icon.**

   The Add Printer Wizard appears.

3. **Click Next.**

4. **Choose Local Printer, and in Windows XP, deselect the option to select the printer automatically. Then click Next.**

5. **Select the same port the existing printer occupies and click Next.**

6. **Select the same manufacturer and printer as the existing printer.**

   If the existing printer came with drivers because Windows doesn't have drivers for this printer, click Have Disk and repeat the steps you performed when you installed the existing printer.

7. **In the next window (see Figure 9-5), select the option to use the existing driver and click Next.**

Figure 9-5: The wizard wants to know whether you're updating to new drivers or you want to use the existing drivers.

8. **In the next window, name the printer to reflect its configuration, and do *not* make it the default printer.**

   Windows automatically names the printer using the same name as the existing printer with (Copy 1) appended to the name.

   You can change the name of this printer to *Color* and later change the other printer to *B&W,* or do it the other way around.

9. **In the next window, you can share the printer (be sure the sharename includes *color* or *B&W,* depending on the printer's name).**

   If you prefer, you can skip the sharing step for now and share the printer later by using the steps enumerated earlier in this chapter.

10. **In the next window, deselect the option to print a test page and click Next and then click Finish in Windows XP; in Windows Vista, just click Finish.**

    Your new printer appears in the Printers folder, along with the original printer.

Renaming the original printer

Rename the original printer by right-clicking its listing and choosing Rename. Enter the new name (*B&W* or *Color,* depending on the name you gave the duplicate printer you just installed).

If you had previously shared this printer, renaming it removes its shared status, and you must share it again. This time, use a sharename that matches the printer name you just created.

Configuring a color printer for monochrome

Now you must change the printer options for the monochrome (B&W) printer (the color printer is already set up to default to color printing). To do this, you need to consult the documentation that came with the printer because there's little consistency in the process required to select Monochrome or Black & White as the default printing mode. Even printers made by the same manufacturer differ in the steps needed to perform this task.

When you know where to find the selection to turn off color printing, right-click the printer's listing and choose Properties. Follow the documentation's instructions to find the right place to do this. For example, Figure 9-6 shows the way to turn an HP DeskJet 500C into a monochrome printer.

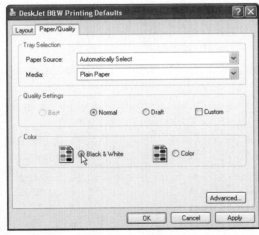

Figure 9-6:
For this
printer, the
printing
preferences
are found
in the
Paper/
Quality tab.

Share the printer, using a sharename that describes its printing defaults, and install the printer on all the network computers by using the steps described earlier in this chapter.

Now instruct everyone in the family that when they select a printer in the Print dialog box, they must select the B&W printer unless they absolutely, positively, have to produce a color document.

Other reasons to clone printers

Making it easy for users to print black and white documents from a color printer is the most common reason to clone a printer. However, I've found numerous other situations in which cloning is a necessity.

Create separate printers for each tray

If you have a printer with two trays, you can load different types of paper in each tray and then clone the printer. After you have both printers installed, disable one tray in each printer (not the same tray in both printers, of course), as shown in Figure 9-7.

Figure 9-7:
Shut down one tray in each computer to keep users from printing documents on your good letterhead or on checks.

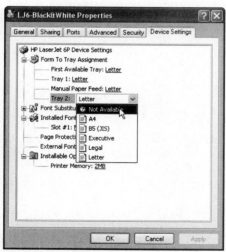

Rename the printers to indicate the tray, or better still, the type of paper. For example, I've set up the following sets of printer names for this scenario:

- ✔ A printer named Checks and a printer named Paper.
- ✔ A printer named Bond and a printer named RegularPaper.
- ✔ A printer named Letterhead and a printer named PlainPaper.
- ✔ A printer named DadLetterhead and a printer named PlainPaper.
- ✔ A printer named Paper and a printer named PhotoPaper

Create separate printers for settings that save toner and ink

All laser and inkjet printers are capable of printing with a variety of dots per inch (dpi). The lower the dpi, the less toner or ink you use.

For ordinary printing, when you just want a record of information, printing at a lower dpi (for example, 300) creates a perfectly readable document. If you're printing an important report for work that has to look more professional, use a higher dpi (such as 1200). Some older inkjet printers have 150 dpi for draft mode and their "better" mode is 300 dpi.

To make it easier for users to print with a lower dpi (because they almost certainly won't remember to take the appropriate steps every time they want to print), create a clone printer named Draft and rename the original printer Professional or something similar. Make the appropriate changes to the printer's settings.

Using a Hardware Print Server

Most network equipment manufacturers offer a hardware device called a *print server*. A print server is a standalone device that holds the network printers you're sharing (instead of using computers as the hosts for printers). A print server can provide some practical benefits, such as the following:

- ✔ **A convenient location.** You can put your printers where they're convenient for all users on the network. If your network computers aren't physically near each other, printing becomes more work for any user who is printing to a remote printer. Well, printing is still easy — it's walking to the printer to pick up the printed document that's tiring.

✔ **Full time availability.** The print server is always on, while computers that hold printers are sometimes shut down.

✔ **Faster printing.** Most print servers have components designed to deliver the data to the printer faster.

Print servers range in price from about $50 to slightly over $100, depending on features (especially the number of printer ports).

Attaching a print server

The print server has two types of connectors: one for connecting to the printer(s), and the other for connecting to your network. When you buy a print server, you must choose a model that matches your printer(s) and your network connections.

You can buy a print server with USB ports, regular printer ports, or both. The range of models includes single-port devices for one printer and multi-port devices for multiple printers (up to four). To connect to your network, print servers are available as Ethernet devices or wireless devices.

The print server plugs into the network the same way a computer does, either by connecting it to a hub, switch, or router with Ethernet cable, or by sending wireless signals (if it's a wireless print server). It's just a network node, like a computer is a network node, so all the computers on the network can access it.

Installing a print server

To a computer, a print server is like a printer. Each computer has to install drivers for the print server, in addition to installing the drivers for the printers attached to the print server.

Each manufacturer supplies a CD that has the drivers. Of course, you can share one computer's CD drive and have each user install the drivers for each computer, instead of walking the CD around the house to each computer. Aren't networks nifty?

The CD that comes with the print server also has setup and maintenance software for the print server. You can use the utilities on the software to check the status of the print server and the status of the printers. You access the print server's utilities through your browser, using the print server's IP address. Each manufacturer provides clear, easy-to-follow documentation.

Troubleshooting Network Printing

Sometimes when you're printing to a remote printer, you get an error message indicating that there was a problem printing to the port. (The *port* is the path to the remote computer that has the printer attached.) Before you panic, thinking that something awful has happened to your network printing services, check the condition of all the hardware.

Check the print server

Computers that have printers attached (called *print servers*) have to be turned on if you want to print from a remote computer. If the computer is turned off, turn it on.

Nobody has to be logged on to a computer to use its shared printer. The Windows operating system on that computer simply must be started. That's a really nifty way to design network printing!

Check the printer

If the computer is turned on and you still get error messages when you try to print, check the printer. Make sure that it's turned on. Check any buttons, indicator lights, or message windows that may be trying to tell you that something is amiss.

Most printers have a "ready" light, a button that lights up to say that everything is cool and the printer is ready to do its work. If the ready light isn't on, follow the instructions in the printer manual to investigate the problem. The most common problems are that the printer is out of paper, a paper jam has occurred, or the cartridge is out of toner (or ink).

Check the network cable

If the computer is on and the printer is fine when you print from the print server, check the network cable between the print server and the concentrator (the best way to check is to replace the cable using cable from another computer). A cable that isn't connected properly can't send data. Also check the cable between the client computer and the concentrator.

Check the firewall

If you use the Windows firewall, or a firewall software application, make sure the firewall is configured to allow access to the printer by remote computers. Be sure the File and Printer Sharing option is selected.

If nothing in your setup seems amiss, your printer is probably dead. Check the manufacturer's Web site for help (unless your warranty is still in effect, in which case follow the instructions for replacement or repair).

Chapter 10

Getting Around the Neighborhood

In This Chapter

▶ Visiting the network's neighborhood

▶ Opening shares to see what's in them

▶ Using shortcuts to move to folders on other computers

*T*o get to resources (files, printers, and so on) from another computer, you have to access that computer across the network. Windows offers several ways to communicate with a remote computer from where you're sitting. (The computer you're sitting in front of, and using, is called the *local computer.*) In this chapter, I show you all the ways to get to remote computers so that you can access the resources on each computer.

In addition, you also find out about shortcuts that are available for working in a network environment. You can use these tricks to make accessing remote computers on your network easier and faster.

Traveling on the Network

The computers on your network are displayed in a network folder, which makes it easy to access them. In Windows XP, the hangout is named My Network Places, and in Windows Vista, the neighborhood's appellation is simply Network.

Calling on My Network Places in Windows XP

By default, Windows XP doesn't put the My Network Places folder on the desktop or on the Start menu, but you can get to it by using the My Network Places link in the My Computer folder. To make it easier to access the My Network Places folder, take the following steps:

1. **Right-click a blank spot on the taskbar and choose Properties from the menu that appears.**

   The Taskbar and Start Menu Properties dialog box appears.

2. **Move to the Start Menu tab of the dialog box.**

3. **Be sure the Start Menu option is selected and click Customize.**

   The Customize Start Menu dialog box appears.

4. **Move to the Advanced Tab.**

5. **In the list box labeled Start Menu Items, scroll to the listing for My Network Places and select it by clicking the check box to insert a check mark (see Figure 10-1).**

Figure 10-1:
Tell
Windows
XP to list the
My Network
Places
folder on
your Start
Menu.

6. **Click OK twice to close the taskbar Properties dialog box and save your configuration change.**

   The My Network Places folder now appears on your Start Menu.

To avoid having to open the Start Menu every time you want to open My Network Places, you can create a shortcut on the desktop or on the Quick Launch toolbar (or both). Click Start, right-click the My Network Places listing, and choose Show on Desktop. Windows XP places an icon for the My Network Places folder on the desktop.

However, the desktop is often hidden by application windows, so it's even more convenient to have a shortcut to My Network Places on the Quick Launch toolbar (and besides, a shortcut on the Quick Launch toolbar works with a single mouse click instead of the double-click required of a desktop shortcut). Using the right mouse button, drag the desktop shortcut to the Quick Launch toolbar. When you release the mouse button, a menu appears. Choose Create Shortcuts Here. Now you have a quick link to My Network Places on the desktop and on the Quick Launch toolbar.

If the Quick Launch toolbar isn't on your taskbar, right-click a blank space on the taskbar and move your mouse to the Toolbars listing to display its submenu. Then click Quick Launch to add that toolbar to the left side of your taskbar.

Click any of these links to open My Network Places, which is shown in Figure 10-2. When you first open My Network Places, it doesn't display the network computers automatically — you have to do a little work to see them.

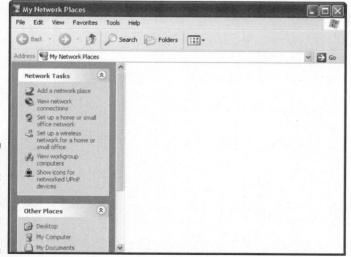

Figure 10-2:
Looking at My Network Places for the first time.

Click the View Workgroup Computers link to display the computers in your workgroup. As shown in Figure 10-3, every computer has a unique name (one of the "laws of networking"), and the computer you're using is included in the display. The computer you're using is called the *local computer,* and all the other computers are called *remote computers*.

Figure 10-3:
View all the
computers
in your
network,
including
the local
computer.

Double-click any computer to see its *shares:* the drives, folders, and peripherals that have been set up for sharing on that computer.

Visiting the Network in Windows Vista

To see your network neighbors in Windows Vista, choose Start⇔Network to open the Network folder shown in Figure 10-4. In Windows Vista, all the computers on your network appear automatically in the Network folder.

Double-click any computer to see its shares and access the files in the shared drives and folders.

Managing the icons in the My Network Places window

In Windows XP, every time you open a share and access a file, an icon for that share appears in your My Network Places window. After a while, the window can become very crowded.

But wait, it's even worse, because by default Windows XP searches the network periodically to see whether anyone has created a share on any computer. Every time a share is added to a computer, an icon for that share appears in the My Network Places folder of every computer on the network. If you have more than a couple of computers on your network, and you share a lot of folders, printers, and drives, it's not long before the folder is absolutely teeming with icons. They're not in any particular order, so it's difficult to find anything — in fact, the folder's contents become totally overwhelming.

Figure 10-4:
Viewing the
Network in
Windows
Vista.

When an icon appears in the folder window, it's there to stay because Windows doesn't check to see whether the share the icon represents still exists. If the share is removed (the folder's configuration is changed so it's no longer shared), the icon remains. If the folder that was shared has been removed, the icon stays. If the computer on which the share lives isn't turned on, the icon remains. This means you might double-click an icon and have to watch an hourglass for a while until you finally see an error message telling you the share can't be found.

Every icon of a share that's in this window is a shortcut — just like the desktop shortcuts you create for frequently used programs. You can, therefore, delete the icons without affecting the shares they represent.

You can also cure Windows XP of the obsessive need to search for and create an icon for every share ever created on any computer by taking the following steps:

1. **Open any Windows folder, such as My Computer.**

2. **Choose Tools⇨Folder Options.**

   The Folder Options dialog box opens.

3. **Move to the View tab.**

4. **In the Advanced Settings list box, deselect the option to search for shares by clicking the check box to remove the check mark (see Figure 10-5).**

5. **Click OK.**

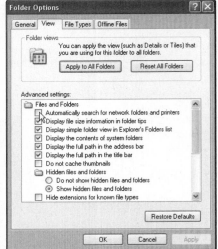

Figure 10-5:
A mouse click lets you tell Windows, "Stop doing that!"

Viewing information about the neighborhood residents

By default, the computers in the network folders are displayed as icons. The name of the computer is displayed under the icon.

When you double-click a computer's icon, the window that opens to display its shares also uses icons as the default view. The name you assigned when you created the share is also displayed under the icon.

When you create a share, you have the opportunity to enter not only a name for the share but also a comment (description). If you want to see the description fields that you or other users have entered, you must change the way the network folder displays computers and shares. The descriptions don't show in the default icons view.

To see the descriptive information about all the components on your network, change the view:

- In Windows XP, choose View➪Details from the menu bar.

- In Windows Vista, choose Views➪Details.

Descriptions are rather important for shares. Most of the time, the share-name makes sense to the person who created the share because he knows what's in the folder or what the printer does (for example, it prints color, has a certain type of paper in the tray, and so on). However, other household members may not understand those sharenames, and giving others more information is an act of kindness.

Figure 10-6 shows the window that appears after double-clicking a computer to see its shares with the Details View selected. The shares that have ambiguous names have useful descriptions.

Figure 10-6:
It's easier to locate the share you need when you know what the contents are.

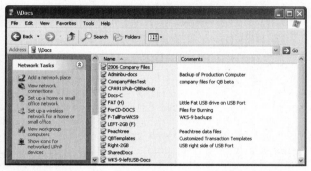

You don't have to change the view every time you open a computer in the network folder because Windows remembers the view you select and presents the same view every time you open that window.

Exploring the neighborhood in other Windows windows

You can view My Network Places in Windows Explorer or in the Computer folder (named My Computer in Windows XP and Computer in Windows Vista). Click the Folders icon to create a two-pane window. Scroll down the left pane to find the listing for My Network Places or Network and click it to see all the computers in the right pane. Or, click the plus sign to expand the listing to display the computers in the left pane.

Say UNC-le: Understanding UNCs

When you access remote resources, you're using a convention called the *universal naming convention (UNC)*. The format for displaying the UNC is like this: \\computername\resourcename. To locate a shared resource (such as a shared folder or printer) you have to navigate through the network to reach the resource, moving to the computer (computer name) and the shared resource (resourcename).

Naming your computers and shared resources

Computers on Windows networks have names. Naming a computer is part of the configuration process when you set up the network features on your Windows computer. You can name your computers whatever you want. Some people use descriptive names (Den, Kitchen, Laptop, and so on); some people use names that reflect the owner or primary user of the computer (Dad, Sis, and so on); and others just give computers names that don't necessarily have any meaning. I have a colleague who named the computers on his home network Zeke and Fred because "when I brought them home and set them up, they looked like a Zeke and a Fred." Hey, whatever works.

In addition to the computer name, you have to consider other names when you work on your network — the share names. Each shared resource has a name, because providing a name is part of setting up the share.

Sharenames are usually a bit more descriptive than computer names because people tend to use the name of the drive or folder that's being shared when they create the share. For example, if you have a folder on your computer named Addresses, you probably named the share Addresses when you configured the folder for sharing.

Understanding the UNC format

When you understand that a computer has a name and a shared resource has a name, using a formatted style to refer to a particular shared resource on a particular computer makes sense. Once upon a time, a computer nerd said, "Hey, let's call that the UNC." And everybody who needed to access shared resources in this way said, "Okey-dokey."

So, if you're working on your network and you open a folder named Budgets on a remote computer named Bob, you're working at a UNC named `\\Bob\Budgets`.

This format may look familiar — it's very similar to the way you use paths when working at the command line or viewing the path in the address bar of My Computer. For example, your Windows files are located in `C:\Windows`, which means that they're on drive C in a folder named Windows. Some important operating system files are in a subfolder named System. The path to that subfolder is `C:\Windows\System`.

In a path, a letter followed by a colon (such as `C:`) indicates a drive. In the same way, in a UNC statement, a double backslash (`\\`) followed by a name indicates a remote computer.

Your own computer has a name, too, because it's on a network. If your computer's name is Bigdaddy, your system files are in `\\Bigdaddy\Windows\System`. Anyone working at another computer on the network uses that UNC to get to that folder.

Displaying UNCs

You can see the path or UNC for any object on any computer when you're working in Windows Explorer, the Computer folder, or the Network folder if you configure those windows to display this information (they don't display the UNC by default). Use the following steps to display path and UNC details in Windows windows:

1. **Open Control Panel.**
2. **Choose Folder Options.**

   In Windows XP, select the Folder Options icon. In Windows Vista, select Appearance and Personalization, and then select Folder Options.

3. **Click the View tab of the Folder Options dialog box.**
4. **Select the Display the Full Path in the Address Bar option.**
5. **Click OK.**

Now, when you select drives or folders on your own computer or on remote computers, you see the full path or UNC statement in the window.

Opening a share by typing the UNC

If you get tired of double-clicking your way through My Network Places, you can open a share on another computer by typing the UNC, as follows:

✔ **In the Run dialog box:** Choose Start⇨Run in Windows XP, or Start⇨ All Programs⇨Accessories⇨Run in Windows Vista. Then type the UNC in the Run dialog box. After you click OK, a window opens, displaying the contents of the share.

What's nifty is that after you do this once, the UNC is saved in the Run dialog box command list. The next time you want to run a UNC, click the arrow to the right of the Open text box and select the UNC from the drop-down list.

✔ **In a Web browser:** You can use your browser to open a share and display its contents in the browser window, as shown in Figure 10-7. Just enter the UNC in the Address bar of your browser window, and press Enter. As with your favorite Web sites, you can add UNCs to your Favorites list (or bookmarks, if you're using Firefox).

Creating UNC shortcuts

If you access a particular UNC frequently, you can create a shortcut to the share on your desktop or your Quick Launch toolbar. A shortcut saves you all those mouse clicks you need to navigate through My Network Places. Follow these steps to create a shortcut:

1. **Open My Network Places.**

   Don't open the window in full-screen mode — you want to be able to get to the desktop.

2. **Navigate to the computer you want to access and double-click its icon.**

3. **Right-drag the share you want to use to the desktop or to the Quick Launch bar.**

4. **Release the mouse button and choose Create Shortcut(s) Here from the menu that appears.**

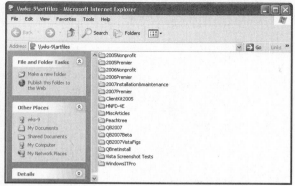

Figure 10-7:
Use your browser to access shares, and add oft-used UNCs to your Favorites list.

Mapping Drives

You can use a feature called *mapping* to more easily access a shared resource on another computer. Mapping means assigning a drive letter to a shared resource on another computer.

The drive letter you use becomes part of the local computer's set of drive letters, and these letters show up in the My Computer (Computer in Vista) and Windows Explorer windows as if they were part of the local computer. The drives you create are called *network drives*.

Understanding drive letters

The computer you use already has at least two drive letters. The floppy drive (if you have one) is A, and the hard drive is C. If you have a second hard drive, it's D. If you have a CD-ROM drive, it also has a drive letter (probably D or E). If you have a peripheral drive (such as a USB flash drive) attached to your computer, a drive letter is assigned to that device, too.

To see the drive letters that your computer is already using, open My Computer (Computer in Vista). All the devices on your computer that have drive letters are displayed.

For example, say that a computer named Eve, located in the kitchen of a house that has a home network, has the following three drive letters that belong to local resources:

- ✔ Drive A is a floppy drive.
- ✔ Drive C is a hard drive.
- ✔ Drive D is a CD-ROM drive.

Drive C is configured as a shared resource named EveDriveC. The hard drive has many folders, of course, and some of them have been configured as shared resources that can be accessed by users on other computers. Eve's shares include the following folders:

- ✔ AddressBook, which has the sharename Addresses
- ✔ FamilyBudget, which has the sharename Budget

The other computer on the network is in the upstairs hallway (in a handy little nook that was just perfect for a computer console). That computer is named Adam, and it has the following resources with drive letters:

- ✔ Drive A is a floppy drive.
- ✔ Drive C is a hard drive.

The hard drive on Adam is a shared resource named AdamDriveC. It has lots of folders, too, and the following folders have been configured as shares:

- ✔ LegalPapers, which has the sharename Legal
- ✔ Letters, which has the sharename Letters

Of course, when Adam looks at Eve, or Eve looks at Adam, those shares are UNC statements. If Adam wants to get to a file named `MyFile` on Eve's hard drive, entering `C:\MyFile` would not work, because even though Eve's drive is named C, that drive letter designation is connected to (mapped to) Adam's local computer.

Mapping a UNC

Even if you have a floppy drive, two hard drives, a CD-ROM drive, and a USB drive, most of the letters of the alphabet are unused. So put the alphabet to work! Turn a UNC into a drive letter. When you assign a drive letter to (in other words, *map*) a UNC, your life gets easier. (Well, your life as a computer user gets easier; the rest of your life is your problem, not mine.) Here are some of the benefits of mapping:

✔ Every object on your computer that has a drive letter is displayed in your computer folder in a logical list, so you don't have to expand the network folder to find a share.

✔ Every object on your computer that has a drive letter can be opened right from the computer folder by double-clicking the icon. This means you can open a local drive or a remote share with equal ease.

✔ You can use an MS-DOS command session and MS-DOS commands to work with any remote storage object (drive or folder) that has a drive letter. For example, to copy documents from a remote folder that you've mapped to drive G to your documents folder, you can type the following at the DOS prompt:

```
copy g:*.doc c:\documents
```

You can map a share only if it has been specifically configured as a share, and you can't map a subfolder that isn't shared (it's just accessible because it's in a shared folder). If there's a folder you want to access frequently enough to map a drive letter for it, you must specifically share that folder.

Follow these steps to map a network drive to a UNC:

1. **Open the network folder.**

2. **Double-click the icon for the remote computer that has the share you want to use.**

3. **Right-click the share you want to map as a network drive.**

   The shortcut menu for the share appears.

4. **Choose Map Network Drive from the shortcut menu.**

   The Map Network Drive dialog box opens, as shown in Figure 10-8. By default, Windows shows you the next available drive letter, starting with Z and working backward.

5. **Select the Reconnect at Logon check box to map this drive automatically every time you start this computer.**

   Reconnecting every time you start the computer is easier than going through all this mapping stuff every day. However, this feature can become a bit complicated; see the section, "Reconnecting mapped drives," later in this chapter, for more information.

6. **Click Finish.**

   The folder for the UNC you just mapped opens in a window, displaying its contents. You can open a file and go to work or map another network drive to a share by repeating these steps.

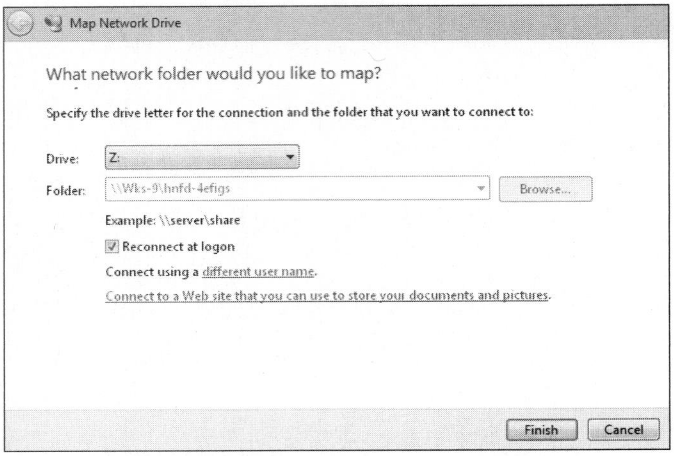

Map Network Drive

What network folder would you like to map?

Specify the drive letter for the connection and the folder that you want to connect to:

Drive: Z:

Folder: \\Wks-9\hnfd-4efigs   Browse...

Example: \\server\share

☑ Reconnect at logon

Connect using a different user name.

Connect to a Web site that you can use to store your documents and pictures.

Finish   Cancel

Figure 10-8:
Choose the
drive letter
you want to
assign to
this share.

If you don't want to see the contents of the share you just mapped, hold the Shift key while you click Finish.

Viewing and using mapped drives

After you map a UNC as a drive, you can move easily to its share by opening the computer folder. All the drives on your computer, including network drives (UNCs that are mapped to a drive letter), appear in the window. Just open the drive and go to work.

Using the example of Eve and Adam (if you haven't yet met Eve and Adam, see the section, "Understanding drive letters," earlier in the chapter), you can see how this works.

Adam has a computer named Adam. On the C drive of that computer is a folder named LegalPapers. He shared that folder and gave the share the name *Legal*. Eve uses files in that folder constantly, and to make life easier, she mapped drive Z to the share. Here's how easy it is for Adam and Eve to access this folder:

✓ When Eve wants a file, she opens drive Z, which is a network drive that is mapped to the UNC \\Adam\Legal.

✓ When Adam wants a file, he opens C:\LegalPapers.

After you've mapped a drive, like real drives, you can get to everything on that drive. For example, Adam also shared his hard drive, giving it the share name AdamDriveC. Eve mapped Y to that drive share, and when she opens drive Y, she sees the same thing Adam sees when he expands drive C in the computer folder.

If Eve finds that she constantly uses files that are in a folder on drive Y (drive C to Adam), but that folder isn't shared, she can't map a drive to that folder. Mapping works only for shared resources. She can ask Adam to share that folder, too, so she can map it. Or, she can continue to expand drive Y and move to that folder in the same way she moves through folders for real drives on her computer, using the computer folder.

Reconnecting mapped drives

When you're mapping a UNC to a drive letter, you can select the Reconnect at Logon option (see the section "Mapping a UNC," earlier in this chapter). This means that every time you log on, Windows verifies the network drive — in other words, it peers down the network cable to make sure that the shared resource that's mapped to the drive is there. This verification slows the logon process, but you probably won't notice a big difference.

Incidentally, the reason that the option is Reconnect at Logon instead of Reconnect at Startup is that the mapped drives you create are part of your personalized profile. If multiple users share a computer, the mapped drives that appear are those that were created by the user who is logged on. If a user named Sandy logs on to the computer that Eve uses, Eve's mapped drives don't exist. Sandy has to create her own mapped drives (which may very well duplicate the mappings created by Eve).

The jargon for mapped drives that are configured to reconnect at logon is *persistent connections*.

Connecting when reconnection fails

You can easily imagine that a problem may arise if you have two computers on your network and both have mapped network drives that are configured for reconnection at logon. The computer that runs the logon procedure first loses, and the computer that logs on second wins!

When the first computer looks for the mapped drive during logon, the second computer isn't yet up and running. The UNC isn't available, so the mapping function fails. Windows displays a message telling you that the mapped drive isn't connected. If your computer can't reconnect to a mapped drive at logon, it's no big deal. The logon process works, and everything's fine. Later, after the other computer is up and running, click the mapped drive's icon in the Computer folder and you'll travel there immediately.

Working with mapped drives in the computer folder

When you map drives for all the network resources you use often, the first thing you notice is that you save a whole lot of time in the computer folder. If you want to copy or move a file, everything you need is right in front of you in the folder window.

Your mapped drives appear in the Computer folder, where they're listed as Network Drives (XP) or Network Locations (Vista). If you click the Folders icon, every mapped drive is listed in the left pane of the window, along with all the drives and folders on your local computer.

If you have a long list of folders on your hard drive and you have to scroll through them to see the other drives on your computer (including mapped drives), save yourself the trouble. Enter the letter of the drive that you want to access in the computer folder window Address bar.

Working with mapped drives at the command line

If you're comfortable working with text commands, you can use those commands on a mapped drive just as if you were working on a local drive.

In a couple of situations, I find that using the command line is faster and easier than using the computer folder window. For example, if I need to rename a group of files that have similar filenames (all the files start with abc), I can accomplish that in one command, as follows:

```
ren abc*.* xyz*.*
```

In the computer folder, I'd have to rename each file separately.

Follow these steps to use a mapped drive in a command prompt window:

1. **Choose Start⇨All Programs⇨Accessories⇨Command Prompt.**

2. **Enter the drive letter for the mapped drive, followed by a colon (for example, Z:).**

   You're now working on the remote computer, and you can perform any command-line tasks.

You can even map a drive from a command prompt. Windows has a command named Net Use. The syntax for creating a mapped drive with the Net Use command is `net use` *x:* *UNC*, where *x* is the drive letter that you want to use and *UNC* is the UNC statement for the shared resource.

For example, to map G to the shared resource named Letters on the computer named Adam, enter **net use g: \\adam\letters** and wait for the response, "The command completed successfully." Now drive G is mapped, and it shows up in your computer folder.

To disconnect the mapped drive, enter **net use** *x:* **/delete**.

Chapter 11

Using Files from Other Computers

*O*ne nifty advantage to a network is that you can work on any file, anywhere, at any time, from any computer. Other users are creating files on other computers all the time. Occasionally, you may want to see one of those files. In fact, you may want to work on one of those files. Perhaps you want your very own copy of a file that currently resides on another computer.

If you find yourself working on different computers at different times, you probably have files of your own on all of them. That can be nerve-wracking. Imagine that you're sitting in front of the computer that you use most of the time, looking for that letter to Uncle Harry. You know you started it yesterday, and today you want to finish and mail it. But where is it? You look through all your document subfolders; you even use the Windows Find command to search for it. It's nowhere to be found. Think back — could you have begun the letter on the computer in the den? And now you're working at the computer in the kitchen?

You don't have to get up and walk to a remote computer to use a file that's on it, whether you or another household member created the file. Let the network do the work by transferring the file from the other computer to the one you're using now.

Working with Remote Files

When you open remote folders to access the files within them, you can do almost anything with those files that you could do if they were on your own computer. For this discussion, I assume that you have full permission to manipulate the files in the remote folder.

Making Windows Explorer easy to access

The easiest way to find, use, copy, or move files is with Windows Explorer because it has two panes: the left pane displays drives, folders, and network computers, and the right pane displays the contents of the item you've selected in the left pane.

You can get this two-pane effect in the computer folder (My Computer in Windows XP or Computer in Windows Vista) by clicking the Folders button, but why use an extra mouse click every time you open the computer folder when you can make Windows Explorer accessible?

Creating a shortcut to Windows Explorer makes it much easier to navigate through your computer and your network.

Creating a shortcut to Windows Explorer in Windows XP

In Windows XP, use the following steps to create a shortcut to Windows Explorer.

1. **Click the Show Desktop icon on the Quick Launch toolbar to minimize any open windows, which makes the desktop visible.**

2. **Choose Start⇨All Programs⇨Accessories.**

   The Accessories menu is displayed.

3. **Right-drag the Windows Explorer menu item to the desktop.**

   When you release the mouse button the right-drag menu appears.

4. **Select Copy Here.**

   A shortcut to Windows Explorer is placed on the desktop.

5. **Drag (with the left mouse button this time) the shortcut to the Quick Launch toolbar.**

   The shortcut is moved from the desktop to the Quick Launch toolbar, where it opens with one click instead of the double-click required for desktop shortcuts.

Creating a shortcut to Windows Explorer in Windows Vista

To place a shortcut to Windows Explorer in the Windows Vista Quick Launch toolbar, use the following steps:

1. **Choose Start⇨All Programs⇨Accessories.**

   The Accessories menu is displayed.

2. **Right-click the listing for Windows Explorer.**

   The right-click menu appears.

3. **Choose Add to Quick Launch.**

   That's it, you're done! A one-click shortcut to Windows Explorer is on your Quick Launch toolbar.

Make Windows Explorer open with drive C displayed

To make Windows Explorer more useful, you have to change the way it opens. By default, this utility opens with the documents folder selected in the left pane, displaying any and all subfolders. For many of us who organize our documents folder with tons of subfolders, it takes forever to scroll through those subfolders, find drive C, and expand it.

Here's how to change the behavior of Windows Explorer so it opens with drive C selected (and expanded), which means that mapped drives and the Network folder are also easier to see.

1. **Right-click the shortcut for Windows Explorer you created using the instructions in the previous section, and choose Properties.**

   The Properties dialog box appears, with the Shortcut tab selected (see Figure 11-1).

2. **In the Target text box, enter a space followed by /e,c: and click OK.**

   Windows Explorer now opens with drive C expanded so you can see all your folders and you don't have to scroll down as far to find the network listings in the left pane.

Figure 11-1:
The
Shortcut
Properties
options
control
the way
Windows
Explorer
opens.

Copying files between computers

You can copy a file from a remote computer to your own computer by either dragging it or using the right-click shortcut menu.

You can use the same techniques to copy files in the other direction, from your computer to the remote computer. Just reverse the processes that I describe here.

Copying by dragging files

If you drag a file from a remote computer to your own computer, you copy it, which means the original file is still on the remote computer, and a copy of that file is on your computer. This process is different from dragging a file from one folder to another on the same drive on your own computer, which *moves* the file instead of copying it. That's because Windows assumes that you don't want to deprive the other computer's user of the file. It's a good assumption.

To make dragging files from a remote computer to your own computer easier, use Windows Explorer or click the Folders button on the computer folder to display drives and folders in the left pane. With that view, you can see both the remote computer and your own computer in a single window.

Follow these steps to copy a file by dragging it:

1. **In Windows Explorer, expand the network listing in the left pane by clicking the plus sign.**

   All the computers in your network are displayed in the left pane.

2. **Click the plus sign next to the remote computer that has the file you need.**

   All the shared drives and folders on that remote computer are displayed in the left pane.

3. **Click the remote folder that holds the file you want.**

   The files in the remote folder appear in the right Explorer pane.

4. **In the left Explorer pane, use the scroll bar on the left pane to position the target folder near the file you want to copy.**

   The *target folder* is the folder into which you want to copy the file. Don't select (click) the folder; just scroll until you can see the target folder in the left pane. You want the files from the remote computer to remain in the right pane. This maneuver just makes it easier to drag the file — the distance is shorter.

5. **Drag the file to the target folder in the left pane.**

   When your mouse pointer is on the correct folder (as shown in Figure 11-2), release the mouse button.

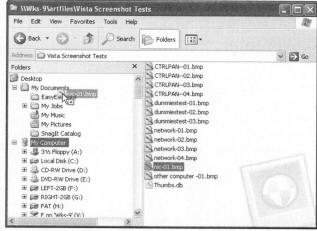

Figure 11-2:
A file from another computer is about to be stored in the My Documents folder on the local computer.

Only folders that have been configured for sharing are displayed when you look at a remote computer in Windows Explorer. If the folder that holds the file you want isn't a shared folder, click the plus sign next to that folder's parent folder, which reveals all the child folders in the left pane. Then select the folder you need.

Dragging between separate windows

Some people find it a bit difficult to drag files within the Windows Explorer window because the objects are small, so your movements have to be rather precise. If you agree, you can drag files from one computer to another over separate windows. In fact, you have several ways to accomplish this, as follows:

1. **Double-click the My Network Places or Network icon on the desktop.**

2. **Double-click the computer and then the shares on the remote computer to get to the window that has the file you want.**

3. **Open My Documents and any subfolders to open the target folder.**

   If you're not putting the file in My Documents, open My Computer (Computer for Windows Vista) instead and double-click the drive and folder(s) necessary to open the target window.

4. **Position the windows near each other.**

   It's okay if they overlap or if they're separated — you just need to be able to get to each window.

5. **Drag the file from one window to the other.**

If you want to copy multiple files, press and hold Ctrl and select all the files that you need. Then drag one of the selected files to the target folder; all the other files come along for the ride.

Copying by right-dragging files

Perhaps you're not very adventurous, and you're afraid that you may move the file instead of copying it. Or perhaps you can't remember whether dragging moves or copies files when you're working with multiple computers. To play it safe, drag with the right mouse button (called *right-dragging*). When you release the mouse button, a menu appears. Choose Copy Here from the menu.

Copying with the shortcut menu

You can use the shortcut menu that appears when you right-click an item to copy a file. This method eliminates the need for a second window. Follow these steps to copy files from a remote computer to your own computer:

1. **Open Windows Explorer.**

2. **Expand the Network listing and then expand the remote computer to select the folder that holds the file you need.**

   The files in the selected folder appear in the right Explorer pane.

3. **Right-click the file that you want to copy.**

   The shortcut menu appears. If you want to copy multiple files, press and hold Ctrl as you click each file. Then right-click any file to see the shortcut menu.

4. **Choose Copy from the shortcut menu.**

   The file (or group of files) is placed on the Windows Clipboard.

5. **In the left Explorer pane, right-click the folder on your local computer into which you want to copy the file.**

6. **Choose Paste from the shortcut menu that appears.**

   The file (or group of files) is copied to your local folder.

Relocating (moving) files

Sometimes you may want to move a file, removing it from the remote computer and placing it on your local computer (or the other way around). Moving files is less common than copying files, but if you used to work on the computer in the den and have decided that you prefer the computer in the kitchen, you may want to move your files to your new computer.

Moving by right-dragging files

You can drag files from the remote computer to your own computer with the right mouse button (called *right-dragging*). If you drag with the left mouse button, you copy the files instead of moving them.

Use the steps that I discuss in the section "Copying by dragging files," earlier in this chapter, to get to the file or folder you want to move. You can use either Windows Explorer or two windows, depending on your comfort level. Then right-drag the file or files you need from one computer to the other. When you release the right mouse button, a menu appears. Choose Move Here from the menu. The files move from the original location to the new location.

Using the shortcut menu to move files

If you don't want to open separate windows to drag files, you can use the file shortcut menu to cut and paste files.

Follow the steps in the section "Copying with the shortcut menu," earlier in this chapter, to select and right-click the file(s) you want to move. Instead of choosing Copy from the shortcut menu, choose Cut. Then right-click the target folder and choose Paste. The files move from the original location to the new location.

Deleting files from remote computers

You can delete a file from a remote computer as easily as you can delete files from your own computer. Just select the file and press Delete. The same thing is true of folders.

Deleting a file or folder from a remote computer is much more dangerous than deleting files and folders on your own computer. The problem is that the Recycle Bin doesn't work across the network. A deleted file or folder is really deleted, so you can't recover it from the Recycle Bin right after you say "oops."

Okay, now I hear you talking to this page. You're saying that when you look at the contents of a hard drive on a remote computer, you can see the Recycle Bin, so I must be wrong. Well, double-click that Recycle Bin to open it. Now, double-click the Recycle Bin on your own desktop. Notice anything strange? The files in the two Recycle Bins are identical.

This is a cute trick that Windows plays on network users. When you open the Recycle Bin on a remote computer, instead of flashing a message that says "Access Denied" or "No Way, Go Away" and refusing to open the folder, the system acts as if you're opening a real Recycle Bin. But you're really opening a copy of your own, local Recycle Bin.

Opening Remote Files in Software Windows

You don't have to take the trouble to copy or move files to your own computer when you want to work with them in a program. You can open and save files on remote computers right from the software. In fact, software that's written for Windows is designed to do this.

Both computers need to be running the same software. In other words, if you want to open a Microsoft Excel document that you see on a remote computer, you must have Microsoft Excel installed on your own computer. (Obviously the remote computer has Microsoft Excel installed or nobody would have been able to create an Excel document on that computer.)

This feature is handy if you don't always work at the same computer. Of course, if you have enough clout to tell whoever is working on your favorite computer to move to another machine, you don't have to worry about this eventuality. And, you should be writing books on effective family dynamics. Most of us with more users than computers in the household have to use whatever computer is available.

Opening distant files

If you work in a Windows program and you want to work on a file that's located on a remote computer, you can accomplish that right from the software. Follow these steps to use a remote file in your software:

1. **Click the Open button on the software toolbar or choose File⇨ Open from the software's menu bar.**

   The Open dialog box appears. The contents of the default document folder are displayed (usually the Documents folder on your own computer).

2. **Click the arrow to the right of the Look In box and select the network listing from the list of locations.**

   The Open dialog box displays the computers that are on your network (see Figure 11-3).

Figure 11-3: The Open dialog box in any Windows software can take you to any resource on your computer or on the network.

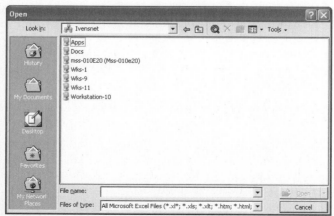

3. **Double-click the icon of the remote computer that you want to access.**

   Icons for the shared drives and folders on the remote computer appear in the Open dialog box.

4. **Double-click the folder that holds the file you want to use.**

   The files located in that folder are displayed in the Open dialog box.

5. **Select the file and click Open.**

   The file loads in your software window, so get to work!

If the file that you need is located in a subfolder of a shared resource, it doesn't appear when you double-click the computer's icon (only the folders that are configured for sharing show up in the display). You must open the shared parent folder and then open the subfolder to get to the file.

This is one of the scenarios in which mapped drives are handy. If you've mapped a drive to a folder on the remote computer, you can get to its contents by using its drive letter (which is listed as one of the drives on your local computer when you use the drop-down list in the Open dialog box). See Chapter 10 to find out about mapped drives.

Saving remote files

If you open a file from a remote computer, saving it doesn't change its original location. Every time you click the Save button on the toolbar, press Ctrl+S, or choose File⇔Save, you save the file in its original location on the remote computer.

The same thing is true for files that you open in software that resides on your local drive — they're saved to the same location every time you save.

Suppose that you open a file that's on a remote computer and work on it in an application, and then you decide that you want to have a copy of it on your own computer. Well, doing that is easier than you may think because you don't have to close the software and use the Copy function that I describe earlier in this chapter. You can work on the document and copy it in one fell swoop by using the features in the software.

The same shortcut action is available for documents that you create on your local computer if you decide that you want to share the file with a user on another computer.

Saving a remote file to the local computer

You've opened a program and loaded a document from another computer on the network by using the steps discussed in the section, "Opening distant files," earlier in this chapter. You work on the document, making creative changes and adding brilliant new text. Then your brain comes up with a thought that matches one of the following ideas:

- ✔ The user who created the document likes it just the way it is. If you prefer the changed document, you should keep it on your own computer.

- ✔ The original document is meant to be used as a template, and you'd prefer to have your own copy of it.

- ✔ You haven't finished working on the document, and reloading it is faster if the file is in your local My Documents folder.

- ✔ You know that you want to continue working on the document, but if the other computer isn't running the next time you need it, you don't want to climb the stairs to the den.

- ✔ You just want your own copy because you just want your own copy.

For any of those common reasons (or for some reason I didn't think of), you can save the file to your own local computer. To accomplish this, follow these steps:

1. **Choose File⇨Save As from the menu bar of your software window.**

   When the Save As dialog box opens, the saving location is the same remote folder that you opened to fetch the file.

2. **Click the arrow to the right of the Save In text box.**

3. **Choose the folder that you normally use for saving files on your local computer.**

4. **Click Save.**

   You can change the name of the file before you click the Save button if you don't want both files to have the same name.

You now have a copy of the file on your local computer, and the original file remains on the remote computer.

Saving a local file to a remote computer

When you work in an application and you create an absolutely terrific work of art, a fantastic poem, or a mathematically brilliant budget that helps your family save 20 percent of your income without any deprivation, you should show it off — er, share it. If you just created the document, you should save it to your local documents folder first because having your own copy of a document is a good idea.

Or, in another scenario, perhaps you're working on the computer in the kitchen because somebody else is working on your favorite computer (in the den). You're sure the next time you want to use a computer, you'll be able to get to the machine in the den. Therefore, it makes sense to save the file on the den computer, where it will be handy when you want to continue working on it.

Follow these steps to save the document on another computer:

1. **Choose File⇨Save As from the software menu bar.**

   The Save As dialog box appears.

2. **Click the arrow to the right of the Save In text box and select the network from the list of locations.**

   Icons for the computers that are on your network appear in the Save As dialog box.

3. **Double-click the icon for the remote computer on which you want to store a copy of your document.**

   The shared folders on the selected computer appear in the dialog box.

4. **Double-click the folder into which you want to save the document.**

   If the folder you want to use is a subfolder of a shared folder, open the shared folder first and then open the subfolder.

   If the only shared resource is the hard drive, open the hard drive and then open the appropriate folder.

5. **Choose Save to copy the document to the remote location.**

   If you want, you can also change the name of the document before you save it to the remote computer.

Uh oh, two documents with the same name

If you have a document with the same name on two different computers, your life could get a bit complicated — well, at least your life as it relates to this document — your real-life complications are probably unrelated to computer networks.

The two files most certainly have different content — you opened the file from one computer, made changes, and saved it on another computer. Here's the problem: If you open the copy on your local computer and use the Save As command to save it in the documents folder on the remote computer (or vice versa), you replace the file that was on the remote computer. In fact, Windows displays a message that asks you if you really want to replace that file.

If you've been working on both files, you don't want to replace one file with the other — you'll lose your changes. The solution is to change the filename, sort of. Make it a rule that every time you use the Save As command on a document that's shared between computers, you append text to the filename. The best text to append is a number. For example, if the original file had the name Budget, the first time you save it on another computer, change the file-name to Budget02. Each time you use the Save As command to change the location of the file to another computer, increase the number.

When you're working locally, just keep saving the file under the same name — you don't need to use the Save As command until you want to change the computer on which you're saving the file.

Eventually, if you work on the document numerous times, you'll probably end up with several copies of the file on each computer. Perhaps the computer in the den has files named Budget02 and Budget04, while the kitchen computer has files named Budget and Budget03.

At some point, open all the copies of the file on one computer at the same time (all Windows software lets you open multiple files at the same time). Cut, copy, and paste parts of the documents into one document to create one masterpiece that contains every change you want to keep. Then delete the other copies.

The same danger occurs if you copy or relocate files instead of opening them in software. Be careful not to replace one file with another if the file that's going to disappear contains data you want to keep.

Understanding documents in use

If you try to open a document that's already open on another computer, the software displays a message telling you that the document is being used. The document may be one that lives on the local computer (the one you're working on) and has been opened remotely by a user on another computer. Or, the document may live on another computer, and a user on that computer is working with it.

Software that is properly written for Windows displays a message telling you that the file is in use and offers to load a read-only copy and then notify you when the person who is using the document closes it (see Figure 11-4).

Figure 11-4:
Somebody
is using this
document,
but you
can have a
read-only
copy of it.

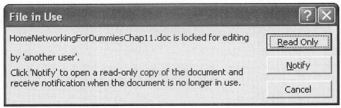

Click the Read Only button to have a copy of the document placed in your own software window. The file is in *read-only* mode, which means that you can't save it on its originating computer using the same name. Actually, read-only means you cannot use the Save command; only Save As works.

Click the Notify button if you want to be notified when the other user closes the file. In the meantime, the software loads a read-only copy of the file in your software window.

It's important to realize that the copy that's loaded in your software window is from the hard drive of the remote computer, not the software window of the remote user. This means that you get a copy of the file the way it looked the last time the remote user saved it, which may have been three minutes ago, yesterday, or last week. That user is obviously still working on the file, but any changes or additions since the last time she saved aren't copied to your software window.

So, now you have a copy of the file in your software window. You can make all the changes and additions that you care to, just as if the file weren't in use.

Eventually, you're going to want to save the file. If you don't remember to use the Save As command on the File menu, an error message appears to remind you the file is read-only. Click OK, and a Save As dialog box appears so that you can save the file under a different name or in a different location. You have the following options:

✔ **Use a different filename and save the file in the original location on the remote computer.** For example, add your initials to the end of the existing filename.

✔ **Save the file to your local computer.** Click the arrow to the right of the Save In text box and select your local hard drive or the My Documents folder.

The problem with the second option is that you now have two files with the same name but different content on the network (albeit on two separate computers). If you think that you and the original user may want to compare and combine the two documents, save the file under a different name when you save it to your local computer.

If you save the file to your computer, using the same filename, and then later copy the file back to the original computer, a message appears asking you if you want to overwrite the existing file. If you click Yes, you replace the file that the first user saved. Now leave home because your life is in danger. This is a dirty trick because you end up overwriting all the work that was saved by the first user.

If you selected the option to be notified when the first user closes the file, a message appears to tell you the file is unlocked and asks if you want to remove the read-only lock (see Figure 11-5).

Figure 11-5:
Making this file read-write instead of read-only means you can save it normally, under its original name — which may not be a good idea.

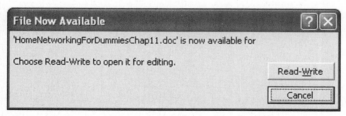

If you click the Read-Write button, the file is reloaded into your software window and all the changes the first user made are added to the file (you have a copy of that person's final saved file). Because you had to open that file as a read-only file, you didn't make any changes to the original file.

If you've saved the file under a different name (with the Save As command) because you wanted to save the changes you made, you can open that file and paste your changes into the original file. However, your contributions to the file will come as a surprise (and not necessarily a welcomed one) to the original user.

Play it safe — close the original file and continue to use the file you saved with the Save As command. Later, you and the other user can discuss the differences and decide whether it's okay to combine the contents of the two files.

Files that should never be opened across a network

Don't open files from programs that automatically save data as soon as you enter it. This is usually true of database programs that aren't designed for multiple users or for which you don't own a multiuser copy. No Save or Save As command is available — as soon as you enter data and move on to the next record, the data is saved automatically. If somebody else is working on the same record, you end up with conflicting data.

Most database programs have safeguards against this behavior — they're built for shared access by multiple simultaneous users. For example, you may be using accounting software that is specially designed for multiuser activities. (One example of this type of software is QuickBooks, but you must purchase the multiuser version.)

However, some single-user database programs may let you open a file that's in use and manipulate it. Then, when you finish entering data and the automatic save process begins, the software, unable to manage multiuser procedures, goes crazy. The software may crash or freeze, or the data may become corrupted.

Play it safe — don't share database files unless you've purchased database software that's built for multiuser access.

Licenses and other complications

Most software that's designed to let multiple users access the files in a peer-to-peer network requires you to install the software on every computer. The data file is stored on one computer, so the data can be shared.

When you buy software that works in this manner, you're actually buying a license to use the software; you're not buying the program itself. That license has terms, and you agree to the terms when you install the software. It is almost always illegal to purchase one copy of a single-user program and then install it on multiple computers on your network. You must buy a separate copy for each computer.

Breaking the license agreement is illegal. It's also immoral. It's no different from buying a can of vegetables at the grocery store, hiding another can in your coat pocket, and paying for only one can at the checkout counter. Just as shoplifting is illegal, so is installing software for which you didn't buy a license. When you set up a home network, your actions are visible to your children. Stealing is not the kind of example you want to set.

How About Including My Macintosh?

This is the part of the chapter in which I'm supposed to tell you how to include a Macintosh computer in the file-trading circle you've established for your PC-based network.

Here's the deal: If you're running OS X on your Mac, it can join your network easily. Otherwise, to move files between a Macintosh and the PCs, you'd have to launch a browser and use the FTP feature to download and upload files.

FTP, which stands for *File Transfer Protocol,* is commonly used to transfer files between Web sites and your computer. FTP uses the Internet's Transmission Control Protocol/Internet Protocol (TCP/IP) to move files. The Web site acts as a server, and your computer acts as a client. If you have the right permissions, you can also upload files from your computer to the Web site. When you're on the Internet, you don't normally have such permissions except on your own Web site, where you use a password to upload the files required for your Web pages.

When you set up a Macintosh, you make sure that the Mac, which is acting as a server, is configured to give you uploading rights. Otherwise, you would only get files from your Mac; you wouldn't send the Mac any files from your PCs.

FTP is just one of the protocols that are part of the TCP/IP protocol. Among the other TCP/IP protocols you use are http (Hypertext Transfer Protocol), for viewing Web pages, and SMTP (Simple Mail Transfer Protocol), which moves your e-mail between your computer and the Internet.

To make it worse, after I figured out how to transfer files between a Mac and my PCs, I found out that the configuration settings and the ability to use the Mac as a server differ among different Mac models and among different versions of the Mac operating system.

After I returned to my chair from my "walk to the wall and bang your head against it" episode, I contacted some Mac network experts, some of whom are well-known authors of books about Macintosh computers.

"I want to network a Mac," I'd say. "Sure, easy," each replied. "Install File and Print services for Macintosh on your Windows domain and on all the servers in your network that will be responsible for Mac client/server processes."

"No, no," I would say. "This isn't in a business network; it's a peer-to-peer home network."

"Sure, easy," came the replies, as long as you're running Mac OS X. When I asked about earlier versions of Mac operating systems, some of them laughed. One person said, "You can't get there from here." But a few experts said that I could buy software to accomplish this. You can buy software for the PCs or software for the Macintosh. You don't need both.

Check with magazines and books that are devoted to Macintosh users to find out about software for incorporating your older Macintosh into your network. Or, check out the programs that I cover next, which were recommended by some Macintosh experts whom I talked to.

Mac, meet Dave

For the Macintosh, buy Dave. Yep, that's the name of the software. It's from Thursby Software, which you can reach at `www.thursby.com`.

This software uses TCP/IP on the Mac, so your PCs can recognize and inter-act with the Mac. In effect, it makes the Macintosh look like a PC to the other PCs that are on the network. It even lets the Mac user log on to the network the way PC users do.

You must be using a Mac with a 68030 or higher processor, and you must have at least 16MB of RAM. The software supports Mac OS 8.6 and higher. You can download a free trial, which is a limited version of the software, before deciding to purchase it (the purchase price is about $150 for a single-user version).

Thursby Software also has a product called MacSOHO that has fewer fea-tures, but it does support file sharing between Macs and PCs. You may want to investigate it.

From a PC LAN to a PC MACLAN

Computer Associates offers a product called PC MACLAN, which is installed on PCs that need to interact with Macintosh computers. To learn more about it, go to `http://ca.miramar.com/Products/PC_MACLAN`.

Part IV
Network Security and Maintenance

"We take network security here very seriously."

In this part . . .

Securing the network is the technical terminology for keeping the bad stuff — including viruses and Internet invaders — away from all the computers on the network. You probably know what a virus is (even if you've never encountered one on your computer), but you maynot know what Internet invaders are. These are malicious people who try to break in to your computer while you're connected to the Internet, a feat that's amazingly easy to do if you don't take the proper precautions. In this part, you find out what steps you can take to keep the bad stuff out of your network.

Maintenance is the technical term for, well, maintenance — I guess there's no better word. Your computers and your network need maintenance to stay healthy — just like your car or your teeth. In this part, you discover techniques and tools you can use to keep things humming along.

Chapter 12

Making Your Network Secure

In This Chapter

▶ Combating computer viruses

▶ Keeping Internet spies out of your computers

▶ Fending off evil-doers

As users, we make mistakes. We inadvertently delete important files (including software files) and perform other accidental actions that can totally mess up a computer.

However, some people deliberately work at the task of destroying computers, and they perform their dirty deeds by installing viruses on your computer. Other nasty folks invade your computer while you're on the Internet, and they get private information from your files (or leave viruses on your computer). Any malicious program that finds its way onto any computer on your network can move to any other computer on the network.

This chapter discusses methods you can use to make sure that the computers on your network have as much protection as possible against the misery these actions can cause. However, the most important ingredient in your scheme to protect your network is a healthy dose of paranoia. Be suspicious. Be very afraid.

All about Viruses

A *virus* is programming code that is designed to cause damage and is disguised to appear to be a normal program. Most viruses are also designed to clone themselves if they find a network environment so that they can move on to the other computers.

Almost all virus infections occur over the Internet, attached to e-mail, attached to a file that you download, or sent over an Instant Message connection. Three major classes of viruses exist, and each class has a number of sub-classes, as rogue programmers devise innovative ways to ply their nefarious trade.

A virus is a program, although it's frequently disguised as something else (for example, it may pretend to be a screensaver). The code in the program is designed to cause harm. In addition, code exists to make sure that the virus is replicated to other drives on your computer, to other computers on a net-work, or to other computers on the Internet.

The severity of the damage a virus leaves behind depends on the viciousness of the programmer. Viruses can erase data, replace program files, and change system files. Some viruses cause enough damage to the operating system files to make it impossible to boot the computer, rendering the machine use-less. Some viruses go to work as soon as you inadvertently start them, but other viruses are programmed to wait until certain circumstances cause their code to be executed (usually a certain date).

Viruses arrive in many categories, and within each category many subcate-gories exist. Covering all of these variants would fill a thick book. In the fol-lowing sections I go over some of the basic virus types so you can learn how to spot (or be suspicious about) problems that may be caused by the most frequently encountered virus types.

File-infecting viruses

File infectors are the oldest virus type, and they've been around as long as personal computers have been around. These viruses attach themselves to program files, which are usually files with the filename extension `.com` or `.exe`. However, some file-infecting viruses don't need the main executable file to infect your system. They can attach themselves to another file type, one that is loaded by the main executable file. Among the file types that pro-grams load (and viruses can use) are filenames with the extensions `.sys`, `.ovl`, `.prg`, and `.mnu`.

When the program is loaded, the virus is loaded as well, and it does its work independent of the program that runs when you open the program file. The program file is just the mode of transportation — the way the virus gets itself loaded into memory.

How to avoid being fooled by Windows

People who know that file-infecting virus types are connected to executable files are frequently surprised when their computers become infected. They're always careful about examining the filenames of e-mail attachments and downloaded files, looking for a file extension that indicates an executable file. When they see an attachment with the file extension `.txt`, they stop worrying and then go crazy trying to figure out how a virus slipped past their guard.

These people have been fooled by Windows. Unfortunately (okay, I'd rather say "stupidly"), Windows doesn't display file extensions by default, so a file that seems to be named `readme.txt` could really be named `readme.txt.exe`. I've never understood the logic (or lack of it) that went into Microsoft's decision to hide file extensions when you're viewing files. To avoid this Windows "gotcha," the first thing to do when you set up a computer is to change the default setting for viewing files so that file extensions are visible. To do this, follow these steps:

1. Open My Computer or another system folder, such as Windows Explorer or Control Panel.

2. Choose Tools⇨Folder Options.

3. Select the View tab.

4. Scroll through the Advanced settings list to locate the Hide File Extensions for Known File Types item and click the check box to remove the check mark.

5. Click OK.

Some viruses can also be programs at the same time. The filename is innocuous, and the filename extension is `.exe`. Opening the file unleashes the virus. This virus type is frequently transmitted to its victims as an e-mail attachment.

System and boot infectors

System and boot infectors infect the code that's placed in certain system areas on a drive. On a floppy disk, they attach themselves to the DOS boot sector. On hard drives, they attach themselves to the Master Boot Record (MBR).

This virus type doesn't launch itself into memory and go to work until the next time you boot your computer. If you boot to a floppy disk — using the infected disk — the virus is activated. If you start your computer normally, the virus loads itself into system memory when the boot files on the MBR load.

After it's loaded into your system memory, the virus can control basic computer operations, and it can replicate itself to other drives on the computer or to other computers on the network. Some boot sector viruses are designed to destroy the computer's ability to boot; others permit startup and then perform damaging processes all over the computer (and any computers that are attached through a network).

Macro viruses

Macro viruses are usually programmed to do the same damage as file-infecting viruses, but they use a different vehicle to arrive at your computer. They don't attach themselves to an executable file, nor do they arrive as a self-contained executable file. Instead, they attach themselves to a document and launch themselves when the document file is opened. Then they carry out their damaging agenda and replicate themselves into other documents.

Macro viruses should really be called VB viruses because they attach themselves to Visual Basic (VB) code, which some programs use to create or run macros. (Macros are automated procedures that you can use to perform tasks in software.) VB files have the extension .vbs.

All the software applications that are included in Microsoft Office use VB code for macros. In fact, almost all the software that you can buy from Microsoft uses VB code for a variety of tasks.

A neat trick is available for avoiding VB viruses, but if you use VB yourself, you can't use it. (Personally, I think avoiding these common viruses is important enough to stop using VB.) The essence of this trick is to make your computer think that VB code is text, and because text files can't execute program code, the VB virus code never executes. The way to implement this trick is to change the association of files with the extension .vbs from Visual Basic to Notepad (the Windows text editor). Here's how to make this change:

1. **Open My Computer or another system folder, such as Windows Explorer or Control Panel.**

2. **Choose Tools⇨Folder Options.**

3. **Move to the File Types tab.**

4. **Scroll through the list of registered file types and select VBS.**

    The file association information about the .vbs file extension is displayed, as shown in Figure 12-1.

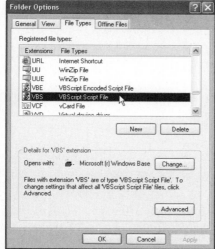

Figure 12-1:
VBS files
are
associated
with
VBScript,
which is an
executable
program.

5. Click the Change button.

The Opens With dialog box appears (see Figure 12-2).

Figure 12-2:
Select
Notepad to
create an
innocuous
association
for VBS
files.

6. Select Notepad and click OK.

7. Click Close.

A strange name for a program, huh?

The name *Trojan horse* comes from Homer's *Iliad*, which tells the story of the Greeks faking out the Trojans during a long, bitter war. The Greeks pretended to give up, and then they offered a giant wooden statue of a horse to the Trojans, calling it a peace offering. What the Trojans didn't know was that the statue was hollowed out, and within it were armed soldiers.

That night, while the Trojans celebrated their victory, the belly of the statue opened and the soldiers emerged, overwhelming the Trojans. Because the rogue code in a Trojan horse program disguises itself as a normal, safe program, somebody (who obviously read Homer) applied this name.

VBS viruses now lack an executable association, which means they can't run. Of course, you can't run VBS macros either, but because most users aren't macro programmers, that's probably just fine.

Some programs that provide the power of macros use their own proprietary method that doesn't run as a program. It's much more difficult for a virus to insert itself within macro code that doesn't use VB. WordPerfect is an example of a program that provides powerful macro abilities without using VB.

Trojan horses

A *Trojan horse* performs the same malicious deeds that viruses perform, but a Trojan horse doesn't qualify as a true virus because it doesn't fit the technical definition of a virus in terms of replication. Trojan horses don't replicate themselves. Of course, if you've been victimized by a Trojan horse, those definitions are piddling.

One problem with a Trojan horse is that it's sometimes difficult to remove the damage it does, even after you catch and remove the Trojan horse file. You almost always have to contact an antivirus software company to get instructions for eliminating the damage the Trojan horse left behind. You may have to undo changes to the Registry, replace system files, or perform other manual tasks to rid your system of the damage.

Most antivirus programs can successfully identify and delete most Trojan horses, but if you find yourself facing continual attacks by Trojan horses, you may want to install a program that's dedicated to this type of virus. Experts give high recommendations to Pestpatroll (www.pestpatroll.com) and Tauscan (www.agnitum.com).

Worms

A *worm* is always a self-contained program, so it never has to attach itself to any other program to launch itself. A worm must be opened manually, at which point it does its damage and replicates itself (often by mailing itself to recipients in an Outlook or Outlook Express address book).

One characteristic of a worm is its ability to propagate itself across drives and computers that are connected via a network. Because they don't need to attach themselves to other programs, worms propagate easily and rapidly. They don't need to find a host file, so they can just plop themselves down anywhere they want and then clone themselves all over your drives (including drives of connected computers). Sometimes each clone that's created carries a different assignment, so when all these copies leap into action, they can do the maximum amount of damage. Worms almost always arrive as e-mail attachments.

If you use Outlook or Outlook Express for e-mail, it's urgent that you pay attention to Microsoft's security alerts, fixes, and updates. Unfortunately, this can be a frequent chore. (Those of us who gave up Outlook/Outlook Express in favor of Eudora tend to get a bit smug about this.)

Antivirus Programs: For Prevention and Cure

An important defense against viruses is an antivirus program. Good antivirus software performs the following tasks:

- ✔ Scans your drive, looking for viruses
- ✔ Checks every executable file as you open it to make sure that no virus is piggybacked onto it
- ✔ Checks your e-mail to find viruses as messages are brought into your inbox
- ✔ Removes any virus code it finds (or deletes the file if it cannot remove the virus)

A number of antivirus programs are available, and the following are the most popular:

✔ Norton AntiVirus (www.symantec.com)

✔ PC-Cillin (www.trendmicro.com)

✔ McAfee VirusScan (www.mcafee.com)

I'm sure that other existing programs are just as good as these, but I've used all of these and can personally endorse them.

Antivirus software has two main components:

✔ **The engine,** or the program itself

✔ **The virus information data files,** which have information about known viruses, making it possible for the software to spot virus files

New viruses are invented all the time (reliable sources put the number of new viruses at 400 per month). Usually, the cures are found quickly. The cures are put into the virus information data files, and you can download those files from your antivirus software vendor (which is not the same as downloading a complete update to the software). Configure your antivirus software to check for updates to the virus information data files on a regular basis (every few hours), or manually check for updates every day.

The antivirus engine/program has the following parts:

✔ **The on-access component,** which runs all the time and automatically checks files as they're received or opened

✔ **The scanning component,** which checks all the files on your computer when you initiate a scan

Antivirus software works by intercepting computer operations, such as reading files or receiving e-mail messages, so that it can scan the files before allowing the operating system to continue with the operation. The scanning process involves the following steps:

✔ Matching the contents of the file against the information that's in the virus data information files. The software looks for a known signature, called a *marker,* which is a string of characters or bytes that's found in every instance of a specific virus.

✔ Looking for unusual file attributes, such as unexpected changes in the size of existing executable files.

✔ Looking for suspicious behavior by using heuristic scanning to sniff out suspicious code (see the sidebar, "Heuristic scanning," for more information).

Heuristic scanning

Heuristic scanning is a way to analyze the behavior of an executable file to try to determine whether the file offers a potential threat. Antivirus software companies use this technique to try to catch viruses that are new and therefore have not yet been added to their virus information data files. Each antivirus software company has its own method for determining a potential threat and for defining "suspicious behavior" during heuristic scans. Heuristic scanning is really a guessing game, but it uses educated guesses.

Heuristic scanning has some side effects, but none of them are serious enough to turn off the feature (most antivirus software lets you turn off the heuristic scanning option). It makes scanning slower, it can sometimes produce false alarms when a good program has code that seems to resemble the code in a virus, and it can miss a new virus that doesn't behave in typical virus fashion. Personally, I think it's best to maintain an attitude of paranoia, so even though the technology for heuristic scanning is not as advanced as it probably will be one day, you're better off letting your antivirus software use this feature.

When the software finds a file that's infected, it flashes a message. Usually, the message asks you to decide how to handle the file. The choices vary depending on the software, but you're usually offered one of the following choices:

- ✔ **Clean the file:** This choice works when a virus has infected an existing file. The software tries to clean the virus out of the file, reverting the file to its original condition. If the software can't clean the file, you're notified of that fact, and you must delete the file. (Use the Delete option in the antivirus software window; don't open Windows Explorer to delete the file.) If the file that you delete is required by the operating system or an application, you'll have to replace it with a copy of the original.

- ✔ **Delete the file:** When you delete the file through the antivirus software window, the file is not sent to the Recycle Bin; it is permanently deleted.

- ✔ **Isolate the file:** Some antivirus programs offer a method for isolating infected files, usually in a folder that the software creates, by locking the isolation folder to prevent any file in the folder from damaging the computer. Later, you can delete the contents of the folder, or you can send the files to the software company (if you're participating in a program that asks you to do this).

The software always identifies the name of the virus it finds, and you should note the name and go to the antivirus software company's Web site to find out more about the virus. You may have to do more than just delete the infected file to clean up your computer, and the company has instructions for any other steps you should take. This is especially true of Trojan horses.

Common Sense: Part of Your Arsenal

If you develop an enhanced sense of suspicion, even paranoia, you're less likely to suffer a virus attack. Therefore, changing your normal friendly, naive personality into that of a suspicious curmudgeon makes sense.

Develop e-mail paranoia

The most common delivery method for viruses is e-mail. That's because rogue programmers have figured out that if they can invade e-mail software, they can automatically send their destructive code to lots of additional victims — they use your address book and send the virus to every e-mail address they find. This practice is why many people end up with virus infections. The virus came from somebody they know (even though that person didn't know he or she was sending the virus).

Therefore, follow these precautions when reading e-mail:

✔ Don't open any files attached to an e-mail message from somebody you know unless you know in advance that those files are coming to you.

✔ Don't open any files that are attached to an e-mail message from somebody you don't know.

✔ Don't open any files attached to an e-mail message if the subject line is strange. In fact, don't even open the e-mail message if the subject line seems weird — some viruses are capable of launching themselves when the message is opened. Just delete the message without reading it.

Develop Internet download paranoia

Be careful about downloading files from the Internet. Here are specific precautions to take:

✔ If you're not sure of the source, avoid downloading the file.

✔ Make sure that your antivirus program is configured to check the files on the download Web site. If your antivirus software can't do that, and you're reasonably certain that the site is safe, take the precaution of having your antivirus software scan the folder you used to save the file before you install the software.

✔ If your kids are downloading multimedia files (music and video), do whatever you need to do to make them paranoid and suspicious. Kids download many of the viruses that attack family computers.

Virus hoaxes

The threat of viruses is real enough to those of us who are nervous about safe computing, but dealing with virus hoaxes makes it worse. People who fall for these stupid hoaxes often end up damaging their systems by following the advice they receive. (I've seen messages that tell me to look for a certain file and delete it immediately, and it's almost always a valid Windows system file.)

People fall for this stuff because they don't have enough technical knowledge to recognize that most of the information doesn't make sense, so I'll give you some helpful hints for identifying virus hoaxes.

Never take technical advice from a chain letter

Anyone who forwards a chain letter without checking the facts first is, de facto, not computer literate. So why would you take advice from this person?

Some virus hoax messages aren't warnings; they're advisories on avoiding the spread of viruses. The most famous example is the "Add !0000 to your address book" chain letter that's been traveling the Internet for a long time. The e-mail message includes a tip for adding the recipient !0000 to your address book (newer versions of this hoax use the recipient AAAAA), explaining that when a virus tries to send itself out to everyone in your address book, the e-mail software will fail on the bogus address, stopping any mass e-mail attempt. The hoax message includes the information that this recipient always appears first in your address book because of the way computers alphabetize lists. It's true that computers alphabetize starting with numbers and move on to letters, but that's the only fact in the message.

Check with antivirus experts

Lots of virus hoax messages are circulating all the time. If you get one, do everyone in your address book a favor — don't click the Forward button in your e-mail software window. Check the facts first by going to your antivirus software vendor's Web site, which has information on virus hoaxes.

How to identify a virus hoax

Virus hoax messages have some things in common, so in this section, I present some guidelines for identifying them.

Look for a plot that reminds you of a soap opera. It's a long, drawn-out story about somebody's cousin who has a brother-in-law who works for a widget manufacturer, which had a customer who was a cosmetic surgeon, who went to some Internet site, and . . . it just goes on and on.

At least one person in the cast of characters of the soap opera is some sort of computer expert; he works at Microsoft or IBM or is the IT director of a major technical company. This is the old "credibility" trick; don't fall for it.

Often, a sentence appears that says "I personally got this virus and it wiped out my machine." You're supposed to assume that "I" is the person who sent you this message (whom you probably know, or else why would your e-mail address be in the sender's address book?). Because this message has probably been traveling around the Internet for a long time, using the Forward buttons of a thousand e-mail software installations, the "I" probably refers to somebody who has either been informed of the facts by one of his recipients and now regrets clicking that Forward button or has died of old age.

The chain letter instructions include an urgent plea to distribute this information immediately to the whole world. This part of the message is usually in capital letters to promote a sense of urgency: SEND THIS MESSAGE TO EVERYBODY IN YOUR ADDRESS BOOK. Or, SEND THIS TO EVERYBODY YOU KNOW, HAVE EVER MET, OR MIGHT MEET IN THE FUTURE.

Firewalls: Defense for Internet Attacks

Some of the people who use the Internet are annoying, or even dangerous, jerks. They're like the kids who destroy property just for the fun of it, or break into homes and steal personal items. Mostly, these jerks are kids — at least emotionally. They're the kind of kids we called "punks" in my salad days (when the word "punk" was the worst insult you could apply to someone). Today, some people call these punks *hackers,* but the real root of *hacker* isn't negative — it used to refer to people who hacked away at programming code, out of curiosity. Frequently, these people improved the code. However, I'll use the current jargon and refer to this danger as *Internet hacking.*

Fortunately, you can protect your network from Internet hackers by running a firewall. A *firewall* is a program that protects computers from users on other networks (remember, the Internet is another network). In fact, a firewall can protect computers from other computers, but if you have a network, you don't want to isolate your computer from the other computers on your network.

Windows XP and Vista both have built-in firewalls, and they automatically reconfigure their settings to accommodate communication among the computers on your network.

Why do you need a firewall?

While you're on the Internet, you're vulnerable to any malicious act that a hacker wants to perpetrate. This is especially true if you're using an always-on connection to the Internet via a cable modem or a DSL device.

When you're on the Internet, your computer has an Internet Protocol (IP) address. That address is needed for communication between you and other computers on the Internet, and data flows in both directions. A malicious hacker can access your computer through that IP address.

Internet hackers select an IP address and then try to connect to that IP address. Most of the time, they have no particular victim in mind. They use software that selects an IP address at random, and then their software tries to access the computer that's linked to that address.

If the access attempt fails, the software picks another IP address. If the attempt succeeds, the intruders have access to your computer and its contents. You won't know that anything is going on, even if you're working at the computer, because everything happens in the background, and the attack doesn't interfere with anything you're doing. Here are some of the common actions performed by intruders:

- ✔ Sending executable files that contain viruses to your computer
- ✔ Renaming or deleting the files that run at startup and are needed to run software
- ✔ Copying your documents to their own systems, where they hope to find personal and sensitive information that they can use
- ✔ Sending enormous files or a massive number of small files, just for the "fun" of filling your hard drive

That's not a complete list, but it should be enough to scare you (which is my intention). Defend yourself by blocking your computer with a firewall.

What a firewall does

A firewall works by watching everything that happens on your computer that has anything to do with activity outside your computer. Unless you say that it's okay, no action can occur between your computer and another computer. That other computer could be on the Internet or on your network.

The firewall blocks communication in both directions — to and from the Internet. The software you use to access the Internet, such as your browser and e-mail program, must be given permission to do its job.

Any computer that tries to access your computer is either stopped dead in its tracks or is stopped temporarily until you tell the firewall to let the computer gain access (depending on the way you configure the firewall's behavior).

When an intruder attempts to reach your IP address, it's really your communication ports that are being examined. Computers send and receive data via ports. You already know about ports because you've connected a printer to a parallel port, attached a modem to a serial port, or attached some device to a Universal Serial Bus (USB) port. Besides these ports, which you can see, your computer contains thousands of *virtual ports.* You can't see a virtual port because it's a software service rather than a physical connector. However, just like a physical port, a virtual port accepts and sends data.

Almost every type of computer communication is programmed to use a specific port. Ports are numbered from 0 to 65536, and the ports between 0 and 1024 are reserved by certain services. For instance, http (the protocol you use when you're visiting a Web page) uses port 80. Ports work by "listening" for data, and when data arrives, the ports automatically open to accept it if the data announces that it's the right data type for the port.

Internet hackers use ports to move data between their computers and your computer. They have access to software that lets them test whether a port on a remote computer is *listening*, which means it's open to an exchange of data and therefore vulnerable to attack. (If it weren't willing to accept data, it wouldn't be listening.)

Some of the software tests only certain ports by pretending to be sending data of a type supported by that port. This technique is called *port scanning,* and it's the most popular method of testing computer vulnerability. The hacking software uses that information to attack, masquerading the data to resemble the appropriate type of data for the listening port.

Firewalls examine the ports to see whether the type of data is appropriate for the port that's being used. This process is called *stateful inspection,* and it involves checking the data that is passing through the port. Stateful inspection can catch data that identified itself as being appropriate for the port by recognizing that the actual data stream contains a false data type — the data doesn't match the type that it pretends to be.

Windows XP firewall

The most important piece of information about the Windows XP firewall is that if you didn't install Service Pack 2 (SP2), you can't use the firewall with your network. Before SP2, the firewall was incapable of distinguishing between local network data traffic and Internet traffic. The firewall blocked everything, so no data could come into your computer from any source, including the other computers on your network.

To see whether your Windows XP computer is running SP2, right-click My Computer and choose Properties. If the text in the System section of the General Tab doesn't display "Service Pack 2" (or a service pack number greater than 2), you need to update Windows.

If you haven't updated your Windows XP computer to SP2, travel to www. microsoft.com and search for the download of SP2. Do that now and then come back to this page to continue learning about firewalls.

Are you back? Okay, now that you've installed SP2, you need to know that the second most important piece of information about the Windows XP firewall is that it doesn't monitor outgoing traffic, it only monitors incoming traffic.

The one-way traffic pattern of the Windows XP firewall may or may not cause you concern. It bothers me, so I turned off the firewall and downloaded a third-party firewall that performs bi-directional inspections. This means that when a program wants to send data from my computer to another computer on the Internet, I have to approve it (for the software I installed, I can tell the firewall "always let this program send data" so I don't have to keep clicking OK). If some intruder is trying to grab copies of files from my hard drive, the software firewall I installed stops him; Windows XP firewall doesn't. This event doesn't occur terribly often, and installing antivirus and other malware prevention programs stops most of these actions, but I'm paranoid about my computer's security.

If you install a third-party software firewall, turn the Windows XP firewall off — don't run multiple firewalls.

When you set up your computer as a member of a network, the Windows XP firewall should automatically adjust its settings to open your computer for data coming from the other computers on your network.

To check the settings of the Windows XP firewall, choose Start➪Control Panel➪Network and Internet Connections. Then click Windows Firewall to open the Properties dialog box for the firewall, which displays the General tab, as shown in Figure 12-3.

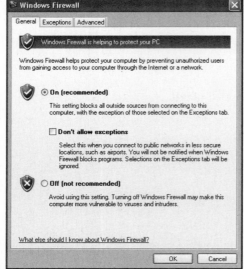

Figure 12-3:
View and edit your firewall settings in the Windows Firewall Properties dialog box.

By default, the firewall is enabled (on) and permits exceptions. These are the normal settings for a computer running in a network environment because the exceptions (covered next) permit the exchange of data between this computer and the other computers on the network.

Firewall Exceptions tab

The Exceptions tab is where you open data streams that would otherwise be blocked by the firewall. You can create exceptions for programs and for ports. To save you the trouble (and the attendant research) of determining which programs and ports need to be opened for common communications, Windows lists some pre-defined exceptions that you can enable (see Figure 12-4).

You can configure exceptions based on program names or on ports. If you select program names, the firewall almost always knows which ports to open, so that's the easiest approach. If the firewall doesn't open any ports for a program you specify, it can mean that the program uses only the ports that are already open, or that the firewall doesn't know which ports the software uses. If in doubt, contact technical support at the software company.

To create an exception for a program, click Add Program. The Add a Program dialog box appears with a list of programs (mostly games you can play over the network and the Internet). If the program you want to add to the exception list isn't there, click Browse to locate the program on your hard drive.

Figure 12-4:
Use the
Exceptions
tab to open
the firewall
for specific
programs
and ports.

To open a port manually, click Add Port. In the Add a Port dialog box, specify whether the port is a TCP or UDP port. Then, enter the name of the service or program that will use this port, as well as the port number. To get the information you need, you have to check the technical specifications of the service or program that needs the port.

You can edit any exception by selecting its listing and clicking Edit. The Edit a Service dialog box opens, displaying the ports used by the selected exception. Editing involves changing the *scope* of a port (or multiple ports), which means defining the network, or part of a network, from which the excepted data stream can originate. To change the scope, select the applicable port and click Change Scope. In the Change Scope dialog box (see Figure 12-5), select one of the available options:

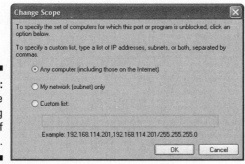

Figure 12-5:
Change the
originating
source of
data traffic.

✔ **Any computer (including those on the Internet):** This option, which is selected by default, means you want to allow data into your computer through this port from any computer, anywhere in the world. Needless to say, this is rather dangerous and you must disable the selection. The only reason to choose this level of traffic is to maintain a Web site (which you wouldn't be doing from a computer running Windows XP). Any computer with a firewall that's been opened this wide should be configured for all sorts of security.

✔ **My network (subnet) only:** If the computer is part of a network, this is the appropriate setting, and it means that traffic is allowed only from IP addresses that match the local network segment (subnet). For example, if the network connection has an IP address of 192.168.0.03 and a subnet mask of 255.255.0.0, excepted traffic is allowed only from IP addresses in the range 192.168.0.1 to 192.168.255.254. If you're sharing an Internet connection, that range matches the range of IP addresses assigned to computers on the network.

✔ **Custom list:** Use this option to specify allowed traffic from one or more IP addresses, separated by commas, or IP address ranges, separated by commas. For example, if the computers on your network have fixed IP addresses, you can determine which computers can or cannot send data to this computer.

Fixed IP addresses are usually found in networks with business-class (expensive) DSL services. Your network computers probably don't have fixed IP addresses; instead, the network connection is configured to obtain an IP address automatically.

Don't use this option if your network computers obtain IP addresses automatically, even if you know the current IP address of a computer you want to include or exclude. That current IP address changes often because it's leased from the DHCP service for a finite period of time (by default, 24 hours). When the lease is renewed, the IP address often changes.

Firewall Advanced tab

The Advanced tab (see Figure 12-6) contains the following sections:

✔ Network Connection Settings

✔ Security Logging

✔ ICMP

✔ Default Settings

Except for Default Settings, each section has a Settings button, which opens additional configuration dialog boxes. The Default Settings section has a button labeled Restore Defaults, which is your life saver if you've messed around with the firewall's configuration and ended up with network communication problems.

The Network Connection Settings dialog box offers advanced options for permitting traffic from the Internet. Because it's unlikely you're running a Web server on your Windows XP computer, you shouldn't change the settings. If you have some reason to make changes, you need a great deal of knowledge about port data types.

The Security Logging feature lets you create a log of the data stream coming into this computer. You can track successful or unsuccessful connections and save the data in a log file. It's not common to need this information, so don't enable logging unless you've been having a network communications problem and a support technician asks you to keep a log.

The ICMP (which stands for Internet Control Message Protocol) settings let you determine the circumstances under which a remote computer receives a message from this computer after the remote computer attempts to communicate. These settings are usually changed to enhance troubleshooting efforts and shouldn't be accessed unless you're working with a support technician.

Troubleshooting the Windows XP firewall

You may find that you can't configure the Windows XP SP2 firewall to match your needs, or the firewall may interrupt network communications. In this section, I give you some troubleshooting tips for the problems commonly encountered in home networks.

Configuration options aren't available

If the options on the General, Exceptions, and Advanced tabs aren't available (they're grayed out), it means you are not logged on to the computer with a user account that has administrative permissions. A user with administrative permissions must log on to the computer to change the firewall options or to change your user account to an administrative account. (See Chapter 8 for more information about setting up user accounts.)

Firewall service may not be running

If you're having trouble communicating with the other computers on the network, or the other computers are having problems accessing this computer, check the configuration options of the firewall. If File and Printer Sharing is enabled, and you can't find any reason for the firewall's apparent blocking of communications, make sure the firewall service is running properly on the computer. Use the following steps to check the service:

1. **Choose Start⇨Control Panel⇨Performance and Maintenance⇨Administrative Tools. Then, double-click Services.**

   The Services console appears (see Figure 12-7).

Figure 12-7:
The Windows XP firewall is actually an operating system service, and it can be checked in the Services console.

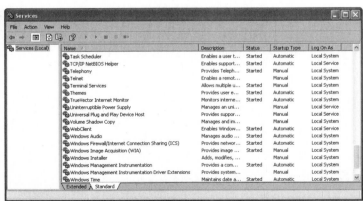

2. **In the right pane, scroll through the list to find the listing for the Windows Firewall (WF)/Internet Connection Sharing (ICS) service.**

3. **Double-click the listing to open its Properties dialog box (see Figure 12-8).**

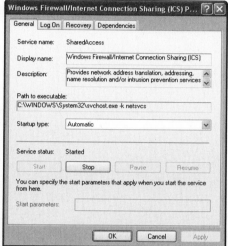

Figure 12-8:
Make sure
the firewall
service
is running
and is
configured
properly.

The Startup Type must be set to Automatic. If it's not, select Automatic from the Startup Type drop-down list.

The Service Status must be Started. If it's not, click Start. After a few seconds, if the service doesn't start, you have a more serious problem. Write down the text of any error messages that appear and call an expert to help you figure out what's wrong with your Windows setup.

Avoid firewall clashes

If you're running a software firewall or you have a firewall-enabled router (covered later in this chapter), turn the Windows XP firewall off. Running multiple firewalls doesn't double your protection; instead, the firewalls usually conflict with each other, which could make your computer vulnerable.

Windows Vista firewall

The Windows Vista firewall is bi-directional, powerful, and can be configured and tweaked in many ways. To view or change the firewall settings, choose Start➪Control Panel➪System and Maintenance➪ Administrative Tools to open the Administrative Tools folder. Double-click Windows Firewall with Advanced Security to display the window shown in Figure 12-9.

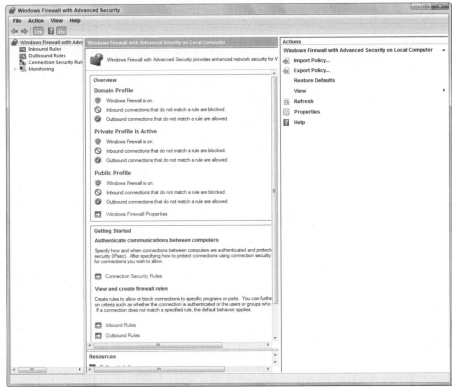

Figure 12-9:
You can
modify the
behavior
of the
Windows
Vista
firewall.

The options are seemingly endless and are very complicated because you're dealing with a more powerful and more flexible firewall. In addition, just like Windows Vista, the firewall is built from the ground up to enforce security rules. As a result, reconfiguring some of the complicated firewall settings can be dangerous unless you have a lot of information about the consequences of your actions.

However, you can view and edit some of the standard properties by clicking the Properties link in the right pane to open the Properties dialog box. The dialog box (shown in Figure 12-10) displays a tab for each of the three available profiles:

✓ **The Domain Profile** is applied when the computer is running on a Windows domain. (See Chapter 1 for a discussion of client/server domains that are usually found in large corporate networks.)

✓ **The Private Profile** is applied when the computer's domain connection isn't in use, such as when the computer is attached to a peer-to-peer network. (Almost all home networks are peer-to-peer networks.)

✔ **The Public Profile** is applied when the computer is connected to a public network, such as hot spots in airports and coffee shops.

Figure 12-10: View and modify settings for the profiles you use for this computer.

There's also a tab for IPsec settings, which you shouldn't use unless you understand IPsec (Internet Protocol Security), which is a complicated subject.

Each profile tab has a set of options that differ depending on the level of security required for the profile. For example, the security should be much tighter when you're on a public network than when you're working on your home network. The following settings appear in each tab:

✔ **State:** Determines whether the firewall is enabled, and also determines the action the firewall takes for inbound and outbound data streams. By default, inbound connections are blocked, and outbound connections are allowed in all three profiles.

✔ **Settings:** Specifies the particulars of all settings for the profile. Click the Customize button to display the current settings (see Figure 12-11).

The following settings are displayed:

• *Display notifications to the user when a program is blocked from receiving inbound communications.* Specify whether you want to receive a message when the firewall blocks an inbound connection for a program.

• *Allow unicast response to multicast or broadcast requests.* Enable or disable the ability of the computer to receive unicast responses to its outgoing requests. (Unicast responses are computer-to-computer messages, usually invoked to report errors.)

Figure 12-11:
Adapt
firewall
behavior to
match the
way you
want to
work.

- *Rule merging.* This section of the dialog box refers to rules that are applied by Group Policy, which is a complicated subject and beyond the scope of this book. It's unlikely you need to concern yourself with these functions to keep your computer safe and secure.

✓ **Logging:** Specifies whether you want to track events in a log file. Click the Customize button to view and modify the options, as shown in Figure 12-12. Usually, it's not necessary to log firewall activity unless a support technician asks you to enable the log in order to get information for troubleshooting.

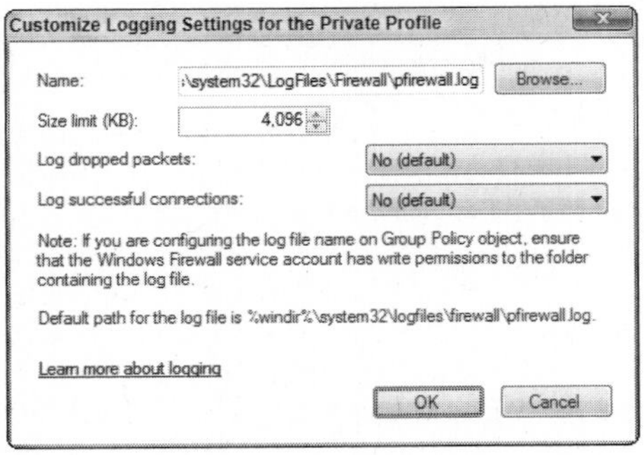

Figure 12-12:
Set logging
options for
creating an
audit trail
of the
firewall's
activity.

Hardware firewalls in routers

If you're sharing an Internet connection, and you're using a cable or DSL modem, the easiest, most efficient, and most powerful way to share the connection is to install a router. In fact, in Chapter 6, I go over everything you need to know to share an Internet connection with a router.

You can buy routers that have built-in firewalls. The firewall-enabled router sits between your modem and the rest of your network, separating the Internet and your network into two independent, unconnected networks (or into two armed camps, which is how I see it when I'm setting up a firewall). The only device that's seen from the Internet is the router, which has a firewall. All the computers on the network are invisible to the Internet.

Several router manufacturers offer routers with firewall protection, and the equipment is available with a wide variety of options. Here are some of the manufacturers who offer hardware firewall devices:

- Linksys (www.linksys.com)
- D-Link (www.dlink.com)
- Belkin (www.belkin.com)
- NetGear (www.netgear.com)

If you've installed a software firewall, or you're using the Vista firewall, disable the router's firewall. This is one case where "the more the merrier" doesn't work. Both software firewalls and the Vista firewall monitor traffic in both directions, something a router firewall and the Windows XP firewall can't do.

Troubleshooting router firewalls

Believe it or not, if your router firewall isn't configured correctly, the symptoms usually appear when you try to access other computers on the network — not when you try to get to the Internet. The firewall in the router is usually automatically set up to let every computer on the network access the Internet because a hardware firewall looks only at incoming data streams, not outgoing communications (which is why I prefer software firewalls or Windows Vista, which do both). If your firewall is blocking incoming ports, your router blocks those ports for all computers on the network. To communicate within your network, you need to make sure the firewall knows it's okay to let data from within the network travel through those ports.

Each manufacturer has a unique configuration tool, along with documentation and instructions for configuring your network. To enter the configuration tool, you must open your browser and enter the router's IP address in the address bar. Here are the IP addresses of the popular routers:

- **Belkin:** 192.168.2.1
- **D-Link:** 192.168.0.1
- **Linksys:** 192.168.1.1
- **Netgear:** 192.168.0.1

All router configuration tools are configured to make you enter a username, a password, or both. If you haven't changed the default username and password, use the entries provided in Table 12-1 to do so. Then, secure the router's configuration tool by creating your own login name and password.

Table 12-1	Login Names and Passwords for Popular Routers	
Manufacturer	*Login Name*	*Password*
Belkin	(Field does not exist)	(Do not fill in)
D-Link	admin (lower case)	(Do not fill in)
Linksys	(Do not fill in)	admin (lower case)
Netgear	admin (lower case)	password (lower case)

Read the instructions from the router's manufacturer and from your ISP to configure the router. You can set basic LAN configuration options or, if necessary, more exotic (and complicated) options.

Don't mess with advanced settings on your router unless you do so under the guidance of a trained professional.

Spyware

Spyware is software that installs itself (without your knowledge) on your computer. Once installed, the software collects information about you, and when you're online, it sends that information to the spyware program's owner. Most spyware fits into either of two categories:

- ✔ Surveillance spyware
- ✔ Advertising spyware

Surveillance spyware scans documents on your computer and can capture your keystrokes as you type. This could be a form you're filling out on a Web site (such as your login password or your credit card number) or the text you enter in a chat window. Government and detective agencies have been known to use this type of software, as have jealous spouses.

Advertising spyware is software that is installed when you're installing other software (usually software you download from the Internet) or that is installed in the background while you're visiting a Web site. It's common for advertising spyware to be included (without telling you) when you install software that's advertised as "free, if you don't mind seeing advertisements when you use it." One of the most pervasive distributors of spyware is software you download to take advantage of peer-to-peer file exchanges (for music and video). Advertising spyware logs information about your computer, and also about you. The information includes passwords, your Web browsing habits, your online buying habits, and so on.

Both types of spyware can also install viruses and worms on your computer. Many of them change your browser settings (such as your home page), and your efforts to correct the changes are temporary — the spyware changes them again.

One of the annoying features of spyware is its connection to pop-up ads. Using the information it collects about you, the spyware initiates pop-up ads whenever you connect to a Web site. The spyware software producer receives income whenever you respond to one of these pop-up ads, so the theory is "the more the better." After a while, using the Internet becomes almost impossible because of the barrage of pop-ups. Regardless of your Internet Explorer controls for your children, the pop-ups often contain pornography.

The only way to remove spyware from your computer is to use software designed for that purpose. The following two programs are well regarded by computer professionals (and I use both of them because I tend to operate in "overkill mode" when it comes to security and privacy):

- ✔ **Ad-Aware from Lavasoft:** www.lavasoft.com
- ✔ **Spybot Search & Destroy:** www.safer-networking.org

Windows Security Center

Windows XP and Windows Vista both provide a Security Center you can use to set up, configure, and view security settings. By default, Windows puts a Security Center icon in the notification area of the taskbar — double-click the icon to open the Security Center window. (You can also open the Security Center window by going to Control Panel and selecting Security Center.)

Both versions of the Windows Security Center display the status of the three important security issues, as shown in Figure 12-13, which is the Windows XP Security Center window:

- ✔ Firewall
- ✔ Automatic Update of Windows
- ✔ Virus Protection

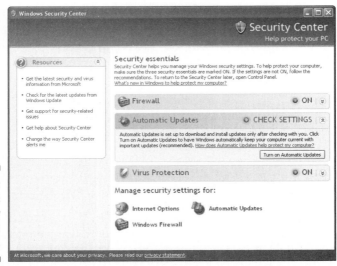

Figure 12-13:
Windows XP Security Center main window.

The Windows Vista Security Center enlarges the scope of its checkup by including additional security concerns, as shown in Figure 12-14.

Both Windows XP and Windows Vista recognize most of the third-party firewall, antivirus, and privacy applications and automatically check the status of the programs found on your computer.

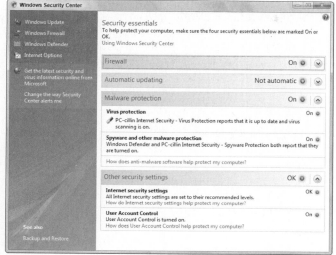

Figure 12-14:
Windows
Vista
Security
Center main
window.

When any part of the security toolbox is missing from your computer, Windows issues a security alert. Sometimes the alert is specious because it means that Windows didn't recognize your malware application.

For example, Windows cannot detect a hardware-based firewall (a router) and will issue a security alert that no firewall is running. Click the Recommendations button and select the option that you have a working application and you will manage it yourself.

Windows Defender

Windows Vista includes Windows Defender, which monitors your computer for spyware. You can configure Windows Defender to work in real time (constantly monitoring your computer) and to scan your computer periodically.

Like antivirus software, Windows Defender needs to be maintained so that up-to-date information about new spyware is available. These update files, called *definitions,* can be downloaded automatically as part of your Windows Update service, or you can download them manually.

Open the Windows Defender folder from Control Panel by clicking Security and then selecting Windows Defender. Click the Tools icon to configure the services and learn more about this software (see Figure 12-15).

Use the links in the Windows Defender window to download updates.

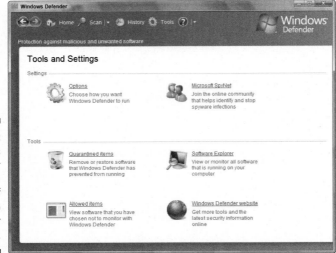

Figure 12-15:
Windows
Defender
offers a
robust set of
tools to
secure your
privacy.

Chapter 13

Disaster Planning and Recovery

● ●

In This Chapter

▶ Avoiding electrical catastrophes

▶ Doing preventive maintenance on your hardware

▶ Devising a backup plan

▶ Restoring after a disaster

● ●

Sometimes, things go wrong with the computer itself — the physical parts of a computer. You can avoid many problems with a little preventive maintenance.

The important consideration, now that you're a network administrator, is that you're protecting your network in addition to protecting each individual computer.

Network computers are connected — they talk to each other, and they interact with each other. Each computer on the network has a physical relationship with the other computers on the network. The computers can pass problems around the network neighborhood in the same way that they can pass files around.

In this chapter, I tell you how to care for your hardware to avoid an epidemic of sick computers. I also tell you how to prepare for the day that your preventive measures fail — because in the end, all hard drives die.

Avoiding Zapped Computers

You know that electricity is dangerous, so you probably avoid sticking your fingers into live light-bulb sockets and electrical outlets. Your computers may not have fingers, but they're sensitive to electricity, too, and it's up to you to protect them from a variety of electrical dangers.

Protecting against electrical surges

An *electrical surge* is a sudden spate of very high voltage that travels from the electric lines to your house and ultimately to your computer. Computers are particularly sensitive to surges, and a real surge can fry your computer. The chips burn up, and your computer becomes a doorstop.

Most of the time, surges occur as a result of a lightning strike, but the danger of a surge also exists if there's a brief blackout followed by a return of electricity. During the return of power, the voltage can spike. (See the section "Protecting against lightning hits," later in this chapter.)

You can safeguard against spikes by plugging every computer on your network into a *surge protector*. The surge protectors that are commonly used look like electrical power strips, usually with four or five outlets. Read the specifications before you buy a surge protector to make sure that it's rated for real surge protection. (Voltage can rise by 10 volts or hundreds of volts, so make sure the surge protector you buy can handle these extreme surges.)

Surge protectors work by committing suicide to protect your computer. They absorb the surge so it doesn't travel to your equipment. (Some surge protectors have reset buttons that bring the strip back to life.)

If a power surge hits any piece of equipment that is attached to your computer by cable, the surge can travel to your computer. Therefore, plugging the computer into the surge protector isn't quite enough; you also have to use the surge protector to power the accessories that are connected to your computer.

Because any surge received by a single computer can travel over the network cable to the other computers on your network, make sure that all the following equipment for each of your computers is plugged into surge protectors:

- ✔ Monitors
- ✔ External modems
- ✔ External removable drives
- ✔ Speakers

Notice that I didn't list printers. Never plug a printer into the same surge protector that your computer is plugged into. (In fact, if you have a laser printer, you should *never* plug it into the same circuit as your computer.) See the section "Protecting Printers," later in this chapter, for more information.

Protecting against telephone line surges

I've seen several large networks destroyed during lightning storms, and in each case, the surge came through the telephone lines, not the electrical lines. This is what happens:

1. Lightning hits the telephone line.
2. The surge comes through the telephone jack in the wall.
3. It travels along the telephone cable from the wall to the modem.
4. It travels from the modem to the computer's motherboard.
5. It travels from the motherboard to the rest of the computer parts, including the network interface card (NIC).
6. The NIC sends the surge out to the network cable.
7. The cable sends the surge back to every NIC on the network.
8. Each NIC sends the surge to its computer's motherboard.

   Every computer on the network is fried!

In most communities, the power company installs lightning arresters on their transformers, which help diffuse the effects of a direct lightning hit on the electric lines. However, I know of no telephone company that protects its phone lines against lightning. When a lightning storm is close, unplug your modem telephone cable at the wall jack and then unplug the computers.

If your telephone company uses fiber optic lines, you don't have to worry about lightning hits that affect the above-ground lines; fiber optic lines don't conduct electricity.

Protecting against lightning hits

If lightning hits your power lines or your house, your surge protector may not be able to protect your equipment against the resulting surge. Thousands or tens of thousands of volts — sometimes more — result from a lightning strike. A surge protector can provide only so much protection, and a direct lightning hit exceeds that limit.

The only protection against lightning strikes is to unplug your computers and all your computer equipment. Stop working. Then walk around the house and unplug other equipment with chips that could fry during a lightning storm (like your microwave oven, VCR, and so on).

Protecting against power loss

When you're running Windows, you *can't* just turn off your computer when you don't want to use it anymore. You must initiate a shutdown procedure by using the Shut Down command on the Start menu. Otherwise, you may have a problem restarting your computer, or you may run into mysterious problems when you try to use software and Windows features after a power failure.

The electric company doesn't know and doesn't care about the need for an orderly shutdown, and if the folks there did know or care, they couldn't do much to warn you about a power failure, giving you time to use the Shut Down command.

You can keep your computers running long enough to complete an orderly shutdown of all your software and the operating system if you have an *uninterruptible power supply (UPS)*. A UPS is a mega-battery that you plug into the wall, and you then use the outlets in the UPS to connect your computer and monitor. If your power fails, your computer draws power from the battery, giving you enough time to shut down everything.

UPS units come in a variety of power configurations (measured in watts). Some have line conditioning to regulate voltage (see the next section "Understanding and fixing low-voltage problems") in addition to the battery feature. Some have software that performs the orderly shutdown for you. (The UPS unit connects to your computer through a serial port to communicate.) This is a nice feature if your power dies while you're away from the computer. The cost ranges from about $75 to several hundred dollars, depending on the wattage and the features you want. The best-known (and, in my opinion, most reliable) UPS units are made by APC. They're available anywhere computer peripherals are sold.

Understanding and fixing low-voltage problems

Sometimes, when everyone in town is using electrical gadgets at the same time, an area's all-around voltage drops. This is called a *brownout*. Computers — especially their hard drives and motherboards — are extremely sensitive to brownouts.

Well before you see the lights flicker, your hard drive can react to a brownout. Most of the time, that reaction destroys the part of the drive that's being accessed, and the result is that your drive develops bad spots — parts of the drive that can't be written to or read from. You can mark the bad spots to prevent the operating system from using those spots to hold data, but if the spots that go bad already have data on them, that data goes bad, too. (See Chapter 14 for a discussion of the Windows tools that can help you find and mark bad spots on your hard drive.)

You can prevent most of the problems associated with bad spots caused by brownouts, and you can overcome those problems that you can't prevent, by purchasing a _voltage regulator_. This clever device constantly measures the voltage coming out of the wall and brings it up to an acceptable minimum; the device sells for about $50 to $100 (depending on how many devices you want to plug into it). Several companies make voltage regulators (try TrippLite, `www.tripplite.com`), and some UPS units have built-in voltage regulation.

If you purchase a voltage regulator in addition to a UPS unit, plug the voltage regulator into the wall and plug the UPS unit into the voltage regulator. If you're using a surge protector, the surge protector is always plugged into the wall, with any other devices plug into the surge protector. The computer is always plugged into the "furthest from the wall" device, to let the protection devices do their thing before power reaches the computer.

Here are some of the causes of low voltage, along with possible fixes:

- **Too many appliances are plugged into the same circuit as your computer.** This is something you can fix. Move stuff around, buy some very long heavy-duty extension cords to get to an outlet on another circuit, or call an electrician and get more outlets connected to empty breakers.

- **An appliance that's a voltage pig (for example, air conditioning and electric heating systems) kicks on, disrupting voltage throughout the house.** Plug your computer into a voltage regulator.

- **Your laser printer (or powerful inkjet color printer) is plugged into the same circuit as your computer.** See the section "Protecting Printers," later in this chapter. You shouldn't plug these printers into the same circuit as your computer. If you have no choice, plug the computer into a voltage regulator. Do not plug the printer into the voltage regulator.

- **The electric company is sending low voltage into your home.** Sometimes, the electric company just can't keep up with demand, and it delivers lower-than-normal voltage to your home. When the voltage really drops, the electric company calls it a brownout. This frequently occurs during very hot weather, when air conditioners in your area are running constantly and working hard. The problem also occurs around 9:00 in the morning on weekdays, as businesses all over town are turning on copy machines and laser printers, and elevators are constantly going up and down.

The solution? Plug your computer into a voltage regulator.

Preventing static electricity damage

Static electricity is responsible for more damaged computers than most people realize. One day, when some hardware component mysteriously dies, you may not realize that you zapped it yourself.

Static electricity charges that zap your computer come from you. You pick up static electricity, carry it with you, and pass it along when you touch any part of the computer. Usually, the keyboard receives your first touch, and even though it's connected to your computer, it doesn't always pass the electricity along to the computer.

However, if you touch the monitor or the computer box, you can pass a serious or fatal amount of electricity to the motherboard (fatal to the computer, not to you) or to any component in your computer (including chips).

You must discharge the electricity from your body before you touch the computer. Touch anything metal (except an electric appliance such as a computer or a lamp). A filing cabinet is good if one is handy. If nothing metal is within reach, attach a metal bar to the desk or table that your computer sits on.

Computers and carpeting create the ideal atmosphere for zapping. New carpeting is really dangerous, followed by carpeting with a thick pile. If you can't pull up the carpeting, go to an office supply store and buy one of those big plastic mats that goes under the desk and your chair. If you don't, each time you move your feet, you'll collect static electricity and eventually pass it to the computer.

Caring for Network Hardware

If you receive an error message while trying to move files between computers or when you open the My Network Places or Network window, it's time to check your network hardware.

The network hardware — the connectors, cable, and NICs — sometimes requires some maintenance. In the following sections, I list the hardware components in the order in which they usually cause problems.

Checking connectors

Cable connectors are the weakest link in the network hardware chain. Because of this, you should check the connectors first when your computers can't communicate.

Ethernet networks

If you wired your network with CAT-5/5e (twisted-pair) cable, you should check the following:

- See if the connectors are properly inserted in the NICs.
- Make sure that the connectors are properly inserted in the concentrator (hub, switch, or router).
- Be sure that the concentrator is plugged in. (A concentrator usually doesn't have an on/off switch — if it's plugged in, it should be working.)

Phoneline networks

Here's what to check if you're using your household telephone line for your network:

- Make sure that the connectors are firmly seated in both the NICs and the wall jack.
- If you're using a splitter (also called a *modular duplex jack*) to plug in both a telephone and the network cable, make sure that the splitter is firmly positioned in the jack.

  Splitters weigh more than the fraction of an ounce that the connector on the end of a phone cord weighs, and sometimes this extra weight pulls the splitter out of the jack just a bit. Frequently, you don't notice this problem when you look at the connection, but if you push on the connector, you notice that it isn't all the way in the phone jack.

  The splitter may have come out of the jack for the following reasons, too:

  - The cable between the splitter and whatever the other end of the cable plugs into (either the telephone jack or the NIC) is taut.
  - The telephone has moved because it was either placed somewhere else or a person who used the telephone walked around while chatting.

Powerline networks

Check the following things if you're using your household electric lines for your network:

- ✔ Check the connector at the computer end to make sure that it's firmly inserted in the port.
- ✔ Check the connector in the wall plug to make sure that it's firmly inserted.
- ✔ Make sure that the connector at the line end is plugged into the wall and not into a surge protector (unless you purchased a special surge protector designed for this purpose).

Wireless networks

Here's what to check if you're running a wireless network:

- ✔ Make sure that all the antennas are unblocked — check to make sure that a computer or access point hasn't been pushed under a metal desk or close to a metal object, such as a file cabinet.
- ✔ If you recently moved a computer, move it back — you may have exceeded the antenna's power.
- ✔ Be sure that you haven't introduced interference into your system. Did you put a cordless radio frequency (RF) device near a computer (such as a cordless phone)?

Checking cables

Make sure that the cables aren't pinched or bent to the point that they can't handle data. Have you ever sharply bent a water hose? The water stops flowing. The same thing can happen to the data flowing through cable.

If you have excess cable, don't twist it into a knot to avoid having it spill on the floor. Gently roll the cable into a circle and use a twist tie to keep it together. (Don't tie it tightly.)

I pounded long nails into the backs of the tables that hold my computers, and I hang coils of excess cable on those nails to keep the cable off the floor.

Checking NICs

It's unusual for a NIC to give up, roll over, and die (unless you had a power surge or did something dumb like stick a bobby pin in the connector). However, sometimes NICs — like all hardware — just stop working. If your NIC has a light on the back panel near the connector, it should glow green. If no light is glowing and you've checked the connectors and the cable, the only way to check the NIC is to replace it. If the new NIC works, the old NIC was bad. If the new NIC doesn't work, recheck your connectors and cable. Take the new NIC back to the store and get a credit (or, now that you have a spare NIC, get another computer and enlarge your network).

If your NIC has two little light bulbs and the red one is glowing, your NIC is working but isn't receiving or sending data. You can be fairly sure that you have a connector or cable problem. Check the documentation that came with your NIC to see the color schemes for the lights — your bulbs may be different colors.

Monitoring Monitors

Monitors require some special attention, and too many people maul and mishandle them. By no coincidence, those are the same people who have to buy new monitors more frequently than necessary.

A monitor's screen attracts and collects dust — I believe it actually sucks it out of the air. You can't avoid monitor dust, but you can remove it by wiping the screen with a soft, dry cloth. It's best to turn off the monitor before cleaning it. (Static electricity, which is responsible for attracting the dust, can build up to explosive levels when you rub the screen.)

If you're a person who points to the screen when you show somebody a beautiful sentence you just composed or a mind-blowing graphic you just created, you probably have fingerprints on your monitor. Fingerprints are oily and don't always disappear with a dry cloth. Office supply stores sell pre-moistened towelettes for cleaning monitors. You just pull one out and wipe the screen. (Remember to close the container's lid to keep the remaining towelettes moist.) They're like the towelettes that you use on infants when you change diapers, although I assume that the moistening agent is different and isn't so gentle on a baby's bottom.

If you want to use the bottle of window cleaner that you keep around the house, spray it on a cloth, not on the monitor; the monitor isn't sealed properly to avoid leaks. Then wipe the moistened cloth across the screen.

You can also use a cloth that's moistened with window cleaner on the keyboard and mouse (the other collection points for fingerprints and dust).

Protecting Printers

You should regularly perform a few maintenance chores to make sure that your printed documents look terrific and that your printers perform without errors:

- ✔ Don't overfill paper trays — doing so results in printer jams.

- ✔ If you have to clean up a printer jam, unplug the printer. Never yank on the jammed paper; pull it steadily and gently.

- ✔ Always clean a laser printer when you change toner cartridges, following the directions that came with the cartridge.

- ✔ Dust is the printer's biggest enemy. Keep printers covered when they aren't in use.

- ✔ Don't put label sheets back into the printer for a second pass. If you used only a couple of labels on the sheet, throw away the sheet. The chemicals on the sheet can damage the internal mechanisms of the printer.

- ✔ Use paper that's compatible with your printer. (Check the documentation that came with your printer.)

- ✔ When you use heavy paper stock, labels, transparencies, or envelopes in a laser printer, open the back door to let the paper go through the printer in a straight path. That way, the stock doesn't have to bend around the rollers.

- ✔ Use the features in the software that came with your color inkjet printer to check the alignment of the color cartridge. (No alignment maintenance is required for monochrome cartridges — you simply replace the cartridges when they run out of ink or dry up.)

Besides protecting your printer, you also need to protect your computer from your printer, especially if you use a laser printer or a powerful color inkjet printer. These printers use a lot of power, and if they're on the same circuit as your computer, you're probably causing minor brownouts for the computer, which can harm your hard drive and your data.

Learning to love canned air

Office supply stores sell cans of air. It's not just air you're buying; it's air that comes out of the can with enough pressure to push dust out of places that it shouldn't be in. The cans come with little straw-like tubes that you can attach to the sprayer so that you can get inside your removable drives, between the keys of your keyboard, and in the paper pathway in your printer.

Spray every opening, pore, and vent in your computer frequently. Built-up dust can interfere with the operation of your computer. CD-ROM drives and floppy drives that stop reading files usually have nothing wrong with them except they are dusty. (Don't tilt the can when you're spraying air — if the can isn't upright, you won't get the power blast that you need, and you may release some unwanted vapors.)

I use canned air everywhere. It's the handiest cleaning tool I have in my house. I spray all the openings on my CD player, television set, radio, and cable box. It works great on the ridges that hold my storm windows and screens, too.

Establishing a Plan for Backing Up Data

If you take the time to establish a plan of attack, you can fight back when disaster strikes. For computers, the best plan of attack is a well-designed plan for backing up your data. Your plan must provide protection for important files and must be so easy to implement that you won't be tempted to skip doing it.

You should back up document files on every computer in your home network every day. Now, here's what you're probably doing: you're nodding your head because you agree that backing up every day is the smart way to run computers. But you won't do it, and you'll be sorry later. People don't back up regularly until they have a disaster and realize how long it has been since they did a backup. That's an awful situation, and it provides the impetus for backing up religiously for a while, until the memory fades.

Deciding what to back up

It's not necessary to back up your entire hard drive because if the drive or the computer dies, you have to reinstall Windows and reinstall your software, so backing up all those Windows files and software files is a waste of time.

It's possible to back up the entire drive, along with the Registry (which means you don't have to reinstall software), but it takes a long time and requires very large media (a DVD or a large external drive). Windows backup applications provide a way to do this, and those applications are discussed later in this chapter.

The important files to back up are the files you created, such as documents, spreadsheets, financial software files, and so on. Because you created them, they're unique in the world and can't be replaced. If you lose them, you have to create them again from scratch (ask anyone who has faced this to learn how impossible it is).

Most of the files you create are saved in your documents folder (called My Documents in Windows XP and Documents in Windows Vista), which is extremely convenient for backup planning.

Some files you create are saved in folders that are created by the software you're using. This is true of financial programs such as Quicken. By default, many of these programs do not save your data in the documents folder (although you can often specify your documents folder as the data folder when you install the software).

All of these programs have a backup program, and you should learn to use it every time you use the software. If you've devised a nightly backup plan that backs up your documents folder, back up these data files to the documents folder.

Back up daily

Computers die. Sometimes only one part of a computer dies, but it's usually one of the important parts, like the hard drive. You have to approach the use of computers with the attitude that one of the machines on your network could go to la-la land, or that a hard drive could go to hard drive heaven, tomorrow.

If you don't plan for the sudden demise of your equipment, the computer fairies figure it out — they notice that you're complacent (they call it smug), and they break something. Computer fairies must be the culprits — nothing else explains the fact that most computers bite the dust the day after the user has finished writing the greatest novel in the history of literature or an important report for the boss that's sure to mean a promotion, and no backup files exist.

Making a backup doesn't prevent the death of a computer. And there's no proof that skipping a backup invites a serious problem — it just seems to happen that way. But just in case, backing up important files every day is imperative.

Configure computers for efficient backups

If something bad happens to one of your network computers, and you haven't backed up, you can reinstall the operating system and all your software, but you can kiss all your documents, including that promotion-earning PowerPoint presentation, goodbye.

The easier it is to back up data files, the more likely it is that you'll perform the task every day. Think about it: If you keep the vacuum cleaner in the hall closet, your house will stay cleaner than it would if you kept the vacuum cleaner in the attic. Convenience is an invaluable assistant.

Store all data files in your documents folder, and make sure that all the people who use the network do the same. If you like to organize files by type, either by application or by some other scheme (perhaps separating letters from spreadsheet documents), create subfolders for each type of file. When you copy your documents folder, you copy all of its subfolders.

Safeguard software CDs and disks

If a hard drive on the network dies, you have to install Windows on the replacement drive. Then, if you have a total backup of your entire drive, including the registry, you can restore that backup and put everything back the way it was before the demise of your equipment. You usually have to do a bit of tweaking, but essentially, the move to the new drive goes pretty smoothly.

If you don't have a total backup of your drive, all isn't lost. As long as you backed up the data files, you can reinstall the operating system, reinstall your software, and then restore the data files that you backed up.

This plan works only if your original software CD or disks are available. Storing the original disks for Windows and the software that you purchased in a safe place is important. I recommend that you use one of those fireproof boxes that you can buy in office-supply stores, or even store them a bank safe deposit box.

If you have software that you downloaded from the Internet, copy it to a CD and put the CD in a safe place.

One of the best safety schemes for storing software CDs off site is to trade CDs with a friend, neighbor, or relative. If you need the software CD, it's available more readily than it would be in a bank safe deposit box.

Safeguard backup media

Backup media should be removable CDs, DVDs, or USB flash drives. Don't back up on the same disk or flash drive that holds your last backup — if something goes wrong during the backup, not only do you not get a good backup this time, but you also destroy your previous backup.

If a fire, flood, or other catastrophe strikes, then after you clean up the mess, you can replace the computers. You can replace and reinstall software, but you have no way to restore all those important documents, accounting information, and other data that you created on your computer unless you have a backup that's stored out of harm's way.

Even if you back up to an on-site device, once a week you should transfer the backup data to a removable device such as a CD or DVD and leave it with a neighbor or at your office. You'll probably be able to find a neighbor with a computer and backup media who wants to do the same thing, so the two of you can trade disks or flash drives.

Backing Up to Network Computers

One easy way to back up your data files is to use another computer on the network. If your network has two computers, each computer uses the other as the place to store backups. If your network has more than two computers, you can pick one of the other computers as the recipient of the backups. In fact, you can back up your data to every remote computer in a frenzy of cautiousness (which is what I do).

This technique works if you operate on the theory that it is highly unlikely that all the computers on the network could die at the same time. The fact is that a fire, flood, or power surge from lightning could very well destroy every computer on your network. If you use remote computers for backing up, you should also back up on some sort of media, whether it is floppy disks, removable-drive cartridges, or tapes, on a weekly or monthly basis. Or, sign up for a backup service with your Internet service provider (ISP). These services work by uploading your backup files to the ISP's servers, where the ISP has reserved disk space for you.

Start by creating a folder for yourself on the remote computer. Make it a shared resource and call it *Fred* (unless your name isn't Fred). To find out about creating shared resources, refer to Chapter 7.

After you create a backup folder, copy your documents folder to the shared folder you created for yourself on the remote computer. You have two methods available for performing this daily task, both of which are quite easy:

✔ Copy your documents by using the computer folder.

✔ Copy your documents by using the Send To command.

I cover both options in the following sections.

Copying documents from the computer folder

To use the computer folder (called My Computer in Windows XP and Computer in Windows Vista) to back up your documents, perform the following steps every day:

1. **Open the computer folder on your own computer.**

2. **Right-click your documents folder and choose Copy from the shortcut menu that appears.**

3. **Select the Network listing (below the drives listings) and double-click the computer that has your backup folder.**

4. **Right-click your personal folder on the remote computer and choose Paste from the shortcut menu that appears.**

If you're making another backup on another remote computer in which you created a folder for yourself for safety's sake (me, cautious?), repeat the preceding steps.

Using the Send To feature

Windows has a nifty function called Send To that lets you select a pre-configured location as the target for copying. The Send To command exists in the menu you see whenever you right-click a folder or file listing in your computer folder. You just select the target location from the Send To list, and Windows takes care of copying the file, without the need to navigate through the network to find the computer and shared folder you created to hold your backups.

Windows pre-populates the Send To folder with commonly used send-to target devices (such as CD drives and other locations).

Send To works best with mapped drives, so you should map a drive to your shared folder. Then, in Windows XP, you can add the mapped drive to your Send To folder.

In Windows Vista, you don't have to take that step because the operating system automatically adds every drive you map to the Send To folder. Chapter 10 has instructions for creating mapped drives for shared folders on remote computers, and after you've created a mapped drive, you can add that drive to your Send To folder.

Adding a mapped drive to the Send To folder in Windows XP

It's easy to add a mapped drive to your Windows XP Send To folder. Open My Computer and navigate to your Send To folder, which is in the following location:

```
\Documents and Settings\<Your Logon Name>\Send To
```

Substitute your logon name on the computer for *<Your Logon Name>*. For instance, Figure 13-1 shows the folders for the user named Kathy, with the Send To folder selected.

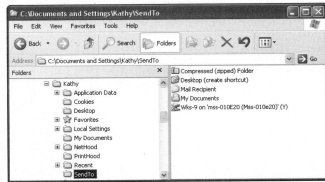

Figure 13-1: Each user on the computer has his or her own Send To folder.

Then take the following steps to add the mapped drive to your Send To folder:

1. **Choose File➪New➪Shortcut.**

   The Create Shortcut dialog box shown in Figure 13-2 appears.

2. **Click Browse.**

   The Browse for Folder dialog box opens.

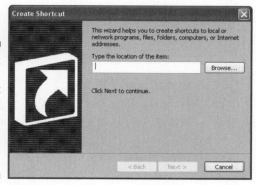

Figure 13-2:
Create a
shortcut
to your
mapped
drive in your
Send To
folder.

3. **Expand My Computer by clicking the plus sign to the left of its listing.**

4. **Select the mapped drive you want to add to your Send To folder and click OK.**

   The Create Shortcut dialog box displays your mapped drive.

5. **Click Next.**

6. **Enter a name for the shortcut.**

   Windows XP enters the name of the folder for the mapped drive, which usually works fine; if you wish, you can change the name.

7. **Click Finish.**

   The mapped drive is now in the list that's displayed when you select the Send To command after right-clicking a folder or file listing.

Copying files with Send To

Now that your Send To folder contains a shortcut to your backup folder on the remote computer, right-click the listing for your documents folder in the Start menu or in the computer folder and choose Send To from the menu that appears. Select the mapped drive that represents your backup folder, and Windows begins copying the files.

Using an external hard drive for backups

One of the best things that's happened to network administrators (that's you, because you set up your home network) is the incredible reduction in prices for large external hard drives. You can buy hundreds of gigabytes of storage for under a hundred dollars.

This means you can back up all the data files from all the computers on the network and still have tons of room left on the drive for storing music files, pictures, and other large files.

Large external hard drives are available in two flavors: A hard drive that you attach to one computer (via the USB port) and share so other computers can use it, or a drive that has an Ethernet connection that plugs directly into your concentrator, making the drive look like another computer on the network.

These drives come with software that does more than configure the drive and install drivers — many come with backup software that is easy to set up and use.

The advantage of an external hard drive that attaches to the computer is the price — these drives are generally less expensive than drives that stand alone on the network.

Drives that don't have to be attached to a computer, and plug directly into the network concentrator, are called *NAS devices* (NAS stands for *Network Attached Storage*). They're always available (which isn't true of a large external drive connected to a computer that may be turned off).

NAS devices are considered "network node" devices, which means they are as much a part/node of the network as the computers on the network. When you open your network folder (My Network Places in Windows XP, and Network in Windows Vista), you see the NAS device along with the network computers (see Figure 13-3).

For either type of external hard drive, the best way to manage the drive as a backup center is to create a folder for each computer or for each user. Then each user can map a drive to the appropriate folder to back up data files.

Periodically (weekly is best), back up each folder on the external drive to a CD or DVD for offsite storage.

All the external hard drives I looked at when I was deciding on a purchase had USB ports, and you can attach any USB device to those ports, including a USB flash drive for creating copies of data files from the external hard drive that you can take with you to another site.

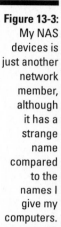

Figure 13-3:
My NAS
devices is
just another
network
member,
although
it has a
strange
name
compared
to the
names I
give my
computers.

On NAS drives, many people use one or more of the USB ports for printers, creating a print server in addition to the data storage on the external drive. Most NAS drives come with a built-in Printers folder and the software needed to install a printer on the device (instead of installing the printer on a computer).

Using Windows Backup Software

Microsoft provides backup software with Windows, and because it's free, many people use it. In this section, I walk you through using Microsoft Backup to ensure a safe computing environment.

Installing the Backup software

In Windows Vista and Windows XP Professional Edition, the backup software is installed automatically. However, Microsoft Backup is not installed during a typical installation of Windows XP Home Edition. Here's how to install Microsoft Backup in Windows XP Home Edition:

1. **Insert the Windows XP Home Edition CD-ROM in the CD-ROM drive.**

2. **Press and hold the Shift key as the CD tray slides closed to prevent the installation program from starting automatically.**

Full backup is the only way to go

One of the configuration options for Windows Backup is to back up only those files that changed since the last backup; this is called an *incremental backup*. The theory behind an incremental backup is that any files that haven't changed are already in a previous backup file, so there's no need to back them up again.

This is a rather inefficient theory. When your drive dies, and you need to put your data back on the new drive, you must go back to your first backup file and restore each backup file in chronological order. This could take hours or days. It also means that you have to save every backup file you ever make.

The purpose of backing up is *not* to make backing up quick and easy — the purpose is to make restoring your data quick and easy so that you can get right back to work after a drive crash or after you purchase a new computer. Incremental backups are not easy to restore.

3. **In My Computer, right-click the icon for the CD-ROM drive and choose Explore.**

4. **Navigate to the subfolder** `\Valueadd\Msft\Ntbackup`.

5. **Double-click the file named** `Ntbackup.msi`.

    The Backup Installation Wizard opens.

6. **Follow the wizard's prompts to install the backup software.**

When installation is complete, the backup tool is on your menu system. When you want to run the program, simply choose Start➪All Programs➪Accessories➪System Tools➪Backup.

Configuring Microsoft Backup

When you use Microsoft Backup for the first time, you need to create a backup job (a set of instructions to tell the software which files to back up and when they should be backed up). You have the following configuration options in a backup job:

✔ The folders and files that you want to back up

✔ Whether you want to back up all the files you've selected or only those that have changed since the last backup

✔ The target media — the location to which you want to save your backup files

To do this, when the Backup Wizard opens, walk through the wizard's windows, making the selections you prefer.

After you configure the backup options, you can give the backup job a name. For example, if you select a full backup, you could name it *full*, whereas you could name a backup of your My Documents folder *docs*. Thereafter, when you start the backup software, you can select an existing job or create another job with a different configuration.

Backups are not like copies. You can't retrieve the individual files from the target media because the entire backup is one big file. The backup software makes a catalog that it displays if you need to restore any files. You must select the individual files from the catalog — you won't see the filenames on the media.

For full explanations of backing up and restoring your computer, read *Windows XP For Dummies,* 2nd Edition, or *Windows Vista For Dummies,* both by Andy Rathbone (Wiley).

Restoring a System after a Disaster

If you've replaced a drive or computer, you can restore all your data because you were wise enough to back it up. Here are the tasks you need to perform:

1. **Install Windows.**

2. **Install the removable media drive you used to make your backup.**

   If you backed up to another computer on a network, install and configure the NIC so that you can get to the remote computer on the network. Then open your computer folder and copy the files from the remote folder to your documents folder.

3. **Install and run the backup software you used to create your backup (if you used backup software).**

   A Restore Wizard opens to walk you through the process of restoring your files.

Using System Restore

Windows XP and Windows Vista offer a component called System Restore. If you have a serious problem with Windows (instead of a dead hard drive), you can restore your operating system to a previous state. Your data remains intact.

System Restore monitors the operating system files and program files you install and periodically writes a copy of the system's setup and configuration to a set of files. That set of files is called a *restore point*. If something goes amiss, you can tell Windows to go back to a previous restore point.

It's beyond the scope of this book to provide detailed information about configuring and using System Restore, but you can find out more about it in other books from Wiley Publishing, including Andy Rathbone's *Windows XP For Dummies,* 2nd Edition, and *Windows Vista For Dummies.*

Chapter 14

Using Windows Maintenance Tools

*W*indows has a virtual toolbox built into the operating system. This toolbox is filled with a bunch of handy programs that you can use to perform maintenance checkups and even repair some of the problems that may crop up with the computers in your network.

One nice thing about a network is that if a computer develops problems, when the first symptoms appear, you can copy all the documents from the computer that's in trouble to another computer. Then, if you can fix the problem, you just move everything back. If you can't fix the problem and have to replace a hard drive (or even a computer), the network has your data files.

Preparing to Run Maintenance Tools

Hard drives collect a lot of files that neither you nor Windows use. These files hang around, taking up disk space and making the maintenance utilities work harder.

Before you use maintenance tools, clean up your hard drive — in fact, you should periodically clean up your hard drive even if you're not about to use a maintenance utility because the cleaner your hard drive is, the faster everything runs.

In the following sections, I go over the manual tasks involved in cleaning a drive of excess files. These tasks can be performed on a semi-automatic basis by a Windows utility named Disk Cleanup, but many users prefer the control they retain when they perform the chores manually, and some users have encountered problems with the Disk Cleanup tool. I discuss the Disk Cleanup tool later in this chapter.

Empty the Recycle Bin

I'm often amazed at the number of files that are stored in some Recycle Bins. People apparently just forget to empty this container. The files in the Recycle Bin are taking up space, just as files in other folders do.

If you hold the Shift key when you press the Delete key to remove files, Windows bypasses the Recycle Bin and permanently deletes the files.

Removing temporary Internet files

Nothing grows faster than the size of the Temporary Internet Files folder except dust bunnies (which I believe are among the Earth's most common elements).

Every time you view an Internet page in your browser, the browser saves the page in a temporary folder to make it faster for you to return to the page. When you close the browser (reducing the odds that you'll be needing those same pages), the files aren't removed automatically. Instead, your browser retains the files until the folder grows beyond a certain size (which you can change) and then removes the oldest files to make room for new files.

The steps you take to remove temporary Internet files and configure the size of the temporary files folder vary, depending on the browser you're using. In the following sections, I cover the common browsers: Internet Explorer 6 (standard in Windows XP), Internet Explorer 7 (standard in Windows Vista), and Foxfire (popular with many Windows users as a replacement for Internet Explorer).

Throughout the following sections, I omit discussions of other features that can be enabled, disabled, and configured in the dialog boxes you see as you empty the Temporary Internet Files folder. These additional options are important, but beyond the scope of this book. For complete explanations, read *Windows Vista For Dummies* or *Windows XP For Dummies,* 2nd Edition, both by Andy Rathbone (Wiley Publishing, Inc.).

Temporary Internet files in Internet Explorer 6

In IE6, use the following steps to remove temporary Internet files and optionally change the size of the Temporary Internet Files folder.

1. **Choose Tools⇨Internet Options.**

   The Internet Options dialog box shown in Figure 14-1 appears.

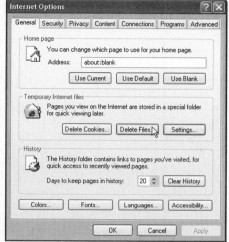

Figure 14-1:
Remove
unneeded
files and
configure
options in
the IE6
Internet
Options
dialog box.

2. **In the Temporary Internet Files section of the General tab, click the Delete Files button.**

   The Delete Files dialog box appears, offering you the option to delete any offline files you've collected (if you use the Work Offline options).

3. **Click OK.**

   An hourglass appears while IE6 deletes the files — if you haven't removed files in a while (or never), this could take some time.

4. **Optionally, change the size of the Temporary Internet Files folder by clicking the Settings button.**

   The Settings dialog box, shown in Figure 14-2, opens.

Figure 14-2:
You can
reduce the
size of the
Temporary
Internet
Files folder
in IE6.

5. **Use the slider bar or the size box to reduce the number of megabytes allowed for the folder.**

6. **Click OK twice to save your new settings and close the Internet Options dialog box.**

Temporary Internet files in Internet Explorer 7

In IE7, use the following steps to get rid of the temporary Internet files and, if you wish, change the size of the folder that holds them:

1. **Choose Tools⇨Internet Options.**

   The Internet Options dialog box appears.

2. **Click the Delete button.**

   The Delete Browsing History dialog box appears, as shown in Figure 14-3.

Figure 14-3:
IE7 has a Delete dialog box that covers all the data types that the browser collects.

3. **In the Temporary Internet Files section of the dialog box, click Delete Files.**

   IE7 displays a message asking you to confirm the deletion.

4. **Click Yes to confirm that you want to delete the files.**

5. **Click Close to return to the Internet Options dialog box.**

6. **If you want to change the size of the Temporary Internet Files folder, click the Settings button in the History section of the dialog box.**

   The Temporary Internet Files and History Settings dialog box appears.

7. **In the Disk Space to Use section of the dialog box, change the MB size.**

8. **Click OK twice to save your new settings and close the Internet Options dialog box.**

Temporary Internet files in Firefox

If you use Firefox, take the following steps to remove temporary Internet files and optionally reset the size of the folder that holds them:

1. **Choose Tools⇨Options.**

   The Options dialog box appears.

2. **Click the Privacy icon in the left pane.**

   The Privacy dialog box opens.

3. **To clear out temporary Internet files, click the Clear button to the right of the Cache listing.**

   Firefox removes the files in the Temporary Internet Files folder — when the job is done, the Clear button becomes inaccessible (sort of an off-white color).

4. **To reduce the size of the folder that holds temporary Internet files, click the plus sign to the left of the Cache listing and enter a new number (see Figure 14-4).**

   Unlike Internet Explorer, Firefox measures the folder size in kilobytes (KB); 1MB equals approximately 1,000KB.

5. **Click OK to return to the Firefox browser window.**

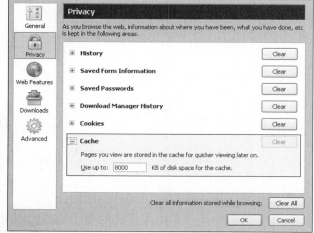

Figure 14-4: Firefox measures the folder size in kilobytes.

Removing temporary Windows files

Windows, software installation programs, and some Internet sites from which you download files use the subfolder named Temp in the Windows folder to store temporary files. Most of the time, they don't bother to clean up the files after they're no longer needed.

Sometimes (but not often), files land in this folder that may be needed in the future, so users get nervous about removing all the files. One rule of thumb to follow is that any file or folder with a .tmp extension (for example, a folder named mcu977.tmp or a file named zzstz.tmp) is safe to remove. (Personally, I always remove all the files in this folder, and in all the years I've been using computers, I've only seen a "missing file" error message that referred to a file in the Temp subfolder once.)

To access the Temp folder, open the Computer folder (My Computer in Windows XP and Computer in Windows Vista), select the Windows folder, and then select the subfolder named Temp.

If all the files in the folder have the extension .tmp, press Ctrl+A to select all files, then hold the Shift key while you press the Delete key on your keyboard (using the Shift key bypasses the Recycle Bin so you don't have to go through a section deletion step to remove the files from the Recycle Bin). If you haven't done this in a while (or ever), it may take a few minutes to remove all the files.

If there are files that lack the .tmp extension, and you're nervous about removing them, take the following steps to select only the files with the .tmp extension:

1. **Choose View⇨Details.**

   Windows displays columns that provide information about each file.

2. **Click the Type column header to sort the files by type.**

   Windows re-sorts the list, putting all the folders first, then individual files by type (the extension determines the type).

3. **In the Folders section of the list, click the first folder with the extension** .tmp **and then hold the Shift key as you click the last folder with the extension** .tmp.

   Windows selects all the contiguous folders with the extension .tmp.

4. **Holding down the Shift key, press the Delete key on your keyboard. Click Yes when Windows asks you to confirm the deletion.**

   Windows deletes all the .tmp folders, bypassing the Recycle Bin (because you used the Shift key).

5. **Below the folder listings, select the first file with the extension** .tmp **and then hold the Shift key as you click the last file with the extension** .tmp.

   Windows selects all the contiguous files with the extension .tmp.

6. **While holding down the Shift key, press the Delete key on your keyboard. Click Yes when Windows asks you to confirm the deletion.**

   Windows deletes all the `.tmp` files, bypassing the Recycle Bin (because you used the Shift key).

Removing Microsoft Word backup files

Microsoft Word has a nifty option in which you can save the last saved version of a document every time you save the document. I spend most of my day in Microsoft Word, and I save constantly (every time I start a new paragraph, I press Ctrl+S). I do this because I will never again let a computer freeze up with an important 20-page document on the screen that hasn't been saved, and my neighbors, who heard my screaming and cursing are grateful for the fact that I save constantly.

If I totally mess up the next paragraph, or I go back to a previously written paragraph and edit it badly or change the formatting incorrectly, all I have to do is close the document (turning down Word's offer to save it first) and open the backup file, which has a pristine copy of the file as it looked when I last saved it.

If you want to enable this feature in Word, choose Tool⇨Options and on the Save tab, enable the Always create backup copy option. The backup copies are saved with the extension `.wbk` instead of the extension `.doc`.

When I exit Word, none of the backup files (the files with the extension `.wbk`) are needed anymore, but there's no way to delete them automatically (at least not in the version of Word I'm using; perhaps newer versions provide that option).

Those backup files pile up, taking up disk space, and I remove them at the end of every day because I don't want to use up disk space on my backup drives.

If you don't use subfolders in your Documents folder, you can get rid of the backup files by changing the folder view to Details and sorting the files by type (as explained in the previous section). Then delete the files of the type Microsoft Word Backup Document.

If you use subfolders to divide your documents by category, deleting backup files from the Documents folder is annoyingly complicated. You have to open each subfolder, and each subfolder of a subfolder if they exist, and select the backup files.

I'm a command line junkie, so I wrote a simple batch file to perform the job for me. I run the batch file at the end of each day, and also before I use any disk utilities. A batch file is nothing more than a program comprised of commands listed in the order in which they're supposed to execute. My "get rid of Word backup files" batch file is easy to create.

In Windows XP, the file has the following contents:

```
del c:\"documents and settings"\kathy\"my documents"\*.wbk
        /s/f/q
exit
```

In Windows Vista, the file has these commands:

```
del c:\users\kathy\documents\*.wbk /s/f/q
exit
```

I'll go over the general rules for creating this batch file so you can create your own.

Batch files are text files, so create your batch files in Notepad, and when you save the file, use the extension .bat instead of .txt. The .bat extension means this is a program, so whenever you double-click a file with the .bat extension, it runs; it doesn't open in Notepad. If you want to open the batch file to view or edit it, right-click its listing and choose Edit.

The format of the first line, which is where the del command is invoked, is

```
del Drive:\UsersFolders\This User's Folder\This User's
        Documents folder\filenames to be deleted
        /parameters:
```

- ✔ del is the command, followed by a space.
- ✔ Drive is the drive letter of the drive that holds your documents folder (usually C) followed by a colon.
- ✔ UsersFolders is the folder that holds user files, including the documents folder. In Windows XP, the folder is named Documents and Settings, and in Windows Vista, the folder is named Users.

  When you use the command line, any folder name or filename that contains a space must be surrounded by quotation marks or else the command interpreter thinks the space represents a parameter to the command.

- ✔ This User's Folder is the folder of the currently logged-on user (using the logon name).
- ✔ This User's Documents Folder is the name of the documents folder, which is My Documents in Windows XP and Documents in Windows Vista.
- ✔ The filenames to be deleted are represented by *.wbk, which means any and all filenames that have a .wbk extension.
- ✔ Parameters are instructions to the command interpreter about how to proceed using the command:

- /s means perform this action on all subfolders.
- /f means delete the file even if it's marked read-only.
- /q means Quiet Mode, or "don't ask me 'OK to delete this file' for every file you find that should be deleted."

The second line of the batch file has a single command, exit, which means close the command window when you're finished.

Here's how to know what the contents of the path (those folders/subfolders entries) should be.

In Windows XP, click the Start button and then right-click the listing for My Documents. Choose Properties, and in the Target tab (which is displayed by default), the path is displayed in the Target field. In fact, it's highlighted, so you can press Ctrl+C to copy the entire path. Then, in Notepad, press Ctrl+V to paste the path into the Notepad document. Remember to insert quotation marks around any part of the path that has spaces in its name.

In Windows Vista, click the Start button and then right-click the listing for Documents. Chose Properties and move to the Location tab, where the path is displayed and highlighted. Follow the instructions in the previous paragraph to copy and paste the path.

Checking Your Hard Drive for Damage

Windows has an error-checking utility that checks the condition of your hard drive, looking for the following specific problems:

- Damaged sections of the drive
- Pieces of files that don't seem to belong anywhere (or the operating system can't figure out where they belong)

If a damaged section is identified, the utility takes files off the damaged section (if possible) and moves them to a good spot on the drive. Then the program marks the damaged section as bad so that the operating system doesn't use it to store files again.

If pieces of files are found and the tool can't figure out where they belong, the software puts the pieces into files that you can look at to see whether you can identify them. However, you usually can't do anything with these files except delete them. Those files are placed in the root of the hard drive (not in any folder), and they're named FILE0000.CHK, FILE0001.CHK, and so on. You could try to read them, but even if they're readable (most of the time they're not text, so you can't decipher them), you can't do anything with them. Just delete them.

Why hard drives develop problems

I bet you're wondering how you get pieces of files floating on your drive. As I explain in the section, "Defragging Your Hard Drive," later in this chapter, Windows keeps track of the location of a file on the hard drive every time you save it. If your computer is running with the NTFS file system, the information about file locations is kept in an index called the Master File Table (MFT). (See the sidebar "NTFS: A file system with muscle.") Some computers running Windows XP run a file system called FAT (more common with Windows XP Home Edition), in which the information about file locations is kept in an index called the File Allocation Table (FAT).

If your computer unexpectedly shuts down while files are open, the operating system has no opportunity to tell the index where all the files or parts of files that are currently in memory came from — their locations on the hard drive. The data is on the drive, but the index doesn't contain any reference for it. This means you may lose parts of any open files, both data and software, because Windows doesn't know how to send them home.

Unexpected shutdowns aren't limited to sudden power failures. If you shut off your computer without going through the Shut Down dialog box, that counts as an unexpected shutdown and can do almost as much damage to your file system as a power failure.

NTFS: A file system with muscle

Instead of a File Allocation Table, which only tracks file locations and has a finite size, NTFS tracks all sorts of information about files and folders in a special file called the Master File Table (MFT). The size of the MFT is dynamic, which means that it's automatically extended when necessary. The MFT is like a robust database, able to store plenty of information about files and folders in your system.

One important piece of information the MFT stores is the permissions that individual users possess to manipulate a file or folder. This means that NTFS can control users' actions, letting some users create or change files, allowing other users to read files but not change or add files, and even preventing users from looking at files. In an NTFS system, when you right-click a file or folder, you see a tab named Security. You can use that tab to specify permissions for specific users who access that file or folder.

Running the error-checking tool

Windows XP and Windows Vista are powerful and protective operating systems, and when a hard drive is running, it can't be locked. To fix file system errors, the Windows error-checking tool locks the drive. But because the drive is in use, it can't be locked. Catch-22!

To get around the problem, if you want to fix errors, the tool offers to run the next time you start your computer. If you've been seeing errors when you attempt to open or save files, you should run the error-checking tool in its fix-stuff mode the next time you reboot.

On the other hand, if you just want to check the disk, looking for bad sectors (and marking them as bad so that files aren't saved there in the future), you can perform that task without rebooting. Of course, the program doesn't perform the important work of fixing the problems it finds.

You should be aware that this process takes quite a bit of time. You may want to start the process at the end of the day. The report will be waiting for you when you go back to the computer.

To run the error-checking tool, follow these steps:

1. **Open the computer folder.**

   In Windows XP, choose Start⇨My Computer; in Windows Vista choose Start⇨Computer.

   The computer folder opens, displaying the drives on your computer.

2. **Right-click the icon for the hard drive you want to check and choose Properties from the shortcut menu that appears.**

3. **Click the Tools tab of the Properties dialog box.**

4. **Click the Check Now button in the Error-Checking section of the dialog box.**

   The Check Disk dialog box opens (see Figure 14-5), displaying options for checking the drive.

5. **Select the Scan for and Attempt Recovery of Bad Sectors option or the Automatically Fix File System Errors option, or both (depending on what you think is necessary).**

   Selecting the option to fix errors means that you must reboot the computer to start the process.

Figure 14-5:
Configure the way you want the error checking tool to perform its task.

6. Click Start.

If you selected only the option to check the bad sectors, Windows begins checking the disk. Now would be a good time to have lunch, clean the bathroom, or take a nap. The process takes many minutes. The larger your drive, the longer it takes. On my 130GB drive that's half filled, it took about an hour to check the disk.

If you selected the option to fix file system errors, the utility displays an error message telling you that it cannot fix errors because the drive is in use. The program then offers to run the next time the system boots. Click OK. If you want, you can reboot your computer immediately to get the task moving.

If you enabled power-management features for your monitor and your screen goes dark while the utility is running, do not press the spacebar or Enter to bring the display back. Pressing either of those keys stops the utility (the safe keys to press are Ctrl or Alt).

Defragging Your Hard Drive

Disk Defragmenter is a program that takes fragments of files and puts them together so that every file on your drive has its entire contents in the same place. This makes opening files a faster process.

Before I discuss the Disk Defragmenter tool, it's important to understand a piece of jargon. Nobody who is hip (well, as hip as a computer geek can be) uses the term *Disk Defragmenter*. In fact, nobody uses the terms *fragmented* or *defragmented*. Instead, when your disk is *fragged,* you "run the *defragger* to *defrag* it." If you're not already a tech geek, at least now you can talk like one.

Files get fragmented (oops, I meant fragged) as a matter of course; the fragging (there — I've redeemed myself) isn't caused by anything you do or any problem with your computer. The more a drive fills with files, the more likely it is to become fragged.

Why hard drives get fragged

After you've used your computer for a while, your hard drive starts to get full. One day, you launch your word processor and open a document that's on your hard drive. That document is 50,000 bytes in size. You add more text to the document, and when you save the document, it's 75,000 bytes. The particular section of the drive where the file was originally stored has room for 50,000 bytes, so the operating system puts 50,000 bytes of your new version back where it was and finds another spot on the drive to lay down the remaining 25,000 bytes.

The sequence of events that takes place goes something like this:

1. Windows makes a note about that file, and the note says something like, "I stuck the first 50K here and put the next 25K there." The note isn't a note, though; it's an entry in the File Allocation Table or the Master File Table.

2. The next time you open the file, the operating system fetches all those fragments, in the right order, after checking the FAT or MFT to see where the pieces of the file are.

3. Because you're never satisfied, you feel compelled to add even more information to the file. When you're finally satisfied (at least for the moment), you resave the file.

4. The operating system puts the first two sections back where they were and then finds another spot for the additional bytes that are needed for your additions and changes.

5. The next time you open the file to add to it or make other changes, more sections of the disk are used to hold the pieces of the file (when will you ever be finished?), and the various file fragments must be fetched from more separate locations.

   This process continues for as long as you keep making changes (which goes on forever if you're trying to write a novel). In fact, this is the standard process that occurs with files that you create and save in all your programs.

So, you're saying to yourself, "Big deal. As long as my computer knows where to get all these fragments so I can obsessively re-edit and add to my documents, why do I care how the process works?" Well, after a while, your system slows as a result of all this searching and piecing together of file fragments. You may notice that loading and saving documents takes a lot longer. That's because your operating system must do all this legwork to fetch and lay down the file parts.

In addition, if file pieces are scattered throughout the drive, when you install software, the installation program won't be able to find the disk space it needs in one place, so the program is installed in pieces. As with data files,

Windows has to pick up the pieces, in the right order, whenever you open the software. This makes loading software slower, and when that's compounded by the slower loading of data files, you're losing a great deal of the efficiency computers are supposed to provide.

Eventually, you need to tell the operating system to pick up all the parts and put them together, putting all the parts of every file in the same location on the drive, making the file contents *contiguous* (all the bytes together in one place). This is what the Disk Defragmenter tool does. Read on to find out how to use this tool.

If you're using NTFS, your drive doesn't frag as quickly as it would with FAT because NTFS is a much more efficient file system. However, you still need to run the defragger occasionally.

How to defrag your drive

The Disk Defragmenter juggles file parts, holding some in memory while it finds room for them and then laying the parts on the drive in a place that has room for the stuff. Although the process may seem tedious (how would you like to search out and find every piece of data that creates a whole document?), the process is pretty pain-free.

Defragging in Windows XP

In Windows XP, you can ask Disk Defragmenter to analyze the drive and see whether it needs defragging. Then you can defrag the drive if the program reports that defragging is needed. In fact, even if the program reports that the drive doesn't need defragging, you can look at a detailed report and decide for yourself whether you want to proceed with the process. Take the following steps to use the Windows XP Disk Defragmenter:

1. **Open the My Computer folder.**

   My Computer opens, displaying the drives on your computer.

2. **Right-click the icon for any drive and choose Properties from the shortcut menu that appears.**

3. **Click the Tools tab of the Properties dialog box.**

4. **In the Defragmentation section of the dialog box, click Defragment Now.**

   The program window opens, displaying all the drives it finds on the computer (including USB flash drives, as seen in Figure 14-6).

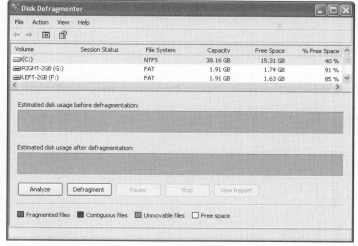

Figure 14-6:
Disk Defrag-
menter can
defrag any
drive on
your system.

5. **To see if a drive needs defragging, select the drive and click Analyze.**

   It takes a few minutes for the program to examine the drive and report back. You can view a detailed report of the drive's fragmentation level.

6. **To defrag the drive, click Defragment.**

   You can take this action if the report says you should, or even if the report says you don't need to but you think the drive is fragged enough to warrant it.

7. **Click the Show Details button to see a full-color representation of your hard drive and its fragmented files.**

   You can watch the pieces of files being put together as the defragging proceeds.

   A message lets you know when the defragging is complete.

Here are a few points about the defragging process:

✔ Technically, you can do work on your computer during the defragging operations, but things go very slowly (because the computer and the hard drive are very busy), and the defragmenter program itself is slowed by your actions. Go grab a bowl of cereal and watch a few commercials instead of trying to work while defragging is underway.

✔ If you must perform some task at the computer during this procedure, click the Pause button in the Disk Defragmenter dialog box. After you finish your work, click Resume. You can also click Stop to end the process.

✔ If you pause or stop the Disk Defragmenter, the response isn't immediate. The program finishes the file that it's currently working on
and updates the FAT or MFT information. Then it responds to your
selection.

After the defragging, you should notice a much peppier response when you
load and save files. Of course, you're going to continue to open and save files,
so the fragging starts all over again; eventually your system will slow, and
you'll have to defrag again.

Defragging in Windows Vista

The default setup for the Disk Defragmenter differs from that of Windows XP.
By default, Windows Vista schedules defragging as a nightly task. You can
change or eliminate the nightly run, and you can manually defrag the drive
whenever you think you should.

To use the Windows Vista Disk Defragmenter, follow these steps:

1. **Open the Computer folder and right-click any drive.**

2. **Choose Properties and move to the Tools tab.**

3. **Click Defragment Now.**

   The Disk Defragmenter window opens to display the current settings.
   (see Figure 14-7).

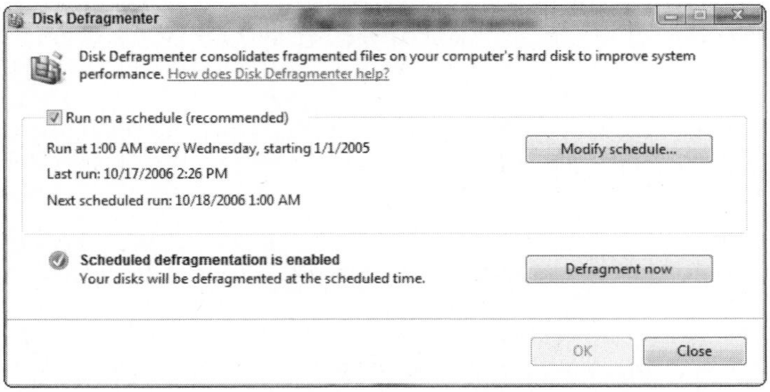

Figure 14-7:
The
Windows
Vista Disk
Defrag-
menter is
config-
urable.

4. **To defragment the drive, click Defragment Now.**

   The program goes right to work, with no user interaction.

5. **To stop a scheduled defragging, deselect the Run on a Schedule option.**

6. **To change the schedule, click Modify Schedule and use the options in the drop-down lists to schedule defragging (see Figure 14-8).**

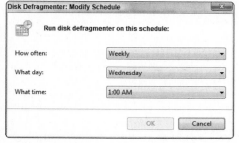

Figure 14-8: Schedule the defragger to suit your needs.

Managing Devices with the Device Manager

The Windows Device Manager is a powerful tool. You can use it to view all sorts of information about the hardware that's in your computer. You can also use it to change the way hardware is configured or the way it behaves.

✔ In Windows XP, open the Device Manager by right-clicking My Computer and choosing Properties. Move to the Hardware tab and click the Device Manager button.

✔ In Windows Vista, open the Device Manager by right-clicking My Computer and choosing Manage. Select Device Manager in the left pane of the Management Console.

All the hardware categories that exist in your computer are displayed, as shown in Figure 14-9.

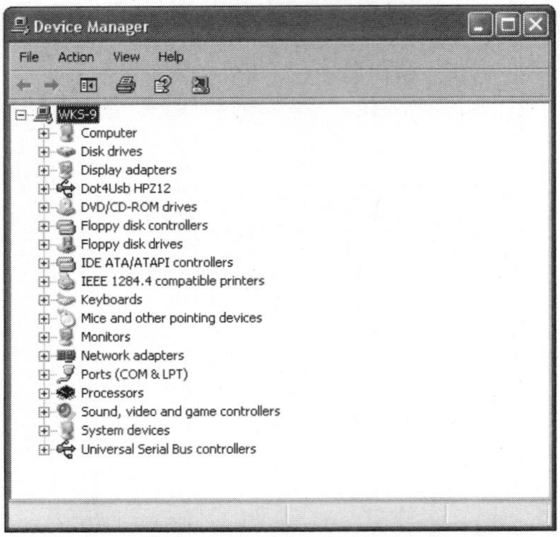

Figure 14-9:
The list of
devices for
your
computer
differs,
depending
on the
hardware
you have.

The following sections describe what you can do with the information in the device listings.

Viewing a specific device

The list that appears when you open the Device Manger window is a list of hardware types, not the actual hardware that's installed in your computer. Click the plus sign to the left of a device type to see the hardware that's installed on your system. You usually see an exact description, sometimes including a brand name and model.

Right-click the listing for the specific device and choose Properties to see information about the device and the way it's configured. The information in the Properties dialog box differs according to the type of device you're examining.

You can change the configuration for some devices right in the Properties dialog box. Just select the setting that needs to be changed and enter a new setting.

Managing device problems

If any device is experiencing a problem, the specific device listing appears when you first open the Device Manager window because Windows expands the device type listing to show you the problematic device. An icon appears in the listing, indicating the type of problem. The icon may be a red *X,* which means that the device has been disabled, or a yellow exclamation point, which means that Windows can't find the device or is having a problem communicating with it (see Figure 14-10).

Figure 14-10:
Windows
Vista has
determined
that no
speakers
are
connected
to my sound
controller
(something
Windows
XP isn't able
to do).

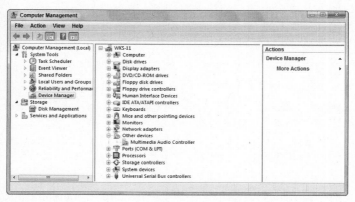

Select the device and click the Properties icon to see a message explaining the problem. Sometimes, the problem isn't so serious, and the device continues to operate. Other times, you may have to reinstall or reconfigure the device. The Properties dialog box usually provides enough information to guide you to a resolution.

Printing a report about devices

It's a good idea to have a list of all the devices in your system and the resources they use. I've found that such a list is handy in the following situations:

✔ If you have to reinstall everything when you replace a hard drive, all the configuration information for each device is available in your list.

✔ If you want to install additional devices, you know which resources on your computer are available by viewing your list.

To print a report on all the devices in your system, click the Print button in the Device Manager dialog box. Select the option to print a summary, unless you want to use a whole ream of paper.

Determining Who's on Your Computer

You can keep an eye on visitors — that is, those users who are working on other computers on the network and who are accessing your computer. To see who's here and what they're doing, take the following steps:

1. **Click Start, right-click My Computer (XP) or Computer (Vista), and choose Manage from the shortcut menu.**

   The Computer Management Console (also called a *snap-in*) opens.

2. **Expand the Shared Folders icon in the left pane.**

3. **Click the Sessions folder in the left pane to see who's visiting this computer (see Figure 14-11).**

   To disconnect a user, right-click the listing in the right pane and choose Close Session from the shortcut menu.

Figure 14-11:
Keep an eye on the people who are using files or resources on your computer.

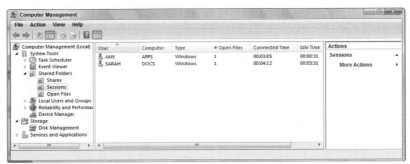

4. **Click the Open Files folder in the left pane to see which files your visitors are using.**

   To close a file, right-click the listing in the right pane and choose Close File from the shortcut menu.

5. **To add a share or modify an existing share, click the Shares folder in the left pane.**

   Then you can use the commands on the shortcut menu that you see when you right-click the folder or right-click any of the shares displayed in the right pane.

Cleaning Up Files with Disk Cleanup

Using the Disk Cleanup tool is like bringing in a housekeeper to clean up all that junk you never use — the stuff that's been lying around taking up space.

In your house, that stuff could be old magazines, newspapers, or clothing that you haven't been able to fit into for years. On your computer, that stuff is files you don't use and probably don't even realize are stored on your drive. Those are the files that Disk Cleanup looks for and offers to sweep out.

Follow these steps to run the Disk Cleanup program:

1. **Choose Start⇨All Programs⇨Accessories⇨System Tools⇨Disk Cleanup.**

   The Disk Cleanup tool takes a few seconds to examine your computer and then opens the Disk Cleanup dialog box, as shown in Figure 14-12. File types that are candidates for safe removal are already selected.

Figure 14-12:
Files that seem safe to remove are pre-selected, and you can select additional file types if you want to clean more aggressively.

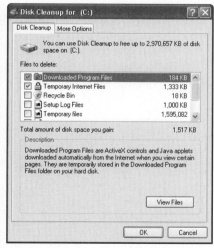

2. **Scroll through the list of file types in the Files to Delete list box and select any additional file types you want to remove. (Click each file-type listing to see more information in the Description box.)**

3. **When you're ready to clean out all this stuff, click OK.**

   Disk Cleanup asks if you're sure you want to delete these files.

4. **Click Yes to proceed, or click No if you suddenly panic.**

Disk Cleanup works similarly in Windows XP and Windows Vista, although there is a small difference in the types of files you can select for removal. For example, Windows Vista offers Hibernation files that are no longer needed. Windows XP has a More Options tab on the dialog box that lets the utility examine installed software and installed Windows components to see if they've been used in the recent past. If not, you are given the opportunity to remove them (which could be a dangerous thing to do, so don't).

Working with System Information

The System Information tool is misnamed because it's not a tool — it's an entire toolbox. It starts off looking like a nifty, handy-dandy tool, but then you discover a menu item named Tools that leads you to more cool tools. In this section, I cover the System Information tool (*SI* for short) and then follow up with sections for some of the embedded tools in its toolbox.

The primary focus of SI is to gather information and diagnose problems. To get started, choose Start➪All Programs➪Accessories➪System Tools➪System Information.

The System Information window opens with the System Summary category selected in the left pane and displays all sorts of technical info about your computer (see Figure 14-13). You can't do anything with this data — it's purely informative.

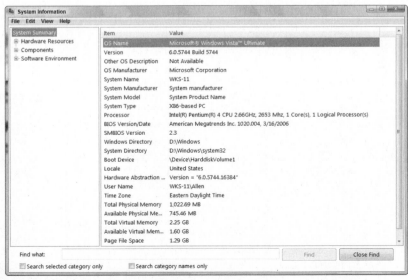

Figure 14-13: Practically everything you'd ever want to know about your computer is displayed in the SI window.

Hardware Resources

Click the plus sign to the left of the Hardware Resources category and select a subcategory to view information in the right pane. The following subcategories are available for Hardware Resources:

- ✔ **Conflicts/Sharing:** This subcategory lists any resource conflicts. It also identifies resources that are being shared by Peripheral Component Interconnect (PCI) devices. This information can be helpful when you're trying to discover whether a hardware conflict is to blame for a device problem.

- ✔ **DMA:** This subcategory displays the status of devices that are using Direct Memory Access (DMA). DMA lets some attached devices (such as a disk drive or a printer) send data directly to the computer's memory. This frees up the processor.

- ✔ **Forced Hardware:** Select this subcategory to see a list of devices that have user-specified resources instead of resources that are assigned by the system. Sometimes this information is helpful when you're having trouble installing a Plug and Play device that should have been easy to install.

- ✔ **I/O:** Selecting this subcategory produces a list of all the I/O addresses (parts of memory assigned to a device) that are currently in use. The devices that occupy each address range are also displayed. You can use this information to avoid the occupied addresses when you're configuring a new device.

- ✔ **IRQs:** Select this subcategory to see a display of the interrupt requests (IRQs) that are in use, along with the devices that are using each IRQ. (An IRQ is a channel of communication that a device occupies.) This subcategory also contains a list of unused IRQs, which is handy when you're configuring a new device.

- ✔ **Memory:** This subcategory displays a list of memory address ranges that are being used by devices. Most of the time, this information is used when you're troubleshooting a device, especially if you call the manufacturer's customer support line. Support technicians often ask for this information.

Components

The Components category contains all sorts of information about your computer's configuration, including information about the status of device drivers as well as a history of all the drivers you've installed. (It's not unusual to upgrade drivers when they become available from manufacturers or from Microsoft.) Information about components in your system is available, including all sorts of highly technical data about memory addresses. Most of the time, the data is incomprehensible, but if you're on the telephone with a support person, this technical mumbo jumbo may be significant. This category also contains a summary of devices that the System Information tool suspects are not working properly.

Table 14-1 lists descriptions of the subcategories in the Components list. Not all categories appear in every version of Windows.

Table 14-1	Components Category Descriptions
Subcategory	*Information Provided*
Multimedia	Has subcategories that contain information about audio codecs and video codecs.
CD-ROM	Contains information about the CD/DVD drives on the system.
Sound Device	Contains information about the sound devices on the system.
Display	Informs you about your video card and monitor.
Infrared	Provides information about infrared devices you've installed.
Input	Has subcategories for information about your keyboard and your pointing device.
Modem	Only in Windows 2000/XP, contains information about attached telephone modems.
Network	Offers information about network adapters, client services, and protocols you've installed.
Ports	Gives you information about serial and parallel ports in your computer.
Storage	Provides data about all the drives and their controllers (SCSI or IDE).
Printing	Tells you which printers and printer drivers (including drivers installed for remote printers) are installed on the computer.
Problem devices	Gives you the status of devices that have problems.
USB	Tells you about the Universal Serial Bus (USB) (also known as Plug and Play) controllers installed.

Software Environment

The Software Environment category covers information about the software that's loaded in your computer's memory. Included are drivers, programs, tasks that are currently running, and all sorts of technical data that's hard to understand. However, the information can be useful to support desk personnel if you're calling for help.

Internet Settings

Only in Windows XP, this category displays information about the Internet Explorer version, the temporary files, and security settings.

Saving system information to a file

You can save all the information that the SI tool provides in a file and then use that file as a reference when you configure new devices or call a support desk. To send the data to a file, choose File⇨Export from the System Information menu bar. A Save As dialog box opens so you can name the file and select the folder in which to save it. The file is a text file, so you can open it and print it from any word processor, as well as Notepad or Wordpad.

Troubleshooting Serious Disk Errors

If your hard drive has a physical problem, you'll probably see one of the following messages (substitute the letter of your hard drive for X):

- ✔ Serious Disk Error Writing Drive X
- ✔ Data Error Reading Drive X
- ✔ Error Reading Drive X
- ✔ I/O Error
- ✔ Seek Error — Sector not found

If you get any of these error messages, your hard drive may have a serious health problem that could even be fatal.

Perform a backup immediately, as explained in Chapter 13 (although some files from the drive may not be readable and won't be backed up). If the backup doesn't work without producing error messages, manually back up as many important data files as you can. Then, take your computer to a computer store to buy a new drive.

Part V
The Part of Tens

The 5th Wave   By Rich Tennant

"You the guy having trouble staying connected to the network?"

In this part . . .

The Part of Tens is a tradition in the *For Dummies* series. In this book, it's also a breath of fresh air and a release from the other chapters, which put you through technical twists and turns, forcing you to concentrate on minutiae and geeky details.

In this part, you discover clever things and fun things that you can do on your network, as well as find out ways to protect your children from the dangerous parts of the Internet.

Chapter 15

Ten Clever Things to Do on Your Network

In This Chapter

▶ Setting up message centers, bulletin boards, and other "communications-central" features

▶ Creating central locations for data that everyone uses

*B*elieve it or not, a networked computer system isn't just about connections, cables, and user profiles. After all that setup stuff is finished, there are a zillion handy reasons for having a home network. Well, perhaps *zillion* is an exaggeration, but it isn't hard to think of ten things, and here they are.

Set Up a Message Center

A computer-based household message center is a place to leave notes for other members of the family. This type of message center is much more efficient than the old system of hand-scrawled notes left on the blackboard in the kitchen, or the less-organized system of dashing off incomplete words and phone numbers on the back of an envelope with your youngest child's crayon. With a message center, you're less likely to run out of room when you take a message for your family members (especially from your teenage daughter's friend Mindy, who just, like, got back from the mall and like can't wait to talk about her, like, new shoes), and even more importantly, no one has to try to decipher your chicken-scratch handwriting.

Creating a shared folder for the message center

Choose one computer to serve as the message center, and then follow these steps to set up a shared folder for messages on it:

1. **Open My Computer.**

2. **Double-click the drive where you want to place the folder.**

   Unless you have multiple drives in the computer, you'll only have drive C.

3. **Choose File⇨New⇨Folder.**

   A new folder icon appears, and the name *New Folder* is highlighted, which means the name is in edit mode. As soon as you press any key, the characters you type replace the name.

4. **Name the folder.**

   Naming the folder *Messages* seems like a good idea.

5. **Right-click the new folder and choose the sharing command from the shortcut menu that appears.**

   In Windows XP, the command is Sharing and Security; in Windows Vista, the command is Share.

   The Sharing tab of the Message Properties dialog box appears.

6. **In Windows XP, select the option to share the folder.**

   In Windows Vista, selecting the Share command automatically shares the folder.

7. **Set permissions for network users.**

   - In Windows XP, click Permissions, select the Everyone Group, and enable Full Control. Then click OK.

   - In Windows Vista, select Everyone from the drop-down list at the top of the window. In the Permission Level column, select Co-Owner and click Share. In the file sharing window that appears, click Done.

Now the share is visible when network users open the network folder and double-click the computer you used to create the message center.

Creating individual message boards

After you create the Messages folder, you're ready to create the individual message-board files for every member of your family. The best way to create a message-center file is to take advantage of a nifty feature that's available in Notepad. Notepad can create a date and time stamp on every entry that's put into a file. Here's how to set up this electronic wizardry:

1. **On the message-center computer, choose Start⇨All Programs⇨Accessories⇨Notepad.**

   The Notepad window opens.

2. **Type .LOG and press Enter.**

   Make sure that the period is the first character on the line and that you use capital letters for the word *LOG* (and no spaces, please).

3. **Choose File⇨Save.**

   The Save As dialog box appears.

4. **Save the file in the Messages folder using your name as the filename.**

   Navigate to the Messages folder and in the File Name box, enter your first name or nickname — Windows automatically adds the extension .txt to the filename. Then click Save.

   The title bar of the Notepad window shows the filename, which is *Yourname*.txt (of course, your *real* name is on the title bar, not *Yourname*).

5. **Choose File⇨Save As, and then save the file under another user name.**

   Use the name of another user. You're creating the same file for another user in your household. Repeat this step for every household member.

6. **When you're finished creating files, exit Notepad.**

Now the message center (the Messages folder on the message-center computer) contains an electronic message board for every user on your network. Everyone on the network can open other users' files to leave messages. And every time you open one of those messages, a time stamp appears.

Testing the message boards

The files you created in the preceding section are designed to work as message centers, noting the date and time of each entry. Make sure that the time-stamp feature is working by opening one of the files. Here's how:

1. **On the message-center computer, open the** `Messages` **folder.**

2. **Double-click a message-board file.**

    The file opens in the Notepad window. The current date and time are pre-entered, and your cursor is waiting for input on the next line, as shown in Figure 15-1.

Figure 15-1:
Is this time-stamp feature cool, or what?

If you don't see a time stamp, you made an error when you entered the original text. Make sure that no characters, not even a space, appear in front of or after the text `.LOG`. Also make sure you entered a period, not a comma (a common error). Make corrections, save the file, and open it again to test it.

Tricks and tips for using the message center

After you have the message center in place, here are some tips for getting the most out of it:

✔ **Leave a blank line at the end of messages.** After you type a message in a user's file, be sure to press Enter to force a blank line to appear before the next automatic time stamp. The blank line makes it easier to separate the individual notes in the file.

✔ **If you don't want to save a message, close Notepad and click No when prompted to save the changes.** If you open another user's file and change your mind about leaving a message (perhaps you opened the wrong file, or maybe you just changed your mind), close Notepad and click No when Windows asks if you want to save the changes you made to the file. If you click Yes, the time stamp remains in the file with no message below it. This will drive the user nuts.

✔ **Use the file to write notes to yourself.** Most of the time, you'll open your message board file just to read the text, not to add text. You can, of course, use the file to write notes to yourself, perhaps entering reminders about tasks or appointments. However, don't enter any information you don't want others to see.

✔ **Clean out old messages to keep message files as small as possible.** You can delete each message as you read it, save some messages for future reference and delete others, or save all the messages forever.

✔ **Delete the time stamp that was automatically added when you opened the file.** Before you save and close your message file, after you've deleted the messages you don't need to keep, remember to delete the time stamp that was automatically inserted when you opened the file.

Don't delete the .LOG entry at the top of the file, or you'll turn off the time-stamp feature.

Hold all my calls! Gaining easy access to the message center

I'm sure everyone in your family gets a lot of phone calls, and I'm sure everyone agrees that the easiest way to do something is the best. That's why you should create a shortcut to the message center for each user on the network. That way, when the phone rings, you don't have to go through the whole folder hierarchy just to find the message center folder.

To create a shortcut, open My Network Places (Windows XP) or Network (Windows Vista) and follow these steps:

1. **Locate the message-center folder and right-click it.**

2. **Choose Create Shortcut from the menu that appears.**

   Windows XP opens a message box that says you cannot create a shortcut here and

offers to create the shortcut on your desktop. Click OK.

Windows Vista automatically creates a shortcut on your desktop.

For even quicker access to the message center (when you're working in software, you can't always see the desktop), drag the shortcut to the Quick Launch bar or drag it to the Start button to put the shortcut at the top of your Start menu.

If multiple users share a computer, each user must log on to the computer and create the shortcut. Desktop shortcuts are linked to the profile of the user who created them. See Chapter 8 for information about user profiles.

Keep a Family Shopping List

Many families keep a shopping list on a blackboard, usually in the kitchen, and everybody in the family adds items to the list. Personally, I don't see the point. Does the person who is heading for the store take the blackboard down and carry it to the store? If not, then the person who's heading for the store has to get a pen and paper and write down everything that's on the blackboard. Hello? Sorry, I'm too lazy for this scheme (and I'm usually the person heading for the store).

The next-best plan is to keep a pad and pen (or pencil, if you have one — I haven't seen a pencil in my house since my kids got out of elementary school) in a central location, like the kitchen. Everybody can add items to the shopping list, and the person (Dad?) who next heads for the store just takes the list with him. Much better, wouldn't you say? Except, in my house, people "borrow" the pad, which always involves moving it to another room. Even more frequently, people take the pen. In fact, putting a cluster of pens next to the pad doesn't work; it's only a matter of a few days before those pens are all in pocketbooks, pockets, and other rooms.

The best place for a family shopping list is in a document on a computer. This list is easy to use and easy to print. Nobody can put the computer in his pocket (or in her pocketbook) and walk away with it, so the list is always available.

Creating the shopping list

To create a shopping list, follow these steps:

1. **Choose a computer to hold the shopping list.**

2. **Create a folder on that computer to hold the shopping list file and then share that folder.**

   Use the steps outlined in the "Creating a shared folder for the message center" section, earlier in this chapter, to create and share the folder.

   If you also set up a family message center, as described earlier in the chapter, you can use that same folder for your shopping list. (It's not necessary to create a time-stamp document for a shopping list.)

3. **Have all the users create shortcuts to the folder on their own desktops.**

   Refer to the section "Creating a shared folder for the message center," earlier in this chapter, for information on how to create shortcuts.

4. **Use the computer that holds the shared folder to create the shopping list file: Open the software, enter the first item on the list, and save the file in the shared folder. You can name the file *Shopping List* or choose something more clever or creative.**

   You can create the file in any software that is available to everyone on the network. Notepad and WordPad come installed on every Windows computer, so either one of those programs will do. If everybody uses the same word processor, you can also use that software.

Using the shopping list

Any person in the household who wants to add an item to the shopping list can open the shortcut to the shared folder, double-click the file to open it, and add athlete's-foot cream, zit zapper, prune juice, or another desperately needed item. Be sure that everyone knows to save the file. Easy, huh?

Always press Enter before you add an item to the list so the item is on its own line. This extra space makes the list much easier to read when the designated shopper prints it.

Managing the list's efficiency and workability is important, or else the concept dies. Then you may have to go back to copying lists from a blackboard. Yuck! When removing items, be sure to remove items from the list; *do not* delete the file. You can either remove all the items on the list and "clean the slate," so to speak, or manually remove only the items you found at the store — and leave "12 pounds of caviar" on the list for next time.

Deletion tips for the designated shopper

Pass on these simple tips to the person who does the shopping for your family, and make sure that if Dad's doing the shopping, he also maintains the list:

✔ To remove everything in the file, press Ctrl+A (which selects all the text in the file), press Delete, and then save the now-empty file.

✔ To remove an individual item, place your pointer at the beginning of the item. Press and hold Ctrl and Shift, and press ↓; this selects the entire paragraph. Then press Delete. Repeat this sequence for other individual items, and save the file.

✔ For multiple items that are listed contiguously, follow the instructions in the preceding bullet but continue to press ↓ to add those items to the selected text. Then press Delete, and save the file.

If you're using Notepad for your shopping file, press and hold Shift while you press ↓ instead of pressing and holding Ctrl and Shift.

Here's some other organizational advice regarding shopping lists:

- ✔ **You can create separate shopping lists for different types of stores.** Your shopping list probably contains food items, paper goods, cleaning supplies, and other items that are available in your local supermarket. Create a file named `hardware` if you tend to purchase nails, tools, propane cylinders, and other hardware-store items frequently. Do the same for other types of stores.

    You could create a file for clothing, but the thought of a single household member shopping for clothing for teenagers makes me laugh. Come to think of it, the thought of sending another household member out with a list of clothing items for me makes me nervous.

- ✔ **You can create shopping lists for special items for each person in the household.** Be careful about naming the files if you're using message files — don't overwrite the time-stamp file for any user. Instead, choose a filename that indicates the contents are a shopping list, for example, `Fred-Shopping` (a dash is an acceptable character in a filename).

    Individual shopping-list files for household members are also great wish lists. Consult another user's shopping file before his birthday.

Collaborate on Documents

If everybody on the network is using the same word-processing software, two of you (or all of you) can collaborate on documents. Common collaborative documents include the annual holiday letter to friends and relatives, a note to a family member who's away at school, or a family wish list for vacations, household repairs, and so on. All modern word processors provide a mechanism for handling multiple-user input. In fact, you can collaborate on documents in several ways, but I discuss only the easiest and most straightforward method here. I'm using Microsoft Word for this discussion because it's the most popular word processor. If you use another product, you shouldn't have trouble figuring out which commands to use to accomplish these tasks — just consult the program's Help system.

The trick to managing a document that has input from multiple users is to configure the document to show each person's input. In Microsoft Word, that feature is called Track Changes (people who use this feature a lot call it *show revisions* or *revisions on*). Follow these steps to use this feature to track changes that are made to a document (I'm using Microsoft Word 2000 in this example — later versions of Word use slightly different commands):

1. **Open the document that you want to edit.**

2. **Choose Tools➪Track Changes➪Highlight Changes.**

   The Highlight Changes dialog box appears, as shown in Figure 15-2.

3. **Select the Track Changes While Editing and Highlight Changes On Screen check boxes.**

   These options enable you to see what changes you're making to the document:

   - All your edits appear in a specific color. If more than one user edits the document, each user is assigned a different color automatically. Everything red came from one user, everything blue came from the second user, and so on.

   - Deleted text isn't really deleted; it has a line through it (called strikethrough).

   - Added text is underlined.

4. **Edit the document by adding and deleting text, as appropriate, and then save the document.**

   Make sure that you save the document with the same filename and in the same folder on the original computer.

5. **If additional people want to edit the document, have them repeat these steps.**

If more than one person has edited a document, you can see the name of the person who made a change by positioning your pointer over any changed text (see Figure 15-3). You can also figure out which color is assigned to each user.

You can accept some changes and reject others, or you can accept or reject all the changes at once. When you accept or reject a change, the text reverts to regular formatting so it looks as if you wrote it. Check the Help files in your word processor to see how to perform these actions. (In Word 2000, choose Tools➪Track Changes➪Accept or Reject Changes and use the dialog box that appears.)

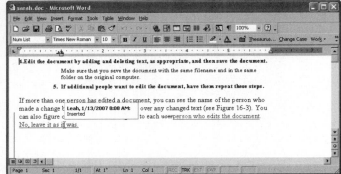

Set Up a Family Budget

Setting up a budget center on a home network is a clever idea, especially for finance-conscious families. A budget center not only gives you a way to see the latest and greatest version of the household budget, but it can also help kids learn how to manage their own money.

Selecting software for your budget

You don't necessarily have to spend money on a bookkeeping program like Quicken. You can prepare your budget using several types of software. Most word processors have a Tables feature that you can use to create lists and columns of numbers, and the software adds up those numbers for you. Spreadsheet programs are designed for budget-type documents.

If you are using a bookkeeping program, you may not be able to separate the budget file from the other data files, but you can usually discover a way to export the budget to a format that you can use in a word processor or in spreadsheet software.

Setting up and using the budget center

After you select the software, set up a shared folder on one computer so that everybody in the household can access the budget files. (Follow the instructions in the section "Creating a shared folder for the message center," earlier in this chapter.) Then save any budgets that you want to share in the budget center folder.

The real budget — the one that you use to run the household — must have a column in which you can enter the actual numbers. But you can also create other specialized budgets, such as a savings plan for a vacation, a new car, or college tuition. Budget regular contributions, and then update the document each time you make a deposit.

If you want to play "what if" games with your budget, copy the budget and save it with a different filename. Then you can change figures in the budget to see how it affects the results. What if you put $100 a month into a mutual fund and reduce other budget categories to make up for that expenditure? You figure out quickly whether the trade-off is worthwhile.

The budget center is also the place to track your investments. And, if you track investments online, you can save financial updates that you download from the Internet in your budget-center folder.

You may want to have one budget-center share for everyone in the household and then create a second share for the "real" budget. Password-protect the second share and give the password to your spouse if you don't want to share it with the kids.

Set Up a Family Document Library

Lots of documents that family members create are of interest to everyone in the family, so it makes sense to create a library where anyone can find these documents.

Follow the instructions in the section, "Creating a shared folder for the message center," earlier in this chapter, to set up a shared folder on one computer so everybody in the household can access the documents. If you want to keep the documents you create on your own computer, you can just copy them to the share you're using as the document library.

Set Up a Download Center

If family members download files from the Internet, it's a good idea to maintain a download center on the network. Here are a few reasons why:

> ✔ **You can run your antivirus software using the download folder as the target.** Running antivirus software on downloaded Internet files is important because many viruses enter computers this way. However, most people don't run virus scans on their computers as often as they should because it takes so much time. Running antivirus software on one particular folder is quick and easy.

> ✔ **A download center avoids duplicates that waste disk space.** If several members of the family want to download a game or a music file, checking the download center first avoids parallel downloading.

Choose the computer with the most disk space for this shared folder. Clean out the folder frequently to get rid of files that are no longer needed or that have been transferred to portable devices.

When you download a file, a Save dialog box opens because you're actually saving the file on your local drive. That dialog box usually has default selections for the folder that accepts the downloaded file, as well as the filename. Use the tools in the Save dialog box to change the destination folder to the network download center. (Don't change the filename.)

Family Blogging

Do you ask your kids, "How was school?", "How was your day?", or "How was the party?" Do you ever get a real answer? Probably not, unless you count "Fine" or "Okay" as a reasonable response. I learned to stop asking, which salvaged my nerve ends.

Why not encourage your kids to blog, and create your own blogs to stimulate their participation? Blogs are the hottest things on the Internet. In fact, lots of people have figured out how to use blogs for both fun and profit.

Blogs are journals (diaries), and the Web-based blogs are kept up-to-date using special software. But you can maintain local blogs by setting up a blog folder for each family member. Each blogger can decide whether to share the blog with other family members. Even if your kids don't share their blogs, the exercise of writing a journal provides a great educational advantage — teachers agree that the more students write, the more they read, and the more literate they become.

If the kids are reluctant to expose their thoughts and activities so blatantly, think about maintaining one family blog. Share the folder that holds the blog document file and encourage everyone to participate anonymously. People can offer thoughts and suggestions about family activities or family problems and can respond to other blog postings.

The best way to keep blogs is to have the latest entry at the top, so you have to remember to press the Enter key at the top of the document to insert a line at the top. Then start typing.

I'm IMming; Are You There?

When you're connected to the Internet, you can use Instant Messages (IMs) to chat with other network users who are also connected to the Internet. Of course, this is much easier if your network Internet connection is an always-on service (DSL or cable).

Microsoft offers several IM programs: Windows Messenger, MSN Messenger, and Windows Live Messenger. Windows Messenger comes with Windows XP, Windows Live Messenger comes with Windows Vista, and you can download MSN Messenger from Microsoft for any version of Windows.

In this discussion, I assume you already have an account on one of the Microsoft Messenger services. If you don't, or if you're not sure how to set up an account and configure it, ask one of the kids, because all kids understand IMs.

If a family member is working on one of the network computers, sending an IM is easier than bellowing when you need to say something (see Figure 15-4).

Figure 15-4: Use an IM to send a quick note.

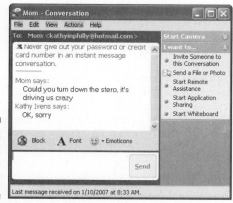

Create a Household Inventory

Fire, flood, hurricanes, tornados, falling trees, robberies, and other household disasters are difficult to cope with, but after the shock wears off, there's the financial side of the catastrophe. You have to deal with insurance companies, tax deductions, and other practical tasks.

Even before a disaster, a household inventory is the only way to know whether you have sufficient insurance. Most people don't realize how much stuff they've collected and how much it's worth until they see it on paper.

An inventory document that tracks the details of everything in the house is easier to set up if everyone has a chance to provide input. You have several choices about the way you set up your household inventory.

- ✔ Create a word processing document; a table works best.
- ✔ Create a spreadsheet document.
- ✔ Buy a program designed for household inventory.

Most people pay attention to the big stuff when they create an inventory of their possessions. Appliances, furniture, and other big-ticket items come to mind immediately. If you have a serious disaster, after you've gone over those items with your insurance company, you're going to find it difficult to resume a normal life if you've only received enough money to replace those items.

How about clothing? How about the stuff that's in the bathroom (like soap, towels, deodorant, makeup, and hair care things)? To insure a complete inventory list, create a section for each room and each person in the household. No detail is too small.

For a word processing table, start a new page for each room (don't forget the basement and garage) and each person. If you create a page break, you can continue to type on the previous pages, and that section will use as many pages as needed while the page break moves along.

To create a page break in Microsoft Word, hold the Ctrl key while you press Enter.

If you use a spreadsheet, create a separate worksheet for each room and each person. Make sure you have a worksheet named "Miscellaneous."

In Microsoft Excel, choose Insert⇨Worksheet to create a new worksheet. To name a worksheet, right-click its tab at the bottom of the window and choose Rename. Enter the name (such as DiningRoom) and press Enter.

For large items, note the date of purchase, cost, serial number, place of purchase, and so on. For small personal items (like the stuff in the bathroom), you just need to list what you generally keep around.

For expensive items, scan the receipt so you have a document that won't get lost, torn, or chewed by the dog. This works best if you create a shared folder for your family inventory so you can store scanned items in the same place as the inventory document.

Make sure everybody works on their specified pages or worksheets to fill in their clothing list, as well as their other possessions (such as toys, including electronic gizmos). Also, everybody should fill in the information about the furniture, fixtures, and other stuff in their rooms.

Every time the document is updated, transfer it to a CD and store it with a neighbor, with a relative, or in a bank safe deposit box.

Create Video Records of Your House

Whether you need documentation of your expensive goods for an insurance claim, or you just want to remember what things looked like before you redecorated the living room, a central repository of household videos can be very handy.

You can take regular photos and scan them, you can take still pictures with a digital camera, or you can use a camcorder and narrate your productions to explain what you're shooting.

Chapter 16

Ten Fun Things to Do on Your Network

In This Chapter

▶ Setting up media centers

▶ Creating central data locations for special (fun) documents

Networks aren't just about being efficient, sharing your Internet connections, and accessing important files that are on remote computers — after a while that's mundane — okay, it's borrrrring.

You can equip your network with gear that brings the fun stuff to the whole household, and that's what I talk about in this chapter.

Play Downloaded Music

If someone (or multiple someones) in your family collects music files, you can listen to those files by sharing the folder in which the files are stored and accessing those files across the network.

The computer you're using must have software capable of playing the music file that's stored on the remote computer, but many PCs come with a variety of media software, so you shouldn't have a problem.

You can start your media software and open the file from the remote computer, or you can copy the file to your own computer and then load it locally. If you have Ethernet cable connecting your network, opening the file on the remote computer usually works quite well. If you have a slower connection (wireless, powerline, or phoneline), the playback is probably going to be very choppy and not very enjoyable. Transfer the file to your computer.

Music files are large, so if you copy a file to your computer, delete the file after you've finished listening. You can copy it again if you want to listen again.

Create a Network Music Collection

To make it easy for everyone to find the CD or downloaded music file they want to listen to while working at the computer, transfer your CDs and down-loaded files to a central location.

The best way to do this is to invest a little money in a central storage device that has tons of disk space available, and there are two types of devices you can look for:

- ✔ A large-capacity external hard drive that attaches to one of the comput-ers on the network (usually a USB device).

- ✔ A large-capacity external hard drive that plugs into the network instead of being connected to a particular computer (called a NAS device — NAS stands for Network Attached Storage).

If you use a USB drive attached to one of the computers, share the drive. If you create folders for music categories (or for each CD), share each folder so users have an easier time finding what they need. (Remember that each share is displayed when you open the shared device in the network folder.) If your family tends to be proprietary by nature, you can create a share for each person's own music collection.

If you have a NAS device, the software that comes with the drive is designed to make it easy for you to set up shared folders. Create a folder structure that matches the way you want to categorize your music.

Convert Music Files

In some families, the music collection is very eclectic technically (and often eclectic by genre) because each family member has a favorite device. If your family is in this situation, you're probably tired of hearing the conversations about the relative merits of WMA, WAV, MP3, OGG, AVI/MPEG, MPC, and so on.

You can get software that converts music files from one format to another so everybody in the family can use the music file regardless of the device and software they prefer. Use your favorite search engine to search the Internet for music conversion software. You'll even find some software that lets you download the utility on a trial basis.

Set up the software on one or more computers (depending on the software license) and store all the music files (pre- and post-conversion) on a large drive (an external humongous drive is best).

Software that converts a CD music track to a hardware/software specific music format is also available.

Create a Network Family Picture Album

Do you have a digital camera in the house? A camcorder? Create an album center by dedicating space on one computer (one with a lot of disk space) or on an external hard drive.

As pictures or video are downloaded, copy them to the album center. You should create folders for each category of pictures (you can invent your own categories).

Create Slide Shows of the Family Album

If you set up a central storage repository of all the pictures your family takes on special occasions, vacations, or just for the fun of it, you can create slide shows of any combination of pictures. You can use a large hard drive in one of the computers on your network or an external large hard drive.

Create a subfolder for each set of pictures that would combine well as a slide show. Junior's birthday party, grandma's retirement party, or a family trip to an adventure park are good subjects for a slide show.

The best way to view a slide show is to copy the subfolder of pictures you want to view to your local My Pictures folder. Open My Pictures, select the subfolder, and make sure the Task List is on the left side of the window. If it's not, choose Tools⇨Folder Options⇨Show Common Tasks in Folders.

In the Task List, select View as a Slide Show. Each picture in the folder appears for several seconds, and a slide show control bar is available so you can move quickly to the next or previous picture.

All of the pictures in the folder are displayed in the slide show unless you select two or more pictures, in which case only the selected pictures appear in the slide show.

 Microsoft's PowerToys include a CD Slide Show Generator you can use to burn images to a CD as a slide show. PowerToys are free and can be downloaded from www.microsoft.com/windowsxp/downloads/powertoys/default.mspx.

Watch Television on Your Computer

If you have the Media Center Edition of Windows on a computer, along with the video hardware required to take advantage of media, you can watch television on your computer.

Okay, this isn't really a network feature, but it's so cool I couldn't resist discussing it, and I figure any family that created a home network is "into" computers enough to appreciate the wow factor of computer/television marriages.

It's actually amazingly simple to hook your TV output to your computer's input and watch TV. You can even record TV shows (if you have enough disk space).

To get started, and to see what's new with Media Center Edition capabilities, visit www.microsoft.com/windowsxp/mediacenter/default.mspx.

Watch Your Computer on Television

The other side of the fun of watching TV on your computer is to throw the output of your computer onto your TV set (or a DVD player). You can let the whole family see that slide show you created of the family photos, or have the family be a "beta test" audience for that slide show you're preparing for work.

All you need to be able to do this is a video controller with a TV Out connector and a cable to connect the TV Out connector to the Video In connector at the back of your television set.

Several manufacturers make video controllers with TV Out connectors, and they work by digitizing the output of your computer and sending that converted signal to your television set.

Believe it or not, sending your computer video to your TV works best if you lower the resolution of your computer to 640 x 480, which would drive you nuts as a permanent setting (everything on the computer screen is large and fuzzy). To reset your computer video resolution right-click a blank spot on the desktop and choose Properties (in Windows XP) or Personalize (in Windows Vista). Select Display Settings and use the slider bar to change the settings.

Play Games over Windows Live Messenger

Windows Live Messenger comes with Windows Vista and can be downloaded for Windows XP (which comes with Windows Messenger, which is not the same thing). Windows Live Messenger was previously named MSN Messenger (and most people still call it that).

A slew of games are available that you can play over Windows Live Messenger — everyone on the network who is logged in to Windows Live Messenger can meet on the Net and let the games begin!

Set Up a Family Web Site

Many ISPs offer Web site hosting services you can use to have a family Web site. Some Web hosting companies also offer low-priced hosting services that are suitable for family sites.

These offerings are less expensive than business Web hosting services, and you can find a wide variety of hosting services for under $10 a month. They don't contain all the nifty high-tech services that businesses need, such as shopping carts, database services, and so on, but you don't need those services for a family site.

You can upload family pictures or your annual "letter to relatives" (commonly called Christmas letters) and send the URL to everybody you know.

Most of these family-based hosting sites provide "click and go" software to help you create your site, and if you want to get fancier, you can learn how to write HTML code (which is the required method of placing text on the Web). Or, you can convert any regular document from Microsoft Word to HTML and upload it to your site.

 Don't put private information on a Web page, and that includes phone numbers and addresses in addition to the information you always think of as private (Social Security numbers and bank account numbers). Anything displayed on a Web page is totally public!

Create an Internet Telephone Switchboard

The popularity of Voice over Internet Protocol (VoIP) telephone services is amazing. (I'd be way over my monthly budget without my VoIP phone because my family and friends are scattered all over the place.) Some of the better (more technically advanced) VoIP providers offer a network-based switchboard service for VoIP for businesses. The standard VoIP service you see in television ads provides a one-phone setup, so anyone who wants to use the phone has to go to that phone (which is near the router).

However, business-class VoIP services are also available, and the ability to use the VoIP telephone is available at every network workstation. It's a PBX (Private Branch Exchange) system, with the PBX switchboard on an Internet server, so it's referred to as an IPBX switchboard.

This service is more expensive than standard home VoIP services, but if you have a lot of out-of-town relatives, friends, and business associates, you should compare your current long distance charges to the cost of a network-based business-class VoIP system.

Chapter 17

Ten Ways to Make the Internet Safe for Children

In This Chapter

▶ Helping children understand what's dangerous about the Internet

▶ Using filters to prevent children from visiting undesirable Internet sites

▶ Setting guidelines for games and violence-oriented Web sites

*P*arents worry about the kind of stuff kids can run into on the Internet, and they're not being paranoid — Internet safety is a real issue. Fortunately, you can do some things to help make the Internet safer for your children, which is good, because you probably can't keep them away from the Net.

Kids love the Internet. In fact, in most households, the kids can find an Internet site faster than the parents. While parents wade through vague searches, due to vague search criteria, kids seem to guess right instinctively. They're at the site they need, reading or downloading, while their parents are still trying to figure out which site holds the stuff they're looking for.

Because you're sharing the Internet across your network, if you're working at a computer while your kids are on other computers, you can't see what your kids are doing.

In this chapter, I discuss some solutions for controlling Internet access. Don't rely on them, because you can only impose them in your own house. Your kids are almost certainly going to access the Internet from friends' houses or from public computers. In the end, there is no substitute for good parenting — discuss the issues openly.

Talk to Your Children about the Internet

Like any other danger, the Internet is less threatening if you have an open and frank discussion with your children about the perils they can encounter online. Approach this subject head-on; you can't pussyfoot around it. You didn't mince words when you warned your kids not to get into a stranger's car — use the same approach to warn your kids about the Internet.

Be aware that just because you have a definition in your own mind about terms like *pornography, hate crimes, child molesters, bomb-making, violent games,* and so on (sorry, but those are some of the dangers on the Internet), your kids may not have a clearly defined notion of their meanings. Depending on the kids' ages, you have to decide what explanations and terminology are appropriate for them. But the bottom line is, you must discuss these issues.

Place Your Computers in the Right Locations

The best way to keep your kids away from the Web sites you don't want them to visit is to provide a deterrent. The best deterrent is sort of a psychological deterrent — one that implies that they could get caught if they don't follow the rules.

My best advice is: Don't put a computer in a child's room. It's a bad idea on several levels, according to many educators and child psychologists who point out that part of a healthy childhood is interaction with other children. Kids who have computers in their rooms tend to spend much more time alone, using the computer (mostly on the Internet), than kids who use computers that are in less-private locations. These are also the kids who spend too much time in chat rooms and have a higher probability of interacting with a predator in a manner that leads to trouble.

Put computers in rooms where it's normal and natural for other household members (especially parents) to walk through those rooms.

Set Controls on Contents

Internet Explorer lets you block Web sites that have content you don't want your children to see. The sites are qualified by rating services, and you can take advantage of these services with a configuration change in Internet Explorer. Open Internet Explorer and follow these steps:

1. **Choose Tools⇨Internet Options.**

   The Internet Options dialog box appears.

2. **Click the Content tab, and in the Content Advisor section, click Enable.**

   The Content Advisor dialog box appears (see Figure 17-1).

3. **Use the slider on the Ratings tab to set limits on the level of the types of content listed in the dialog box.**

   The more you slide to the right, the more liberal your controls become (the opposite of the way political blocs work).

Figure 17-1:
Use the
Content
Advisor to
control
access to
Web sites.

The Ratings tab displays RSACi as the rating service. This service is the Recreational Software Advisory Council, which no longer exists. It's been merged into the Internet Content Rating Association (ICRA). ICRA is an international organization that's dedicated to making the Internet safer for children while respecting the rights of content providers.

Password protect your settings

Even very young children can figure out how to access the Ratings dialog box and move that slider to the right. Therefore, you must lock your settings by requiring a password to override the configuration changes you make.

The lock is on for all users, even the parents. Give the password to the adults in the house but not to the children. Make sure adults who write down the password hide the piece of paper that holds the password.

To set a password that protects your configuration settings, move to the General tab (see Figure 17-2).

Figure 17-2:
The General tab has options for locking your content control settings.

The two options at the top of the General tab set the controls. The first option is Users Can See Sites That Have No Rating. If you select the check box, users can view any Web site that has not been self-rated. This almost guarantees that users will see objectionable material because not all Web sites subscribe to ratings. If the check box is clear, users cannot view any unrated Web page, no matter how benign the content may be.

The second option, which is selected by default, is Supervisor Can Type a Password to Allow Users to View Restricted Content. This means that the adults in your house can use the password you create to view any site on the Internet. If you clear the check box, even you won't be able to view Web sites that don't pass your content configuration controls.

To use a password, click Create Password to open the Create Supervisor Password dialog box, shown in Figure 17-3.

Figure 17-3:
Create a
password
the kids
can't guess.

Enter a password and then enter it again to confirm it. Enter a hint to help you remember the password if you forget it. When you're finished, click OK.

If you use a different browser, you can download software to protect your children against objectionable sites. You can get information and software at www.icra.org (the site for the Internet Content Rating Association).

Use Windows Vista parental controls

Microsoft has provided a robust set of parental controls within Windows Vista. You can apply the controls to any account configured as a Standard User, which means you should make sure your children didn't create user accounts that are in the Administrator category. If any of your children are configured as Administrators, you can automatically change the account type to Standard User when you impose parental controls. Use the following steps to access the parental control features:

1. **Choose Start⇨Control Panel.**

   The Control Panel opens, listing the categories for configuring the computer.

2. **In the User Accounts and Family Safety category, click the Set Up Parental Controls for Any User link.**

   Windows displays a list of all users.

3. **Click the username of the child for whom you want to set controls.**

   If the user is configured as an Administrator, Windows displays a message explaining that the account type has to be changed to impose controls and offers to perform the task. Click Yes to change the user's account type to Standard User.

4. **In the Parental Controls window, shown in Figure 17-4, establish the controls you need and click OK.**

   Click each control's title to learn more about the controls. The explanations are clear and easy to understand.

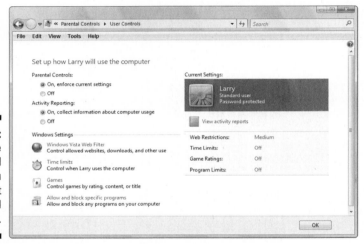

Figure 17-4:
Select the
parental
controls you
feel best
suit you and
your child.

Create Your Own Site Filters

In Internet Explorer, you can create your own Web site filters, which are useful in the following circumstances:

✔ You don't want to use a rating service.

✔ The rating service you use permits access to a site you don't like.

✔ The rating service you use blocks access to sites you feel are appropriate for your children.

Use these steps to create a list of sites that you want to filter for:

1. **Open Internet Explorer and choose Tools➪Internet Options.**

   The Internet Options dialog box appears.

2. **Click the Content tab, and in the Content Advisor section, click the Enable button.**

3. **Click the Approved Sites tab (shown in Figure 17-5).**

Figure 17-5:
You can create your own list of allowed or forbidden sites.

4. **Enter the URL for a Web site you want to filter for; then click the Always or Never button. Repeat this step as many times as you want.**

   If you click the Always button after entering a URL, that site is always accessible, even if you're using a rating service that disallows it. Furthermore, sites designated as Always never require your password. Sites designated as Never require a password.

5. **When you're finished, click OK to close the dialog box and save your changes.**

   If this is your first time using this feature, you're prompted to create a password.

Use Software to Filter Sites

A number of programs are available that control and/or monitor Internet activities. Here are several programs that have received reasonably good reviews, along with their URLs:

- **Net Nanny:** www.netnanny.com
- **Cyber Patrol:** www.cyberpatrol.com
- **Cyber Sentinel:** www.securitysoft.com

These programs work similarly to the rating services by filtering access to Web sites. The advantage you gain by using software is the ability to configure the software to create the filters. Your children's ages and interests and your own general attitude about censorship can be reflected in your configuration choices.

For a comprehensive list of filter software, go to www.safetysurf.com.

Use ISP Restrictions

Several ISPs offer built-in control features for children. In this section, I provide an overview of the restrictions available from popular ISPs.

AOL parental controls

If you use AOL, filtering doesn't take place via the AOL browser; filtering is built into the user's screen name. When you create a username for your child, you can designate an age group. Your choices are Kids Only, Young Teen, Mature Teen, and Unrestricted Access (intended for the parents). These categories determine to what extent AOL filters Web content and activities. Although some of the settings can be customized, the following describes the default limitations:

- The Kids Only category (usually considered to cover up to age 12) blocks instant messages.
- The Young Teen category (ages 13 to 15 or 16) provides IM access, but blocks the ability to exchange files.
- The Mature Teen category limits chat features and Web surfing, but permits all IM features.

You can use the Parental Controls feature to restrict e-mail so that kids can send or receive e-mail from only a selected group. You can also control when and for how long your child can log in to AOL. This is a good way to manage teenagers who seem to spend too much time online.

Limits imposed by the parental controls for AOL apply only to features built into the AOL software. Most children figure out that they can launch the "real" browser instead of the browser built into AOL, so even if you use AOL, you should follow the recommendations earlier in this chapter for limiting your browser. Kids also figure out how to sign up for IMs outside of AOL (such as Microsoft Messenger). To resolve these problems, you can turn on AOL's Internet Access Controls, which prevents the use of non-AOL software.

MSN parental controls

At MSN, the parental control categories are the following:

- ✔ **Teen** (described as ages 13 to 17), which provides access to IMs and most of the Web
- ✔ **Preteen** (ages 9 to 12), which has some restrictions on Web access, as well as limits on e-mail and IMs
- ✔ **Young child** (under age 9)

Within each age category, parents can adjust IM settings as follows:

- ✔ **No Access,** which blocks all use of Microsoft Messenger
- ✔ **Restricted Access,** which allows IMs from people on the child's contact list (parents can approve the child's contact list)
- ✔ **Full Access,** which has no restrictions

MSN also has a parental control that lets you block file downloads. In addition, MSN will e-mail reports to parents about their children's activities. The reports don't include the text of the child's conversations, but they will tell you which Web sites were visited and the online identity of everyone the child communicated with using MSN Messenger and MSN e-mail.

You can enable the recording of online IM conversations. Sign into your child's account, choose Tools➪Options, and then click the Messages tab. Select Automatically Keep a History of My Conversations. Because this setting is within the child's account, not a parental control, your child can disable it if he or she realizes it's enabled.

The parental control settings apply to MSN software. MSN lets you control the use of other browsers, but it does not let you stop your child from using non-Microsoft IM programs.

Comcast parental controls

For cable broadband subscribers using Comcast, a wide set of parental controls is available. (Incidentally, since Comcast has been buying other broadband services, such as AT&T, you may be a Comcast customer soon.) Comcast's parental controls include the following features:

- ✔ Web site content filtering, with customized exceptions.
- ✔ E-mail messages that report visited Web sites.
- ✔ Specific restrictions for each child account.
- ✔ Limits on time of day and length of online sessions.

Other ISPs, such as Earthlink, also provide parental controls. Call the customer support or sales department to learn more about your ISP's offerings.

ISP E-mail Filtering Features

Most ISPs now offer e-mail restrictions designed to protect your children's mailboxes from offensive e-mail. The restrictions are implemented by filtering the mail that arrives. The filters are automatic, based on criteria set up by the ISP. You can get more information about the filtering process from your ISP's Web site.

Most ISPs also offer filtering for spam, and because a great deal of offensive mail arrives as spam, enabling the spam filters for your family's mailboxes usually works to avoid offensive content in your kids' mailboxes.

Be Wary of Chat Rooms

Kids love chat rooms. They make virtual friends. They get a chance to create a persona and become the person they'd like to be. Reality and truthfulness are in short supply in chat rooms.

Chat rooms abound on the Internet, although many parents aren't aware that they exist outside of AOL. Many chat rooms are dedicated to special interests and topics, but most kids hang out in generic chat rooms, some of which are organized by age group.

One concern for parents is that the language used in chat rooms can be offensive, violent, and (to many parents) disgusting. But most of the time, language *per se* isn't dangerous. The inherent problem with chat rooms is that you don't really know whom you're chatting with. Neither you nor your children have any way of verifying that a person is indeed who he says he is. Your son may think he's chatting with a 12-year-old boy when in fact he's chatting with an adult who's posing as a young boy. Predatory adults — mostly child molesters — often hang out in chat rooms and try to befriend young children. The organizations devoted to finding missing children point out that some missing children were lured from their homes to meet chat-room friends.

The best advice is to "pick your battles," and when you're weighing the subjects, the people in the chat room pose a larger threat than the language in the chat room. Make sure that your children follow these safety tips:

✔ Use a generic, asexual screen name that doesn't indicate your age or location. Often, online handles reflect some physical or other characteristic, but for children, that's a no-no. If you're an esoteric parent, you can have a lot of fun picking strange names. (How about *Orange, Wallpaper,* or *Lantern* for screen names?)

✔ Never reveal your real name, address, or telephone number to any chat-room acquaintance. Don't even reveal the region you're from, the name of your school, or the name of your Little League team. With enough personal information, nefarious types can piece together more than you realize.

✔ *Never* accept an invitation to meet a chat-room acquaintance.

Find Acceptable Sites for Your Children

One way to control what sites your children visit is to steer them toward sites that you've picked out and approved. The Internet contains tons of great sites geared for kids — not just homework helpers (oh, Mom, borrrring), but for games, puzzles, books, and other interests. Here are some recommendations from some young acquaintances of mine:

- Girls who read books by Judy Blume recommend www.judyblume.com.

- Every kid I spoke to reports visiting http://harrypotter.warner bros.com. One of my granddaughters tells me she loves the games on this site.

- Kids (mostly girls) whose mothers introduced them to their own favorites report enjoying the Nancy Drew site at www.mysterynet. com/nancydrew/kids.

For parents who are overwhelmed at the thought of trying to ferret out new sites for their kids, here are a couple of places to look for ideas:

- **Parent News** (www.parent.net): This site covers lots of topics of interest to parents, including Web safety, good Web sites, and parenting hints unrelated to computers.

- **FamiliesConnect** (www.ala.org/ICONN/familiesconnect.html): This site, run by the American Library Association, provides great info for parents about Internet issues.

Set Guidelines for the Level of Violence in Computer Games

Almost every time the headlines announce a tragic shooting by a teenager, usually at a school, the background information on the accused includes the fact that the child was devoted to violent computer games — some of which are available for children to play interactively on the Internet.

No research exists that shows that a perfectly normal kid can be turned into a mass murderer as a result of a violent game. But the experts are polarized and locked into extreme positions, and parents have a hard time knowing whom to believe. Violent games are fascinating and popular, especially among boys (according to research), so knowing where you stand as a parent is essential. Here's what you need to do:

- Talk to your children about violence in *all* media, such as movies, music, television, and computer games. Make sure that the boundaries you set are clear to your children, and listen to their opinions.

- If you decide to let your kids play video games, develop guidelines for your children. These guidelines should explain your own value systems and your own definitions of, and reaction to, violence. For example, some parents object to anything that's connected to guns, whereas other parents explain that hurting another person isn't amusing. By setting guidelines, you can send your kids off to gameland with some moral and emotional equipment, which can help them put their activities into perspective — this is a game, not life.

✔ If you decide that some of the games are indeed extremely violent, you have every right as a parent to forbid your kids to buy or play them. Get familiar with all the games that are popular with kids so you're credible in the eyes of your kids.

One of the best ways to stay on top of computer games is to use your favorite search engine to search the Internet for "reviews of games."

One excellent site is **The American Library Association** (www.ala.org/parentspage/greatsites).

Many sites offer links to additional sites, and most of those sites offer newsletters that you can subscribe to in order to keep up with the latest games.

Index

• *Y* •

• *Z* •

BUSINESS, CAREERS & PERSONAL FINANCE

0-7645-9847-3

0-7645-2431-3

Also available:
- Business Plans Kit For Dummies
  0-7645-9794-9
- Economics For Dummies
  0-7645-5726-2
- Grant Writing For Dummies
  0-7645-8416-2
- Home Buying For Dummies
  0-7645-5331-3
- Managing For Dummies
  0-7645-1771-6
- Marketing For Dummies
  0-7645-5600-2

- Personal Finance For Dummies
  0-7645-2590-5*
- Resumes For Dummies
  0-7645-5471-9
- Selling For Dummies
  0-7645-5363-1
- Six Sigma For Dummies
  0-7645-6798-5
- Small Business Kit For Dummies
  0-7645-5984-2
- Starting an eBay Business For Dummies
  0-7645-6924-4
- Your Dream Career For Dummies
  0-7645-9795-7

HOME & BUSINESS COMPUTER BASICS

0-470-05432-8

0-471-75421-8

Also available:
- Cleaning Windows Vista For Dummies
  0-471-78293-9
- Excel 2007 For Dummies
  0-470-03737-7
- Mac OS X Tiger For Dummies
  0-7645-7675-5
- MacBook For Dummies
  0-470-04859-X
- Macs For Dummies
  0-470-04849-2
- Office 2007 For Dummies
  0-470-00923-3

- Outlook 2007 For Dummies
  0-470-03830-6
- PCs For Dummies
  0-7645-8958-X
- Salesforce.com For Dummies
  0-470-04893-X
- Upgrading & Fixing Laptops For Dummies
  0-7645-8959-8
- Word 2007 For Dummies
  0-470-03658-3
- Quicken 2007 For Dummies
  0-470-04600-7

FOOD, HOME, GARDEN, HOBBIES, MUSIC & PETS

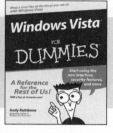

0-7645-8404-9

0-7645-9904-6

Also available:
- Candy Making For Dummies
  0-7645-9734-5
- Card Games For Dummies
  0-7645-9910-0
- Crocheting For Dummies
  0-7645-4151-X
- Dog Training For Dummies
  0-7645-8418-9
- Healthy Carb Cookbook For Dummies
  0-7645-8476-6
- Home Maintenance For Dummies
  0-7645-5215-5

- Horses For Dummies
  0-7645-9797-3
- Jewelry Making & Beading For Dummies
  0-7645-2571-9
- Orchids For Dummies
  0-7645-6759-4
- Puppies For Dummies
  0-7645-5255-4
- Rock Guitar For Dummies
  0-7645-5356-9
- Sewing For Dummies
  0-7645-6847-7
- Singing For Dummies
  0-7645-2475-5

INTERNET & DIGITAL MEDIA

0-470-04529-9

0-470-04894-8

Also available:
- Blogging For Dummies
  0-471-77084-1
- Digital Photography For Dummies
  0-7645-9802-3
- Digital Photography All-in-One Desk Reference For Dummies
  0-470-03743-1
- Digital SLR Cameras and Photography For Dummies
  0-7645-9803-1
- eBay Business All-in-One Desk Reference For Dummies
  0-7645-8438-3
- HDTV For Dummies
  0-470-09673-X

- Home Entertainment PCs For Dummies
  0-470-05523-5
- MySpace For Dummies
  0-470-09529-6
- Search Engine Optimization For Dummies
  0-471-97998-8
- Skype For Dummies
  0-470-04891-3
- The Internet For Dummies
  0-7645-8996-2
- Wiring Your Digital Home For Dummies
  0-471-91830-X

* Separate Canadian edition also available
† Separate U.K. edition also available

SPORTS, FITNESS, PARENTING, RELIGION & SPIRITUALITY

0-471-76871-5

0-7645-7841-3

Also available:

- Catholicism For Dummies
  0-7645-5391-7
- Exercise Balls For Dummies
  0-7645-5623-1
- Fitness For Dummies
  0-7645-7851-0
- Football For Dummies
  0-7645-3936-1
- Judaism For Dummies
  0-7645-5299-6
- Potty Training For Dummies
  0-7645-5417-4
- Buddhism For Dummies
  0-7645-5359-3

- Pregnancy For Dummies
  0-7645-4483-7 †
- Ten Minute Tone-Ups For Dummies
  0-7645-7207-5
- NASCAR For Dummies
  0-7645-7681-X
- Religion For Dummies
  0-7645-5264-3
- Soccer For Dummies
  0-7645-5229-5
- Women in the Bible For Dummies
  0-7645-8475-8

TRAVEL

0-7645-7749-2

0-7645-6945-7

Also available:

- Alaska For Dummies
  0-7645-7746-8
- Cruise Vacations For Dummies
  0-7645-6941-4
- England For Dummies
  0-7645-4276-1
- Europe For Dummies
  0-7645-7529-5
- Germany For Dummies
  0-7645-7823-5
- Hawaii For Dummies
  0-7645-7402-7

- Italy For Dummies
  0-7645-7386-1
- Las Vegas For Dummies
  0-7645-7382-9
- London For Dummies
  0-7645-4277-X
- Paris For Dummies
  0-7645-7630-5
- RV Vacations For Dummies
  0-7645-4442-X
- Walt Disney World & Orlando
  For Dummies
  0-7645-9660-8

GRAPHICS, DESIGN & WEB DEVELOPMENT

0-7645-8815-X

0-7645-9571-7

Also available:

- 3D Game Animation For Dummies
  0-7645-8789-7
- AutoCAD 2006 For Dummies
  0-7645-8925-3
- Building a Web Site For Dummies
  0-7645-7144-3
- Creating Web Pages For Dummies
  0-470-08030-2
- Creating Web Pages All-in-One Desk
  Reference For Dummies
  0-7645-4345-8
- Dreamweaver 8 For Dummies
  0-7645-9649-7

- InDesign CS2 For Dummies
  0-7645-9572-5
- Macromedia Flash 8 For Dummies
  0-7645-9691-8
- Photoshop CS2 and Digital
  Photography For Dummies
  0-7645-9580-6
- Photoshop Elements 4 For Dummies
  0-471-77483-9
- Syndicating Web Sites with RSS Feeds
  For Dummies
  0-7645-8848-6
- Yahoo! SiteBuilder For Dummies
  0-7645-9800-7

NETWORKING, SECURITY, PROGRAMMING & DATABASES

0-7645-7728-X

0-471-74940-0

Also available:

- Access 2007 For Dummies
  0-470-04612-0
- ASP.NET 2 For Dummies
  0-7645-7907-X
- C# 2005 For Dummies
  0-7645-9704-3
- Hacking For Dummies
  0-470-05235-X
- Hacking Wireless Networks
  For Dummies
  0-7645-9730-2
- Java For Dummies
  0-470-08716-1

- Microsoft SQL Server 2005 For Dummies
  0-7645-7755-7
- Networking All-in-One Desk Reference
  For Dummies
  0-7645-9939-9
- Preventing Identity Theft For Dummies
  0-7645-7336-5
- Telecom For Dummies
  0-471-77085-X
- Visual Studio 2005 All-in-One Desk
  Reference For Dummies
  0-7645-9775-2
- XML For Dummies
  0-7645-8845-1

HEALTH & SELF-HELP

0-7645-8450-2

0-7645-4149-8

Also available:

- Bipolar Disorder For Dummies
  0-7645-8451-0
- Chemotherapy and Radiation
  For Dummies
  0-7645-7832-4
- Controlling Cholesterol For Dummies
  0-7645-5440-9
- Diabetes For Dummies
  0-7645-6820-5* †
- Divorce For Dummies
  0-7645-8417-0 †

- Fibromyalgia For Dummies
  0-7645-5441-7
- Low-Calorie Dieting For Dummies
  0-7645-9905-4
- Meditation For Dummies
  0-471-77774-9
- Osteoporosis For Dummies
  0-7645-7621-6
- Overcoming Anxiety For Dummies
  0-7645-5447-6
- Reiki For Dummies
  0-7645-9907-0
- Stress Management For Dummies
  0-7645-5144-2

EDUCATION, HISTORY, REFERENCE & TEST PREPARATION

0-7645-8381-6

0-7645-9554-7

Also available:

- The ACT For Dummies
  0-7645-9652-7
- Algebra For Dummies
  0-7645-5325-9
- Algebra Workbook For Dummies
  0-7645-8467-7
- Astronomy For Dummies
  0-7645-8465-0
- Calculus For Dummies
  0-7645-2498-4
- Chemistry For Dummies
  0-7645-5430-1
- Forensics For Dummies
  0-7645-5580-4

- Freemasons For Dummies
  0-7645-9796-5
- French For Dummies
  0-7645-5193-0
- Geometry For Dummies
  0-7645-5324-0
- Organic Chemistry I For Dummies
  0-7645-6902-3
- The SAT I For Dummies
  0-7645-7193-1
- Spanish For Dummies
  0-7645-5194-9
- Statistics For Dummies
  0-7645-5423-9

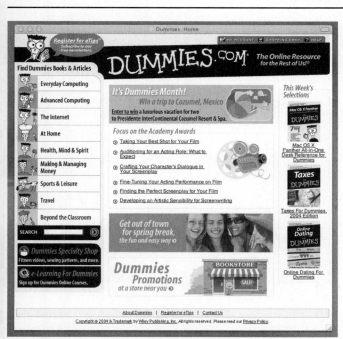

Get smart @ dummies.com®

- **Find a full list of Dummies titles**
- **Look into loads of FREE on-site articles**
- **Sign up for FREE eTips e-mailed to you weekly**
- **See what other products carry the Dummies name**
- **Shop directly from the Dummies bookstore**
- **Enter to win new prizes every month!**

* Separate Canadian edition also available
† Separate U.K. edition also available

Available wherever books are sold. For more information or to order direct: U.S. customers visit www.dummies.com or call 1-877-762-2974.
U.K. customers visit www.wileyeurope.com or call 0800 243407. Canadian customers visit www.wiley.ca or call 1-800-567-4797.